Betty Crocker's
Living
with Cancer
COOKBOOK

Hungry Minds™

New York, NY • Cleveland, OH • Indianapolis, IN

Published by

Hungry Minds™
909 Third Avenue
New York, NY 10022
www.hungryminds.com

Copyright © 2002 General Mills, Inc.,
Minneapolis, Minnesota

All rights reserved. No part of this book may be reproduced
or transmitted in any form or by any means, electronic or
mechanical, including photocopying, recording, or by an information storage and retrieval system, without permission in
writing from the Publisher.

Betty Crocker, Bisquick, Cheerios, Corn Chex, Fiber One,
Multi-Bran Chex, Rice Chex, Total, Wheat Chex and Wheaties
are registered trademarks of General Mills, Inc.

Boost is a registered trademark of Mead Johnson & Company.

Carnation and Instant Breakfast are registered trademarks of
Société des Produits Nestlé S.A.

Coumadin is a registered trademark of DuPont
Pharmaceuticals Company.

Ensure and Pedialyte are registered trademarks of Abbott
Laboratories.

Orabase is a registered trademark of Colgate-Palmolive Co.

All other trademarks are the property of their respective owners.

For general information on Hungry Minds' products and
services please contact our Customer Care Department within
the U.S. at 800-762-2974, outside the U.S. at 317-572-3993, or
fax 317-572-4002.

For sales inquiries and reseller information, including discounts,
premium and bulk quantity sales, and foreign-language trans-
lations, please contact our Customer Care Department at
800-434-3422, fax 317-572-4002, or write to Hungry Minds, Inc.,
Attn: Customer Care Department, 10475 Crosspoint Boulevard,
Indianapolis, IN 46256.

Library of Congress Cataloging-in-Publication Data

Crocker, Betty.
    Betty Crocker's living with cancer cookbook / Betty Crocker.
      p. cm.
    Includes index.
    ISBN 0764565494 (alk. paper)
      1. Cancer—Diet therapy—Recipes. 2. Cancer—Treatment—
Complications—Diet therapy—Recipes. I. Title.

    RC271.D52 C76 2001
    641.5/631—dc21   2001039226

Manufactured in China

10 9 8 7 6 5 4 3 2

Cover recipe photos (from left to right): Fruit Parfaits (page 60),
Angel Hair Pasta with Avocado and Tomatos (page 114), and
Cantaloupe and Chicken Salad (page 120)

General Mills, Inc.

Betty Crocker Kitchens

MANAGER, PUBLISHING: Lois L. Tlusty

EDITOR: Cheri Olerud

NUTRITIONIST: Elyse A. Cohen, M.S., L.N.

RECIPE DEVELOPMENT: Betty Crocker Kitchens

FOOD STYLISTS: Nancy Johnson, Cyndy Syme, Karen Linden

Photographic Services

PHOTOGRAPHER: Valerie J. Bourassa

Oncologists

Kris Ghosh, M.D.
Gynecologic Oncologist
Beth Israel Deaconess Medical Center
Harvard Medical School

Linda Carson, M.D.
Gynecologic Oncologist
University of Minnesota Medical Center

A special thank you and acknowledgement to four friends who not only shared recipes and quotes
but also shared their enthusiasm, advice, inspiration and the wisdom they gained as they learned
to cope with cancer:

Judy Overbeek

Mary Wiser

Anne Rislove

Susan Sullivan

A special thanks to the following individuals who provided tasty recipes and insightful quotes:
Theresa H., Pat Y., Randie N., Susan S., Marie E., Anne R., Catherine H., Lois K., Marilyn T.,
Patty N., Mary W., Joan K., Ellen T., MaryElaine W., Kathy S., Joyce K., Carol N. and Judy O.

Hungry Minds, Inc.

PUBLISHER: Jennifer R. Feldman

EXECUTIVE EDITOR: Anne Ficklen

COVER AND BOOK DESIGN: Edwin Kuo

INTERIOR LAYOUT: Holly Wittenberg

MANUFACTURING MANAGER: Kevin Watt

PHOTOGRAPHY ART DIRECTOR: Brent Bentrott

NATURE AND FLOWER PHOTOGRAPHY: Zane Kuo, M.D.

For consistent baking results, the Betty Crocker Kitchens recommend
Gold Medal Flour.

For more great ideas visit **www.bettycrocker.com**

*H*aving a diagnosis of cancer rearranges your life and its priorities. Many things change for you, including what used to be the simple tasks of cooking and eating.

The side effects of cancer treatment can turn eating from a pleasure into a daily challenge. Inspired by the questions of our patients and their families' cooking and eating challenges, we collaborated on Betty Crocker's Living with Cancer Cookbook, *to offer helpful tips for the unique dietary needs of cancer survivors as well as tasty recipes that are simple to prepare. The book also offers general nutrition guidelines for cancer survivors, eating tips for patients undergoing radiation or chemotherapy, and recipes that have been suggested and used by cancer survivors.*

Sound nutrition is perhaps most important to cancer patients, whose very survival is linked to a well-balanced diet. Unfortunately, cancer and the side effects of cancer treatment can make sound nutrition a difficult hurdle to overcome. That's where these recipes come in—they contain the necessary nutrition and address the issues unique to different cancer treatments.

Betty Crocker's Living with Cancer Cookbook *is a collection of recipes from the trusted kitchens of Betty Crocker and the home kitchens of real people—our survivors—whose experiences make* Betty Crocker's Living with Cancer Cookbook *so practical and useful. Detailed nutrition information with each recipe helps you select the recipes that meet your individual needs.*

Quality of life remains the focus for cancer survivors. Good eating and good nutrition are the cornerstones for maximizing the quality of life during and after cancer. Betty Crocker, for many years, has been the name that people count on for healthy cuisine, easy recipes and great taste. We hope Betty Crocker's Living with Cancer Cookbook *will bring back the joy of eating to you and those you love!*

KRIS GHOSH, M.D.

LINDA CARSON, M.D.

Key to Common Side Effects

The four most common symptoms in cancer treatment are NAUSEA, MOUTH SORES, DIARRHEA and CONSTIPATION. Eating the right foods can help these symptoms, and to make it easier to find foods that work for you, we have marked recipes that are especially good for these symptoms. Remember, any of the recipes in this book will help you during cancer treatment—your personal preference is always the best indicator of what recipe is best for you.

n	**Nausea**
m	**Mouth Sores**
d	**Diarrhea**
c	**Constipation**

Table of Contents

Bring Back the *Joy of Eating*

Although your life is changing and you are extremely frightened, a diagnosis of cancer does not have to take over your life. You may feel that way at first, but that feeling need not stay. Some cancer survivors have told us they prefer to focus on the future and their life after cancer because doing so offers hope.

One way to regain control in your life is to plan what to cook and eat every day. Nutrition and eating well are absolutely essential to your recovery and quality of life.

Included in this book are secrets of survival from cancer patients. These individuals share the small hints and the big ideas that worked for them as they navigated their cancer diagnosis and treatment. They offer bits of advice and wisdom they found to be helpful in their personal struggles to thrive and that brought back the joy of eating for them.

Be Prepared for a Roller Coaster Ride

If you've recently learned that you—or a loved one—has cancer, you may wonder how you, your friends and family can possibly cope. Living with cancer and its treatment can be compared to a roller coaster ride: from day to day, you never know what to expect; the ups, downs and side curves are unknowns. Not knowing the outcome is also very scary.

UNDERSTANDABLY, YOU ARE EXPERIENCING many thoughts, emotions and feelings that are overwhelming. It's normal to feel a lack of control over your life. Take the time you need to accept your or your loved one's diagnosis. Talk to your doctor, dietitian, nurse, counselor, member of the clergy, family and friends. Seek out information to learn everything you can about the disease, treatment and side effects, and learn what you can do for yourself.

As different as each person's DNA, cancer affects people in different ways. Your—or your loved one's—experience with cancer is an individual challenge, a personal roller coaster ride. As you are presented with options, you must decide what is right for you. The plan that's effective for one individual may not work well for another. And rather than follow a road map that may have been developed for someone else, it's best to create your own plan. Trial and error, your own energy level and listening to your body are the best guides to determine what works for you. If you are supporting someone during this time, try to help by gathering information, or taking notes when you meet with doctors, providing child care during medical visits, and discussing possible options for treatment.

In this section, the focus is on the nutritional needs of individuals with cancer and ways to help you meet these needs. Information on eating out, grocery shopping and special diets is also included. In addition to discussing a traditional medical perspective, some of the alternative, or complementary, therapies are also included.

In Chapter 1, you'll find a helpful Coping with Side Effects guide that includes expert medical advice on ten common side effects, a recipe to help each particular side effect and a list of the top recipes in the book that are helpful for the four most bothersome side effects. Following that are seven chapters of recipes to use in planning your meals and mini-meals, including foods that your whole family can help you prepare and enjoy, or that you can prepare to help your loved one with cancer.

Though primarily written for the newly diagnosed cancer patient, this cookbook is also for families and friends and those survivors who remain in treatment for an extended period of time. Because the needs of each cancer patient are unique, we invite you to use this cookbook as a guide. You may adopt the information and recipes that meet your needs and skim over the remainder. We hope this book will bring back the joy of eating for you and those you love.

So What Is Cancer All About, Anyway?

In the beginning, understanding the basics about cancer and treatment and what you can expect is important. Here are the answers to some frequently asked questions:

WHAT IS CANCER?

Cancer is the abnormal growth of cells—any cells—in the body. The foods we eat, our genetic makeup and the environment we've been exposed to all impact your risk of developing cancer. In fact, scientific research estimates that as much as 20 to 40 percent of cancer cases are related to diet.

HOW IS CANCER TREATED?

Treatment of most cancers requires several approaches. Depending on the type and stage of cancer, treatment may include surgery, radiation, chemotherapy or some combination of all three. The success of any treatment is related to the overall health of the survivor. A positive attitude, a sense of humor, courage, having a support system of friends and family and many other factors can have a tremendous impact on your healing and happiness.

WHY ME?

Though it is very common to pose the question "Why me?" (as almost every newly diagnosed cancer patient does), there is no exact answer. Individually, each patient must seek out answers to his or her own personal satisfaction. Asking the question "Why me?" is a normal response to grief about cancer, and it is the beginning of healing.

According to experts, grief has six stages. As we work through our grief, we move through these stages. And as the word *stage* implies, we may be in more than one grief stage at a time or we may move in and out of these stages in different orders, depending upon how we work through our grief. Eventually, as we heal, we reach acceptance, which allows us to move forward with our lives.

Here's a quick overview of the grief stages as they may relate to cancer:

Shock and Denial. To protect us, our brains use shock, numbness and denial to cope with the traumas we experience, whether the traumas are physical or emotional. And for many, a cancer diagnosis is trauma. During this stage, denying the diagnosis of cancer is common. You may feel as though the diagnosis is a bad dream from which you will awaken and realize isn't true. You may go about your daily routine in a very surreal or disconnected way.

Bargaining. When physical or emotional pain becomes unbearable, engaging in some form of negotiation is typical. Consciously or unconsciously, you may try to negotiate with a higher power, your spouse, your friend, your doctor or whomever you see as being able to help cure cancer and rectify the potential outcome. Bargaining is really an attempt to postpone your grief.

Anger. You may become angry about cancer—angry with yourself, family members, doctors and even the world. You may play out your anger as hurt, frustration, fear, helplessness or guilt. The reasons and targets of anger are as unique as the individuals dealing with them. You may even surprise yourself with your rage. To help you cope, ask others to listen to how angry you feel about cancer.

Guilt. You may blame yourself or others and often may feel helplessly guilty about a cancer diagnosis. You may say to yourself or others, "If only I had or hadn't done this." Or you may think, "What could I have done to prevent cancer?" Unfortunately, there may be nothing you can do or could have done to prevent or change a cancer diagnosis.

Depression. A sense of helplessness and the reality of a cancer diagnosis sinks in deeply and you feel depressed. Symptoms of depression often include loss of appetite,

feelings of worthlessness, an inability to enjoy anything, insomnia or difficulty concentrating and making decisions. If depression is lasting a long time, you may want to speak about how you feel with a caring friend, or go to a mental health professional if you feel that's the care you need.

Acceptance. One day, you notice that the sun is shining and you have more good days than bad. You have hope, and you can begin to enjoy life again. At first, acceptance can be so subtle that you may not even recognize it. With time, you realize that there is life with cancer and, hopefully, life after cancer.

As you work through the stages of grief, recognizing and talking about your feelings is healthy, regardless of which stage you're in. Talking to others about how you feel is key to healing. And as you heal and accept cancer, you can begin to move on.

WHAT RESOURCES ARE AVAILABLE TO HELP ME?

Continue to rely on your doctor as your first resource throughout your treatment. Other professionals who may be able to assist you are oncology nurses, dietitians and counselors. And you may find talking with other cancer survivors to be useful. If speaking with a cancer survivor would be helpful for you, ask your doctor for the names of survivors with the same type of cancer you have who have agreed to share their experiences. If you find their comments helpful, you may also want to share comments about your journey with newly diagnosed patients.

A cancer support group comprised of others who are going through experiences similar to your own can be an important source of support and strength. Ask your doctor to provide you with a contact or information about where and when local support groups meet. Organizations such as the American Cancer Society have an endless number of resources to share, from answering questions on hot lines to providing wigs and clothing for survivors to wear, to a website full of useful and helpful information. See page 248 for additional resources.

HOW QUICKLY CAN LIFE RETURN TO NORMAL?

Depending on the type and stage of cancer you have and the kind of treatment you are undergoing, the time it takes can vary considerably. Then again, realizing that you may have to accept a "new normal" may be crucial to your self-esteem and your survival. Talking to your doctor and to other cancer survivors will give you some perspective, but realize that each type of cancer, each survivor and each situation is unique.

WHAT CAN I EXPECT FROM TREATMENT DAY TO DAY?

According to one cancer survivor, "Expect the unexpected." The common side effects of chemotherapy include fatigue, nausea, vomiting and diarrhea. As you undergo treatment, you will most likely experience days when you feel quite ill, days when you feel a bit better and days when you feel almost like your normal self. Tracking your own side-effect patterns relative to your treatments will give you some sense of what to expect, but realize, too, that your course may change. And there is a small percentage of patients who are fortunate enough to have little or no side effects at all.

Focus on and enjoy the days you feel well. On those days when you feel ill, remember that you will feel better again and your energy will return. As another survivor said, "This, too, shall pass."

Take Control of Your Life

Most cancer survivors say the best way to deal with your own recovery is to take charge. That means taking control of your life, control over your cancer and control over treatment options and potential side effects. So much about survival depends upon your outlook. Choose to educate yourself and learn as much as you can in order to make wise choices that are right for you.

Although each course is individual, survivors say there are six universal themes that are key to coping with and living with cancer.

1. EAT NUTRITIOUS FOODS.

The link between diet and health continues to grow stronger with each new study published. In fact, the American Cancer Society estimates that more than 35 percent of new cancer diagnoses are related to diet. In addition to affecting physical health, food plays a major role in your mental health and well-being. The food you eat affects your energy level and how well you sleep and think. In your cancer battle, you may find that as your energy level drops, food will bring it back up. One survivor said, "During cancer treatment, eating was a tool to ward off both physical and mental fatigue."

Cancer patients have increased nutritional needs. And sound nutrition has a tremendously positive impact on healing. During treatment, your body has a greater need for calcium, iron, magnesium and potassium. This increased need is based on two reasons: (1) Your body is fighting the disease, which requires more energy and more nutrients than usual, and (2) your treatment kills cells, both cancerous and healthy cells, thereby disrupting the nutrient balance in your body.

Food can help you regain strength and vitality, but how do you know what to eat and how much? Eating can make you feel worse, so how do you know which foods to avoid? Fortunately, eating well does not have to mean preparing complicated foods or gourmet recipes. The simpler and easier the recipes are to prepare, the better—and the more likely you are to have the energy to eat.

One cancer survivor feels that eating well is the most important factor in her own healing: "Eating is a time of enjoyment and socialization. It goes beyond food. It is a ritual that brings people together for support, communication and pleasure. It is a way for us to feel 'normal' with family and friends."

2. REMAIN POSITIVE AND HOPEFUL.

"Keep a positive attitude, because it will help you physically and mentally," says another survivor. Though being "up" all the time is not possible, finding at least one thing to be thankful for each day can lift your spirits and give you courage. With a little practice, you will find more and more things you can appreciate.

To achieve the hopeful part, you can try to face your worst fears. Being able to identify what it is that you fear most may be helpful. Do you fear death? Leaving others behind to live out their lives while you are gone? Perhaps you fear life—if there's pain and discomfort. Whatever your fears are, trying to face them and coming to terms with them is very helpful for healing.

Once you've worked through your fears, it is possible to have hope and to go on living. Although imagining this seems difficult at first, some survivors say they think about having cancer as being presented with a gift, a unique ability to grow, to build inner strength and to make positive changes in their lives.

3. USE PRAYER, MEDITATION AND RELAXATION TECHNIQUES.

Studies among patients in hospitals have indicated that there is a strong connection between healing and prayer. Having faith in a higher being, one who can help guide you through difficult times, is beneficial to many survivors. Spiritual connections, whether through prayer or meditation, can provide comfort, stress relief and focus for many people. For these reasons, prayer and meditation can be extremely beneficial to those who are sick. Even knowing that others are thinking about you in their prayers can provide relief. You are not alone. If you aren't comfortable with the concept of a higher being, practice relaxation techniques and realize that you are connected with all parts of the universe—the trees, waterfalls, the birds—those things that give you comfort.

4. REMEMBER TO LAUGH.

Laughter is like internal jogging. It promotes better blood circulation, lowers blood pressure, relieves pain and stimulates the release of certain hormones that can have a calming effect. Laughing and smiling are contagious and can have a profound, positive effect on healing. One survivor said, "People must think cancer patients don't have a sense of humor. My family doesn't say anything funny to me anymore." Laughing at yourself or telling a joke can help ease tension, especially for family or friends who may not know what to say during this

particularly difficult time. Letting others know you want to laugh and need to laugh may help ease their discomfort as well as yours.

Isolating yourself from others during this difficult time may be tempting, but don't! Staying in touch with family and friends is very helpful to cancer survivors. Everyone needs support, and who better to provide support than people who know you and care about you? Cancer survivors offer advice to other survivors and their families: "Surround yourself with those you love!" "Just keep talking and sharing." "Join a support group!" "You don't need to do this completely on your own."

"This is one time when it's okay to be selfish. Concentrate on yourself and getting well." "Don't be afraid to ask for help!" Advice from survivors includes tips on letting others help. Many cancer survivors find that asking for assistance isn't as hard as they think it might be. Anticipating the asking seems to be the hardest part, especially for those of us who pride ourselves on self-sufficiency. You may be surprised to find that friends and family are willing to help in any way they can; they just need guidance on where to put their efforts.

Find ways to be especially good to yourself, and include as many of the following options as you can each day and each week:

Exercise daily. Thirty minutes of walking or light exercise is recommended each day to improve appetite and strength and to reduce fatigue. Try doing light housework, walking around the house or climbing the stairs. Because some days you will feel more energetic than others, be sure to exercise whenever you feel up to it. Many survivors have found that even a few minutes of exercise or activity stimulates their appetite. Your own energy level and how you feel are your best gauges to the frequency and amount of exercise that's right for you.

Enjoy nature. Take a walk through the woods, picnic outside or stop to listen to the birds. Immersing yourself in nature will refresh and nourish you. Nature can be very

healing for body, mind and soul. If you can't go outside, relax by an open window and breathe in the fresh air, or gaze at nearby trees, faraway cloud formations or a fresh snowfall. Listen to the sounds of flowing water, even if it means simply running a bath!

Celebrate! Celebrate simple accomplishments, such as reaching treatment hurdles or survival milestones. Take time to set the table and use the good china, just for fun. Put flowers or a plant on the table to represent life. Ask a friend to drop off some colorful balloons to create a party atmosphere. Plan a backward dinner where the whole family is silly and eats dessert first, then the main meal.

Express yourself. Express your feelings, thoughts, hopes and frustrations in a journal. Write, type on the computer or record your thoughts by whatever means works best for you. You may be surprised by what's going on in your head and heart. Being able to share your feelings releases tension and aids healing.

Try something new. Some survivors find that trying something new is rejuvenating. It's one way to lessen fears and boost spirits. Try a new food, a new body stretch or even a new adventure. Experience life to keep yourself feeling alive. One survivor who describes herself as "not too athletic" took up yoga for the first time and found she really enjoyed the stretching and breathing. Yoga helped her tune into her body in a new, healthy way.

Rest. No matter what time the clock says, if you're tired, take a nap. Sleep is your body's way of shutting down to recharge, to regain energy and start anew. Try to sleep well at night by slowing down before bedtime and limiting caffeine late in the day. And if you need to snooze during the day, allow yourself this wonderfully healing renewal.

Use relaxation techniques. Find a comfy spot and listen to calming music or try deep breathing to relax. Use meditation—even for a short time—by repeating a simple word or sound to focus your energy and center yourself. Visualize being in pleasant surroundings enveloped in healing light and warmth. Stretch out on the bed or floor and let the tension ease out of your body. If you're feeling up to it, have a gentle massage, or take a yoga class.

Foods Rich in Essential Nutrients

Potassium	Calcium	Iron	Magnesium
TOMATOES	MILK	READY-TO-EAT CEREALS (FORTIFIED WITH IRON)	GREEN LEAFY VEGETABLES
BANANAS	YOGURT	HOT CEREALS (FORTIFIED WITH IRON)	NUTS
ORANGES	ORANGE JUICE (FORTIFIED WITH CALCIUM)	SPINACH	SOYBEANS
FRUIT JUICES	TOFU	RED MEATS (BEEF, PORK)	PEANUT BUTTER
VEGETABLE JUICES	SALMON (WITH BONES)	PEAS	READY-TO-EAT CEREALS (FORTIFIED WITH IRON)
	SARDINES	NUTS	HOT CEREALS (FORTIFIED WITH IRON)
	SPINACH	GREEN LEAFY VEGETABLES	BANANAS
	BROCCOLI		FISH
	CHEESE		

Eat Well and Enjoy Food

Eating well means keeping your body healthy through the foods you eat. Making nutritious food selections, enjoying eating and maintaining a healthy body fit together. It takes some planning, but the payoff is well worth the effort.

You may have questions about which foods to eat now that you've been diagnosed with cancer. You may wish to consider these factors when making your food selections:

Choose foods you like. Eating will be easier if you're eating foods you like, even if it means eating for breakfast what you'd normally eat for dinner. If the food is appealing to you, enjoy it.

Select foods with healing nutrients. Potassium, calcium, iron and magnesium are nutrients beneficial for your body, especially during healing. For easy planning, the recipes in this cookbook list how much of each of these nutrients they contain.

Ask your doctor. For your particular type of cancer or treatment, there may be some do's and don'ts for success that others may have learned from past experiences. Check with your doctor to be sure you're on the right track.

The Importance of Sound Nutrition

Planning meals and eating can be real challenges when you aren't feeling well, and sound nutrition has perhaps never been more important to your life than right now—your very survival may depend on it. Keep these important nutrition basics in mind as you plan and eat your meals.

BALANCE IS KEY

Eating a balanced diet including a variety of foods each day helps ensure that you get the fuel and all the vitamins and minerals your body needs. The fuel, or energy your body requires, comes from calories. And calories come from balanced sources of carbohydrates, protein and fat.

Carbohydrates provide quick energy and are your body's favorite fuel source. That's why the bulk of your calories (about 55 to 60 percent) is made up of carbohydrates. Foods such as breads, cereals, pasta, rice and potatoes are all examples of carbohydrates, along with simple sugars, honey and fruits. Easy to eat, these foods provide calories that can help sustain you through treatment and healing.

Food Guide Pyramid

If you combine the fuels of carbohydrate, protein and fat with vitamins and minerals, you build a balanced diet and the Food Guide Pyramid can show you the way.

The Food Guide Pyramid emphasizes variety in your food choices from five major food groups and shows you the proportions in which to eat them. Foods are grouped together based on the nutrients they supply and the number of servings you need daily.

For example, the Bread, Cereal, Rice and Pasta Group is at the base of the pyramid. It has the largest number of servings per day, compared to the other food groups. To eat well, start at the bottom of the pyramid and work your way up.

Following the Food Guide Pyramid can indeed aid in your healing. Remember the points below as you plan healthy meals for yourself and your family.

1. **Eat at least five servings of fruits and vegetables daily.** This five-a-day plan assures you're getting ample amounts of vitamins A and C, folic acid and potassium—all nutrients necessary for a healthy body. If eating fruits and vegetables is difficult, try sipping juices or eating applesauce or pureed fruits from the blender.

2. **Get plenty of protein.** Choose lean protein sources of meats (beef and pork), poultry, fish, dry beans, eggs and nuts. In addition to protein, these foods provide B vitamins, iron and magnesium. Dairy foods, such as milk and yogurt, also provide protein and much-needed calcium.

3. **Be sure to get enough whole grains and fiber.** Choose foods from the base of the pyramid, particularly whole-grain cereals and breads that are often fortified with nutrients such as B vitamins, iron and magnesium and that contain fiber to keep foods moving through your digestive tract.

4. **Drink plenty of water and other liquids.** Experts generally recommend eight to ten glasses of water and other liquids daily for healthy

Fats, Oils & Sweets Group
Use sparingly

● Fat (naturally occurring and added)
▼ Sugars (added)
These symbols show fats, oils and added sugar in foods.

Milk, Yogurt & Cheese Group
2-3 servings

Meat, Poultry, Fish, Eggs, Dry Beans & Nuts Group
2-3 servings

Vegetable Group
3-5 servings

Fruit Group
2-4 servings

Bread, Cereal, Rice & Pasta Group
6-11 servings

SOURCE: U.S. Department of Agriculture, U.S. Department of Health and Human Services.

individuals. And that holds true for cancer survivors, too. Beverages such as milk, juices and herbal teas also count, but remember to quench your thirst with plenty of plain water as well.

5. **Eat a variety of foods.** Emphasize foods that come from plant sources, such as breads, cereals, grains, rice, pasta, fruits, vegetables, legumes and dry beans. But don't forget about protein and dairy foods. You need a variety of foods

providing many nutrients to give your body all the benefits it requires.

6. **Include foods loaded with nutrients that aid recovery.** Because of your increased needs, be sure you get enough calcium, iron, potassium and magnesium. Include milk, yogurt and cheese for calcium. Eat protein foods (see number 2 above) and whole grains (see number 3 above) for iron and magnesium. Eat fruits and vegetables for potassium (see number 1 above).

Protein helps build new cells. It makes hormones and enzymes that keep your body functioning and makes antibodies to fight off infection. Protein comes primarily from animal foods, such as meats, fish, poultry and dairy sources, along with some plant foods such as dry beans, vegetables, rice and pasta. As your body fights the cancerous cells, it needs plenty of protein to keep going.

Fat helps to build new cells, shuttle vitamins through your body and make certain hormones that regulate your blood pressure, along with other vital functions. Fats come from oils, butter, margarine, nuts and sweets (such as chocolate and ice cream). Experts recommend that no more than 30 percent of calories should come from fat. But as you progress through your treatment, you may find you need a bit of extra fat to maintain your weight. When adding fat, try to stay away from fried or greasy foods because they may be difficult to digest.

Vitamins help release energy from the fuel sources of carbohydrate, protein and fat. Your vision, hair and skin, as well as the strength of your bones, all depend upon the vitamins that come from the foods you eat. The more variety you have in your diet, the more likely you are to get all the vitamins your body needs.

Minerals help your body with many functions under the surface. Of particular importance during cancer treatment, certain minerals may be needed in greater than normal amounts. Iron, for example, a mineral that carries much-needed oxygen to your body cells, is in great demand. Calcium (key to strong bones and teeth) and potassium (important for proper nerve and muscle function) are also required in greater amounts than usual by cancer survivors.

Surgery and chemotherapy deplete the body of many essential vitamins and minerals. The Foods Rich in Essential Nutrients chart on page 13 shows food sources that can help provide some of these important minerals. Check with your doctor or dietitian to be sure your diet is supplying sufficient quantities of nutrients or to see if you require supplements. It's best not to take vitamin and mineral supplements on your own, without the supervision of your doctor or dietitian.

Enjoy Cooking, Shopping and Eating

With this emphasis on the increased need for certain nutrients, what needs to change in your diet, if anything, isn't always clear. Less clear is how to handle family meals and what you do with grocery shopping when battling cancer. Read on to learn more hints to help you and your family cope.

SHOULD I MAKE CHANGES TO MY EATING ROUTINE?

Much of the answer to this question depends upon your current eating habits, the particular kind of cancer you have, the treatment you are undergoing, any side effects you experience and the foods your body will tolerate. It is best to discuss any potential dietary changes with your dietitian and doctor.

There will be times when you won't be hungry, so eat whenever you can, even if it's only a small portion. If you crave a specific food, go ahead and eat it. If a regular-sized meal looks unmanageable, try eating several smaller meals or snacks throughout the day. Avoid eating just before bedtime because lying down after eating may cause nausea. A short brisk walk after dinner may help digest your food.

HOW DO I COOK FOR MY FAMILY?

If cooking for your family has always been part of your daily life and you enjoy it, by all means continue. Simply plan what to eat, allowing for any dietary limitations. Then apply the sound nutrition advice from the previous pages and follow the simple tips below to ensure success:

Plan menus together. Though patience and planning are needed to choose meals that satisfy everyone, family members want to feel they are doing something to help. And greater success is achieved when tasks are shared among the family.

Save your strength. Overcoming fatigue can be a challenge. Focus on the tasks you enjoy and those that are manageable for your level of energy. Take advantage of offers to help from friends and family members by allowing them

to assist in food preparation and cooking, especially when you're feeling tired.

Season foods to your tastes. Separate a serving or two after cooking each dish. Then season, spice or salt the smaller serving to *your* tastes! By adding extra flavor this way, one recipe can appeal to all members of the family.

Enjoy eating. Just talking with and enjoying your family or friends in a pleasant environment can lead to successful eating. You don't have to be elaborate. Set the table, adjust the lights, play soft music, light candles or light a fire. Then sit back, eat and enjoy each other's company.

Give up the cleanup. When the meal is over, let family or friends clear the table and clean the kitchen. That way,

Radiation (Radiotherapy) Remedies

Radiation is recommended for some types of cancers. If you'll be undergoing radiation treatments, you'll want to know these facts:

1. Fatigue is the most common side effect from radiotherapy and can last for months after treatment.

2. Other side effects from radiotherapy depend upon where the radiation is directed. If you have radiation in the stomach area, a common side effect is nausea. If you have radiation in the pelvic area, a common side effect is diarrhea.

3. A low-residue/low-fiber diet is recommended during abdominal and/or pelvic radiation. Ask your doctor for a list of low-residue and low-fiber foods. Also refer to pages 19 to 20 for a list of these foods, and look through this cookbook for recipes that are flagged as "low fiber" and "low residue."

4. Eat foods that contain high concentrations of iron, and eat these foods with an orange or another food high in vitamin C so the iron in the food can be more easily absorbed. Many of the recipes in this cookbook are flagged as being high in iron. Also, ask your doctor if you need iron supplements to keep your iron stores high; preventing anemia can help the radiation work better.

everyone plays a vital role and is contributing to the workload. Use your time to catch up on a little rest.

HOW DO I GO GROCERY SHOPPING?

Shopping when you have cancer can be difficult, particularly when you don't feel well, you're overcome by fatigue or food sights and smells nauseate you. Take advantage of grocery stores and Web sites that offer home delivery. Or have family and friends pick up several items for you while they are doing their own shopping.

If you must go to the grocery store yourself, try these tips to make the most of your shopping trips:

Shop in the morning or at times when you feel less fatigued.

Make a detailed grocery list so you aren't tempted to binge shop. Visit smaller grocery stores and park close to the building.

Visit only those aisles of the store that are necessary. Do the rest in a separate trip.

Purchase prepared foods to ease food preparation. Bagged salads, baby-cut carrots, deli items and meat that's boned and trimmed of fat can make things easier for you at home.

Buy convenience foods that stay fresh for a long time. Pastas, rice mixes, canned tuna and soups keep on the shelf for a long time.

Shop at farmers' markets whenever you can. Open air promotes less nausea than closed-in grocery stores.

And when you do have assistance in the grocery store, try these suggestions:

Buy large quantities of foods to decrease the number of shopping trips.

Purchase lots of produce. Fresh fruits and veggies are heavy to carry, but they are loaded with vitamins A and C, folic acid and other important nutrients.

Minimize extra walking by asking family members to come along with you. They can run back for items you missed.

Delegate carrying the grocery bags and putting the food away to an able-bodied family member or friend.

HOW CAN I STOCK MY KITCHEN AND PANTRY?

When you return home from grocery shopping, store your foods where they stay fresh the longest. To minimize smells and flavor changes, throw out questionable food items right away and keep packaged fresh foods only to their expiration date. Because food flavors and smells often become stronger over time, you may want to turn over this freshness duty to another household member, especially if you're experiencing nausea.

To make cooking for the family easier for you:

Keep your kitchen well stocked.

Organize your refrigerator and freezer so you and others can find foods easily.

Ask family and friends to prepare meals.

Use simple recipes that can be prepared quickly and easily. Many easy recipes are contained in this cookbook.

Enlist help from others to rinse and cut fresh fruits and vegetables for easier eating.

Prepare only foods that you and your family enjoy.

Break up food preparation tasks, and rest when you can. Start some of the preparation early in the day when you have more energy.

Use timesaving kitchen appliances such as a slow cooker, rice cooker, food processor and microwave oven that keep food odors contained.

Cherish leftovers. Cook more food than you need for your immediate meal, and refrigerate or freeze unused portions for another time.

Plan and prepare foods ahead of treatment times. If food preparation is difficult for you during chemotherapy, for example, rely on foods that have been cooked ahead of time and frozen, or ask friends or family to help out. Some of the recipes in this cookbook can be made ahead and refrigerated or frozen.

Keep foods covered and sealed and take out the trash at the end of each meal to reduce lingering food odors.

HOW CAN I EAT OUT?

Eating out is a great alternative to cooking. It can offer even more food choices than eating at home and eliminates the preparation and cleanup.

To ease your concerns, ask these important questions at the restaurant or phone ahead:

How is the food prepared?
Limit fat and, therefore, the amount of fried or greasy foods you eat. High-fat choices can induce nausea and are difficult to digest. The best choices include broiled and grilled meals, because the flavor of the food is preserved without adding extra fat.

What ingredients are used in a particular dish?
Explain what you cannot eat, because a dish may contain hidden ingredients such as onions, garlic, or spices that could cause discomfort. Knowing ahead of time about problem menu items and avoiding them is better than sending dishes back to the kitchen.

How hot or spicy are the foods?
Some cancer patients can tolerate highly spiced foods and even prefer them, and others desire mild foods. Spice level, sweetness and saltiness can often be tailored to your taste. Just let your server know what you need.

Can I order a small portion?
Try to order à la carte items or lunch-size portions if possible. Select different kinds of foods and flavors when available. New food adventures often lead to greater success in finding foods that you enjoy.

Am I familiar with this restaurant or cuisine?
Choose restaurants you know, if that eases your concerns. Or try new ones that sound appealing to you. Either way, request seating that's far away from the kitchen to avoid cooking smells that may cause nausea.

Is outdoor seating an option?
Choose outside or patio dining whenever you can, weather permitting. Nature is known to be beneficial in the healing process, so be sure to indulge. Fresh air can help settle your stomach, and pleasant surroundings can enhance your overall eating experience.

After-Surgery Suggestions

You or your loved one has just experienced cancer surgery, and you probably feel tired and concerned about how you will cope. Read on for the most important things to do after cancer surgery:

1. Ask your doctor to explain the surgery that was performed. Did surgery involve the removal of tissue or organs? Were part of your intestines or colon removed, and will that affect the foods you can or cannot eat?

2. Ask if you need to be on a special diet and about any foods you may or may not be permitted to eat. Find out how long the dietary restrictions will last, either short term or long term.

3. Ask if you need specific vitamins or mineral supplements. Some nutrients must be supplemented after intestinal surgery, and others may help healing.

4. Eat six small meals per day. Small meals, rather than three large meals, are more easily tolerated after surgery. Try to eat half the normal serving size you ate before surgery. See Easy Menus, page 234.

5. Regular bowel movements are important after surgery to help get your system moving again. Talk to your doctor if you have not had a bowel movement within a 24-hour period after surgery.

6. Protein foods are needed for restoring strength and building new cells. Include lots of protein-rich foods (found on page 15) in your diet every day.

7. Vitamin C, calcium, iron, magnesium and potassium are essential healing vitamins and minerals. Make sure that you eat foods that contain these nutrients. For a list of good food sources, turn to page oo.

8. Start walking or doing light activity or simple exercises as soon as you feel up to it. Movement will help restore your appetite and the regularity your healing body needs. Before starting exercise, consult your doctor regarding any restrictions.

Can I have the recipe?

When you find a restaurant dish that appeals to you, request the recipe. Then try it at home and share the new food with family and friends. If others enjoy it, too, add it to your meal planning.

Will I be rushed through the meal?

Getting ready and dining out does require some extra effort. If eating has been taking longer because of discomfort and you're concerned about feeling rushed, call ahead to be sure you can have a leisurely meal. Request a table that isn't on a tight reservation schedule so you can take your time eating and enjoy yourself.

Can I order dessert first?

Yes, indeed! You're dealing with enough stresses related to cancer right now, and you certainly deserve a break. When eating out, choose to dine at a restaurant with a sense of humor and fun. If it's a stuffy place, you may want to select another restaurant that's more comfortable for you. And remember, dessert can offer many calories per bite, so indulge!

Special Diets

Depending on the type of cancer you have and your treatment plan, you may need to follow a special diet at different times during treatment. Check with your doctor or dietitian to clarify any eating restrictions or questions you may have. And follow the advice you've been given to ease discomfort and aid in your healing.

Some dietary restrictions involve terms such as *fiber* and *residue*. Fiber and residue may not be food descriptions you thought much about before your cancer diagnosis. To help aid your understanding, let's define the two words. Sometimes used interchangeably, the terms *fiber* and *residue* do have different meanings.

Fiber describes the type of carbohydrate in a food that isn't broken down before passing through to your stool. Sometimes people refer to fiber as providing roughage or bulk. For a diet to be high in fiber, it must contain foods that supply substantial amounts of fiber, totaling at least 25 to 35 grams daily. Check the Nutrition Facts on packaged food products or check the recipe nutrition information for the fiber content of foods you eat.

Residue is the material left in the colon after digestion. It includes intestinal cells and breakdown products including fiber from the foods you eat. Increasing the amount of fiber you eat will increase residue and, therefore, the amount of stool you produce.

High-fiber foods are also high-residue foods. And low-residue foods are low in fiber. However, some low-fiber foods contain residue, too. For example, milk is low in fiber but high in residue. The components in milk have a considerable effect on stool production, even though milk contains no fiber.

Information about residue is not listed on Nutrition Facts labels, nor is it usually included in recipe nutrition information. However, any recipe in this cookbook that is low residue is listed that way. Check out the information below to find foods that fit your individual dietary needs.

Foods for Special Diets

LOW RESIDUE

Some survivors, particularly those who have had stomach or colon cancer, find that a low-residue diet works well for them. If your doctor or dietitian has recommended following a low-residue diet, follow the suggestions listed below.

These foods are allowed on a low-residue diet:

- **Beef and pork**
- **Chicken and turkey**
- **Fish and seafood**
- **Eggs**
- **Milk, no more than 1 to 2 cups per day**
- **Potatoes**
- **Cooked spinach, asparagus, beets, eggplant, green beans and rutabaga**
- **Canned tomato paste and jarred tomato sauce (no seeds, no onions)**
- **Avocado (limit to 1 serving per day)**

- **Cooked or canned applesauce, fruit cocktail and pears**
- **Nectarines, peaches, cantaloupe and honeydew (limit fresh to 1 serving per day)**
- **Fruit and vegetable juices and purees**
- **Pasta (white) and couscous**
- **White bread and crackers**
- **White-flour pancakes**
- **Cooked oatmeal, cornmeal, farina, hot wheat cereal, and cream of rice cereal**
- **Egg and rice noodles**
- **Plain cakes and cookies**
- **Graham crackers**
- **Saltine crackers**
- **Broth and bouillon**
- **Butter**
- **Gelatin**
- **Italian fruit ice**

Avoid these foods if eating a low-residue diet:

- **No whole grains, coarse wheat and bran**
- **No seeds, nuts, dried fruits and fruit skins**
- **No coconut, popcorn and marmalade**
- **No apples, berries, citrus, pears and plums**
- **No watermelon, pumpkin and prunes**
- **No rice**
- **No peas, carrots, tomatoes and squash**
- **No broccoli, cabbage, cauliflower and rhubarb**
- **No dairy products**

HIGH RESIDUE

If you don't have any restrictions on the amount of residue in your diet, you may eat a high-residue diet and also include the foods listed under "low residue" above.

LOW FIBER

If you have been advised to follow a low-fiber diet, eat only foods containing less than 1 gram of fiber per serving. The amount of fiber in each recipe is included in this book. And you can read the Nutrition Facts labels to determine the fiber content of packaged food products.

Low-fiber foods include white bread, clear broth, clear liquids (tea, carbonated beverages), saltine crackers, fish, eggs, chicken, beef and flavored gelatin to name a few.

HIGH FIBER

To follow a high-fiber diet, the more fiber you eat, the better. Experts recommend at least 25 grams of fiber daily. To get enough fiber each day, be sure to include:

10 servings of whole-grain breads, cereals, bran, rice, pasta and other whole-grain products

5 to 8 servings of vegetables and fruits, especially those with edible skins, seeds and hulls

2 to 3 servings of legumes (dried peas and beans) and nuts for protein

LIQUID DIET

A liquid diet is often prescribed for hospital patients immediately following surgery because it is soothing and easy to digest. It can also be helpful for times when you may be experiencing bouts of nausea, vomiting or diarrhea or when you're having difficulty chewing.

A clear liquid diet is comprised mainly of liquids and provides only about 500 calories per day. For this reason, a liquid diet is a short-term regimen only. Clear liquids do not provide enough calories and nutrients to maintain good health or to aid in long-term healing.

A clear liquid diet includes the following items only:

Tea, clear beverages and carbonated beverages

Clear fruit juices(such as apple and grape)

Broth

Flavored gelatin

No milk or milk beverages

No fruit juices with pulp

Sometimes cancer survivors may require a liquid diet, but it need not be only clear liquids. Check with your doctor or dietitian to see if a liquid diet with the addition of nutritional beverages, blended smoothies or shakes may be appropriate for you to increase calories and nutrients.

NEUTROPENIC DIET

Cancer treatment can affect your immune system. Cancer survivors undergoing either bone marrow transplant or chemotherapy may be at risk for infection when their white blood cell count is below 500 cells per cubic millimeter of blood. If your white blood cell count is too low and you've been placed on a neutropenic diet, omit the following foods from your diet to reduce risk of infection:

No raw or undercooked meat, chicken, pork, fish or shellfish.

No raw eggs (no Caesar salad, homemade ice cream, cookie dough or cake batter). Use pasteurized egg products as a substitute.

No unpasteurized or raw milk products.

No honey, nuts or fruit or vegetable juices.

No raw vegetables or fruits (except peeled, washed, thick-skinned fruits such as cantaloupe, honeydew melon, watermelon, oranges and bananas).

No outdated products (out-of-code, past sell-by or use-by dates) or moldy products.

No aged cheeses (such as Brie, blue, sharp Cheddar, Stilton, feta, Mexican hot cheese and Camembert).

Mind-Body-Spirit Connection to Healing

In conventional medicine, the mind-body connection is not the focus of the treatment. We rely instead on things outside of us, such as medications and surgery, to cure ailments. This is typical of cancer treatment practices today. Complementary, or alternative, medicine or

therapies place more emphasis on using the inside, our thoughts and emotions, as an integral part of healing and overall wellness.

COMPLEMENTARY THERAPIES

Listed below are treatment options that could be tried in addition to your current treatment options. In the United States, 10 percent of all cancer patients will try at least one alternative therapy during the course of their treatment. Some claims of complementary therapies are poorly documented or unproven, but others are supported by years of scientific research. The Office of Alternative Medicine, established almost fifteen years ago, has collected volumes of research data on complementary practices and is helping to establish guidelines for scientific testing for safety and effectiveness of these therapies.

Connecting the brain, the physical body and good health as tools for wellness is easier in many complementary therapies. Many of the therapies listed here began thousands of years ago, in cultures spanning the globe, from Europe to China and India to Egypt. The treatments use herbs, needles or body manipulation as a means to heal ailments. Before you venture out to try them, read on for details about what they are and how they work. If you have questions about blending these therapies with your current medications or cancer treatment plan, be sure to check with your doctor.

ACUPUNCTURE

Part of traditional Chinese medicine, *acupuncture* is an ancient art and science of healing. The word *acupuncture* comes from two Latin words: *acus,* meaning "needles," and *punctura,* meaning "pricking." Like its definition, Chinese acupuncture involves the insertion of needles into specific points on your body.

Based on the belief that energy flows between body organs along channels, or *meridians,* healing occurs when the flow of energy in the entire body is balanced. The energy is called *chi,* or *qi* (pronounced CHEE). Chi changes with your mental, physical and spiritual well-being and is made up of two opposing forces called *yin* (the shady side of the mountain) and *yang* (the sunny side).

Worldwide scientific evidence exists to support that acupuncture is a successful treatment for headaches, lower back pain, angina, dementia and arthritis and for relief of other ailments or imbalances.

AROMATHERAPY

Aromatherapy, or scent therapy, was developed by ancient Egyptians and is the use of "essential oils" to increase relaxation, improve mood and enhance circulation. Essential oils are the concentrated forms of natural oils extracted from petals, leaves, roots, resin, bark, rinds, stalks, stems and seeds of various plants.

After they're extracted, essential oils are applied externally, inhaled or used in compresses or lotions. They are also used in soaps, candles, perfumes, potpourri, bath salts, massage oils, antiseptic solutions, sprays and shampoos.

AYURVEDA

One of the oldest forms of medical practice, *Ayurveda* (pronounced I-YUR-VAYDA) originated in ancient India. It is based on the concept that energy, called *prana,* keeps the mind and body alive. Each of us is made up of five elements: air, water, earth, fire and space. These five elements are organized into three constitutional states called *doshas,* which govern our physical, mental and emotional processes. These doshas are *vata,* representing space and air; *pitta,* for fire and water; and *kapha,* encompassing water and earth. Each of us is a combination of all three doshas, but usually one of them dominates.

Ayurvedic practitioners observe, ask questions about your lifestyle, spirituality and physical health, touch you, and take pulses at different places to determine the diagnosis and assess the status of your doshas, depending upon which elements are out of balance. You are then further categorized based on the dietary changes needed to rebalance your doshas.

Most Ayurvedic remedies are diet-based, using foods, herbs and spices to regain balance by strengthening or weakening the doshas. In addition, other remedies and behavioral changes, such as minerals, gems, yoga postures and breathing, meditation, detoxification processes or hydrotherapy and massages, may be advised to reestablish the elements.

Chemotherapy Considerations

Chemotherapy, the most common type of cancer treatment, affects no two people the same way. Much of what happens depends on how you respond to the treatment, the particular drug or drugs you are taking, the dosage and the type and stage of the cancer.

Consider these suggestions to help make your experience with chemotherapy one that works in the best way for you:

1. Ask your doctor what kind of drugs you are receiving. Ask about potential side effects and interactions that may occur with other medications or foods you eat. Then you'll know what changes you need to make.

2. Raise questions about how the drug is administered and what potential side effects are associated with it. You'll be prepared for how you may feel and the changes your body may experience during and after treatment.

3. Whenever you have nausea, be sure to take the nausea medication provided to you because it generally will help you feel well enough to eat. If the medication isn't helpful, call your doctor right away and discuss alternate medication.

4. Your body is already tired just from having cancer, and chemotherapy adds to that feeling of fatigue. To help ease the tiredness, rest often and try to do some activity every day. More ideas about handling fatigue are provided on page 28.

5. Expect the common side effects of chemotherapy. You will probably experience at least some of the following typical side effects: decreased appetite, mouth sores, dry mouth, changes in the taste of foods and constipation.

6. Vitamin and mineral stores in the body become depleted while you undergo chemotherapy. Ask your doctor if you need to take any nutrient supplements (especially iron, which can help reduce fatigue) or switch from the supplements you regularly take.

Neutropenia occurs when the white blood cell count drops to a dangerously low level. This usually happens about seven to fourteen days after receiving chemotherapy. During this time, you are at higher risk for infections, and you should avoid certain foods. For a list of these foods, see page 20.

BODYWORK

Bodywork is a catchall term for many different techniques that treat ailments and promote relaxation through proper movement, posture, exercise, massage and other body manipulations. Shiatsu and massage are two types of bodywork practiced more commonly in the United States.

Shiatsu, a traditional healing method from Japan, uses a form of acupressure, or finger pressure, on specific body sites to increase circulation and improve energy flow. The technique involves locating *acupoints,* sites on your body specific to certain tissues. Pressure is applied to these points for two to ten minutes until a pulse is felt. Then the pressure is released slowly. Acupressure techniques can be used in physical therapy and in various types of bodywork and massage.

Massage is the manipulation of soft tissues to relieve sore muscles and promote relaxation. It is used to reduce tension, improve circulation, aid in healing injured soft tissues, control pain and promote overall well-being. Massage can stretch tissue, increase your range of motion and reduce certain kinds of swelling.

HERBAL MEDICINE

Herbs come from plants, mainly the leaves, stems, flowers, twigs, roots, seeds, bark, fruit and saps of a variety of different plants. We typically think of herbs as substances that impart flavor to our foods, but some of these herbs also have medicine-like qualities.

In fact, many modern medicines are derived from plants discovered long ago to have medicinal properties. Though herbs can be predecessors to modern medicines, they are not regulated by the Food and Drug Administration (FDA), so use caution when obtaining them. You can buy herbal remedies in the form of capsules, tablets, powders and concentrated liquids (called *tinctures* or *extracts*), and they can be prepared using fresh or dried ingredients and can be steeped or infused, as in making a tea.

For your own safety, experts suggest you purchase prepared herbal medicines from reliable sources, because those grown or concocted yourself may be inconsistent

or contain natural variations that can be toxic. Trained professionals in the fields of botany, Ayurvedic medicine, naturopathy and traditional Chinese medicine can be helpful in selecting the herbs, form and potency that are appropriate for you.

Herbal medicines are usually milder and may act more slowly than conventional medicines. Certain herbs, such as borage, chaparral, coltsfoot, comfrey, Ma Huang (ephedra), germanium and yohimbe should not be used because they are potentially harmful, causing liver disease, rises in blood pressure and kidney damage. Check with your doctor to be sure that the herbs you take don't interact with your medications or treatment regimens.

MEDITATION

Quiet forms of contemplation, mindfulness or meditation have been recognized worldwide for their effectiveness at establishing a sense of peacefulness, inner calm and relaxation. Developed in Eastern cultures, most techniques require closing your eyes and focusing on a single thought, word, image or sound and allowing other thoughts to float away. Traditionally used as a spiritual exercise, meditation has been helpful for people with chronic pain, panic attacks, high blood pressure and respiratory problems such as asthma and emphysema because meditation slows the heart rate and regulates breathing.

NATUROPATHY

Naturopathy originates from the traditions of early European health spas. Emphasizing preventive care, naturopathy takes advantage of your body's own natural healing powers. It avoids many of the traditions of conventional medicine and teaches healthful lifestyle habits. Naturopathic treatments vary by practitioner and encompass many elements, such as massage, physical activity, herbal remedies, natural foods, acupuncture and *hydrotherapy* (water treatments).

YOGA

Yoga is an ancient practice and philosophy first developed and practiced in India. The word *yoga* is derived from the ancient Sanskrit word *yuj,* meaning "union." Yoga is based on balancing the mind, body and spirit by using exercises, ethical beliefs and dietary restrictions.

Many different types of yoga are practiced worldwide. Western versions of yoga typically practiced in the United States include both body positions and movements, called *postures,* and breathing exercises, in addition to dietary practices. The postures, called *asanas,* are used to stretch and strengthen muscles; the breathing exercises, called *pranayama,* help with relaxation and stress relief. Yoga experts advise that you start slowly with basic breathing techniques and simple postures before moving on to the more advanced exercises.

SUMMING IT UP

As you can see, the wide variety of complementary medicines and therapies from different parts of the world focus on different principles. All are available to you as you make the connection between your mind and body and wellness. Be sure to check with your doctor if you have any questions about your conventional medication or treatment plan or about one of these complementary therapies.

Beyond Treatment

Congratulations! You've made it through your treatment and have started to move on with your life. Cancer survivors have told us that treatment effects, particularly fatigue, may last for a period of time after treatment is complete. To minimize fatigue and continue your healing, you may wish to incorporate some basic principles about food and lifestyle that may help as you continue on your healing path.

The ABCs for a Healthy Lifestyle

The new Dietary Guidelines for Americans, developed in May 2000 by the U.S. Departments of Agriculture and Health and Human Services, can help you take action for good health and develop a healthy lifestyle. Three basic messages, or ABCs, of a healthy lifestyle are aiming for fitness, building a healthy base and choosing sensibly.

At first, following all of the ABCs, and in that particular order, may be difficult for some cancer survivors. If so,

survivors may be better served by starting with B, building a healthy base, then incorporating C, choosing sensibly, and returning to A, aiming for fitness, after they are feeling better.

AIMING FOR FITNESS

As you probably know, obesity is linked to many diseases. Carrying extra weight may place you at greater risk for developing high blood pressure, heart disease, certain types of cancer, diabetes, stroke, arthritis and difficult breathing. Choosing a lifestyle that helps you aim for a healthy body weight and an increased level of activity may be helpful for maintaining good health in the long run.

Experts recommend monitoring body weight regularly by stepping on the scale every few weeks. Work with your doctor or dietitian to determine your *Body Mass Index* (BMI), a measure that links your height and weight to potential health risks. If you find you weigh more than you would like to, there is no better time than after treatment to take off excess weight. (During treatment is not a good time to try to lose weight, because your body is concentrating on fighting cancer cells.) But it's best to lose the weight gradually. Aim to lose about 10 percent of your weight in about six months—or about one-half to two pounds per week. Losing weight and maintaining a healthy weight should become part of your everyday lifestyle.

Being physically active on a daily basis can help you take off and keep off weight, strengthen and tone muscles and increase your flexibility. Aim for at least 30 minutes of physical activity daily. You don't have to do it all at the same time. Keep track of the times you go up and down the steps, walk through the parking lot and lift things, such as groceries. All these activities count and add up to your total activity for the day.

BUILDING A HEALTHY BASE

The Food Guide Pyramid on page 00 is a wonderful visual guide to remind you of the variety and amounts of foods you need to rebuild your healthy base. Use plant foods such as fruits, vegetables and grains as the mainstay of your diet. These foods supply much of the carbohydrate energy you need, along with many of the vitamins and minerals.

Plant foods make up the foundation, or base, of the pyramid and should be the focus of eating. Scientific research has shown that whole grains (such as whole wheat and whole-grain oats) and cruciferous vegetables (those in the cabbage family such as broccoli, kale and Brussels sprouts) contain fiber, vitamins, minerals and other natural components that may help prevent disease. Dark green vegetables (including spinach and broccoli) and orange-yellow fruits and vegetables (such as carrots, winter squash, sweet potatoes, cantaloupe and oranges) are rich in antioxidants (vitamins A and C) and folic acid, which are also important for maintaining a healthy body.

To these plant foods, add small amounts of lean cuts of meats, poultry, fish, eggs and low-fat dairy foods and legumes (dried beans and peas) to balance out your diet. Variety is vital to a balanced diet that supplies the nutrients needed for health. Keeping the portions to a reasonable size is key to helping maintain a healthy body weight.

Some of us choose to follow a vegetarian diet for religious, spiritual or cultural reasons. The Food Guide Pyramid can help you balance your diet by emphasizing plant foods (grains, vegetables and fruits) and adding legumes (dried beans and peas), nuts and seeds to provide protein, vitamin E, fiber and carbohydrates.

CHOOSING FOODS SENSIBLY

Fats supply energy. Too much fat supplies more energy than we need. Besides adding to weight gain, some fats, particularly saturated fats from animal sources in the diet, can increase risk of coronary heart disease by raising blood cholesterol levels. Unsaturated fats, however, such as monounsaturated and polyunsaturated fats mainly from plant foods, do not raise blood cholesterol. Experts recommend you choose unsaturated fats over saturated fats.

Reading the Nutrition Facts label on food packages and the nutrition information included with recipes can help you choose foods that are low in saturated fat and cholesterol. Remember too that experts recommend eating no more than 30 percent of calories from fat. To figure that out, keep track by adding up all the grams of fat you ate for the day and multiplying the total by 9 calories per gram to give you FAT CALORIES. Then divide the

FAT CALORIES by the total number of calories you ate for the day. Multiply by 100 to get the number to a final percent. The final number should be less than 30 percent.

Choose beverages and foods that limit your intake of sugars. Limiting sugars helps keep teeth free from decay and helps ensure you're getting enough foods that supply plenty of healthy nutrients, not just sugars and calories. Again, read the Nutrition Facts to determine the amount of sugars in foods and help you select sensible food choices for life. To decrease dietary sugar, limit soft drinks, fruit punch, lemonade, candy and ice cream.

Select foods and prepare foods with less salt. Scientific research shows that we may be able to reduce our risk of developing high blood pressure by consuming foods that are lower in salt and sodium. In the body, sodium helps to control fluid balance and blood pressure. For some individuals, high levels of sodium in the diet can be associated with higher blood pressure. No one knows for sure who will develop high blood pressure, but limiting salt and sodium is recommended for healthy individuals. Look for low-sodium canned soups and vegetables, and go easy on cheese, salty snacks, pickles, olives, mustard and ketchup to decrease the sodium in your diet. Alcoholic beverages are harmful when consumed in large quantities because they can impair judgment and lead to dependency and other health problems. If you drink alcoholic beverages, do so in moderation. More than one drink per day for women or two drinks per day for men can increase risk of auto accidents, high blood pressure, stroke, violence, suicide, birth defects and cancer. Heavy drinkers also run the risk of malnutrition because they often substitute alcoholic drinks for nutritious foods.

Onward and Upward

Aiming for fitness, building a healthy base and choosing sensibly are keys to establishing a healthy lifestyle. From time to time, though, thoughts of cancer returning to your body are bound to be on your mind. Risk of cancer recurrence is highest in the first five years after treatment, so staying in tune with your body and following up with your doctor regularly are important. Even with the sound nutrition and healthy lifestyle practices offered here and throughout this book, no single food or practice can be a guarantee against cancer recurrence.

To feel your best, remember to eat a well-balanced, low-fat diet and drink plenty of water. Be sure to get some exercise every day and continue to do the activities you enjoy. Spend time with people you love and care about. Listen to your body and get plenty of rest, especially when you feel tired. Taking care of yourself is the very best thing to do right now—and for the future as well.

Cranberry Herbal Tea Granita (page 35)

Creamy Seafood Risotto (page 41)

Coping with Side Effects 1

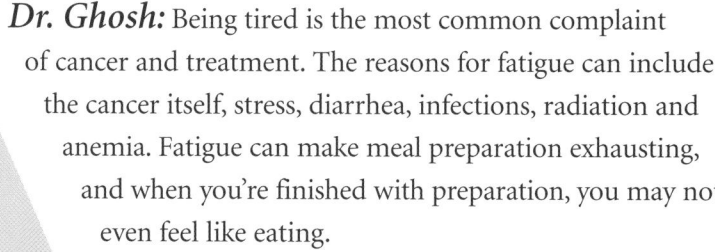

Why am I too tired to eat anything?

Dr. Ghosh: Being tired is the most common complaint of cancer and treatment. The reasons for fatigue can include the cancer itself, stress, diarrhea, infections, radiation and anemia. Fatigue can make meal preparation exhausting, and when you're finished with preparation, you may not even feel like eating.

Make it easy on yourself during the times when you are most fatigued by taking a break from cooking. For easy meals and snacks, keep plenty of time-saving foods on hand.

Here are some tips to overcome fatigue:

Prepare simple meals or snacks, and use time-saving convenience foods whenever possible.

Take iron or vitamin supplements.

Nap during the day and get quality sleep at night.

Invigorate yourself by going for a walk or a swim.

These foods require little or no food preparation and are recommended during times of greatest fatigue:

Fresh fruits and vegetables

Potatoes, especially refrigerated and mixes

Eggs

Canned fruits, vegetables, soups, tuna, legumes, chili and beans

Cereals and grains (bread, bagels, pasta, rice, oatmeal)

Snacks (chips, crackers, popcorn, pretzels)

Bakery items (muffins, pastries, cookies)

Dairy foods (cheese, yogurt, milk)

Beverages (fruit juices, cider, milk, sports drinks, nutritional beverages, lemonade, herbal teas, bottled water)

"Yogurt and fortified cereal team up to make this protein-loaded, high-iron smoothie enjoyable any time you need an extra energy boost." —DR. GHOSH

Berry-Banana Smoothie

2 servings (1 cup each)   PREP: 8 min

1 cup vanilla, plain, strawberry or raspberry yogurt

3/4 cup Cheerios® or another round oat cereal

1/2 cup fresh strawberry halves or raspberries or frozen strawberries

1/2 cup milk

1 to 2 tablespoons sugar

1/2 banana, sliced

1 Place all ingredients in blender. Cover and blend on high speed 10 seconds; stop blender to scrape sides. Cover and blend about 20 seconds longer or until smooth.

2 Pour mixture into glasses. Serve immediately.

High in calcium, iron, vitamin C and folic acid; good source of fiber

1 **SERVING:** Calories 255 (Calories from Fat 25); Fat 3g (Saturated 2g); Cholesterol 10mg; Sodium 210mg; Potassium 550mg; Carbohydrate 51g (Dietary Fiber 3g); Protein 9g % **Daily Value:** Vitamin A 8%; Vitamin C 46%; Calcium 28%; Iron 18%; Folic Acid 24%; Magnesium 12% **Diet Exchanges:** 2 1/2 Fruit, 1 Skim Milk

Why does food have a metallic taste?

Dr. Ghosh: Unfortunately, chemotherapy, radiation treatments and even medications can change the flavor of foods and beverages in your mouth. Chemotherapy commonly causes a bitter, metallic taste especially when eating high-protein foods like meats. Dry mouth may also lead to changes in taste.

To improve the taste of your food, try these hints:

Rev up your taste buds by eating strong-flavored or spicy foods. Spice and strong flavors hide "off" tastes, too.

Smell your food before eating to entice your appetite. Taste and smell are so closely linked that much of what you taste is actually what you smell. And foods that smell good will generally taste good to you, too.

Dazzle your taste buds by eating either hot food or cold food. Skip the just-warm food because it may taste blah.

Refrain from using flatware that contains silver. Opt for stainless steel or plastic utensils instead.

Rinse your mouth frequently.

Brush your teeth often.

Drink cool liquids.

Suck on sour hard candy.

Boost the flavor of foods by adding sugar, herbs, wine, lemon or pepper.

"The citrus flavors along with herbs and spices in the following recipe may help you to disguise a metallic taste in your mouth." —DR. GHOSH

Spicy Citrus Chicken

6 servings   PREP: 15 min • MARINATE: 3 hr • BAKE: 45 min

6 boneless, skinless chicken breast halves (about 1 3/4 pounds)

1/2 cup unsweetened grape juice or red wine

1 tablespoon grated orange peel

1/2 cup orange juice

1 tablespoon grated lemon peel

1/2 cup lemon juice

2 tablespoons chopped fresh cilantro

1 1/2 teaspoons chopped fresh or 1/2 teaspoon dried oregano leaves

1 teaspoon ground cumin

1/2 teaspoon salt

1/4 teaspoon crushed red pepper

2 medium green onions, chopped (2 tablespoons)

Orange slices, if desired

1 Place chicken in shallow glass or plastic dish. Mix remaining ingredients except orange slices; pour over chicken. Cover and refrigerate at least 3 hours but no longer than 24 hours.

2 Heat oven to 375°. Spray rack in shallow roasting pan with cooking spray. Remove chicken from marinade; place on rack. Reserve marinade. Bake uncovered 35 to 45 minutes, brushing with marinade every 15 minutes, until juice of chicken is no longer pink when centers of thickest pieces are cut. Discard any remaining marinade. Serve with orange slices.

Low fiber

1 SERVING: Calories 165 (Calories from Fat 35); Fat 4g (Saturated 1g); Cholesterol 75mg; Sodium 560mg; Potassium 280mg; Carbohydrate 5g (Dietary Fiber 0g); Protein 27g % Daily Value: Vitamin A 0%; Vitamin C 8%; Calcium 2%; Iron 6%; Folic Acid 2%; Magnesium 6% Diet Exchanges: 4 Very-Lean Meat, 1 Vegetable

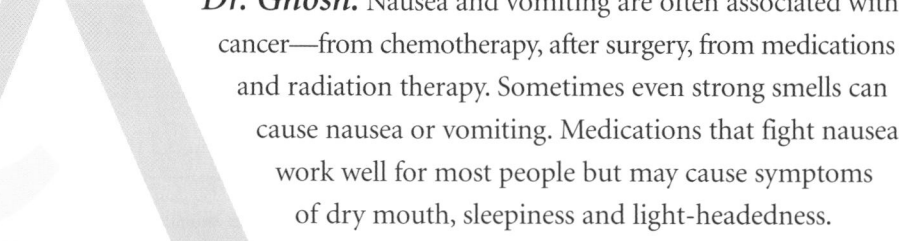

Why do I feel nauseated all the time?

Dr. Ghosh: Nausea and vomiting are often associated with cancer—from chemotherapy, after surgery, from medications and radiation therapy. Sometimes even strong smells can cause nausea or vomiting. Medications that fight nausea work well for most people but may cause symptoms of dry mouth, sleepiness and light-headedness.

Here are some helpful hints to relieve nausea:

Use a kitchen fan or open the windows when cooking.

Keep pans covered to reduce cooking odors. Eat small, frequent meals slowly.

Serve food cold because cold foods have less of an aroma.

Avoid spicy, greasy or rich foods.

Choose dry, salty foods such as dry toast, crackers and pretzels.

Choose sugar-sweetened beverages over sugar-free drinks, because sugar slows digestion and doesn't tend to cause nausea.

Drink chilled beverages because they go down easier.

Consume foods separate from beverages by at least an hour, if you are not troubled by dry mouth.

Sit up or stay up for at least 90 minutes after eating.

Specific foods that may help include clear liquids, carbonated drinks, yogurt, sherbet, angel food cake, hot wheat cereal, rice, oatmeal, boiled potatoes, noodles, canned peaches or other soft fruits and vegetables.

"The following cool drink, which contains a combination of beverages to replenish needed nutrients, may help ease feelings of nausea."   —Dr. Ghosh

Refreshing Lemon-lime Drink

8 servings (1/2 cup each)   PREP: 5 min

1 can (12 ounces) frozen limeade or lemonade concentrate, thawed

1 cup chilled lime- or lemon-flavored sports drink

1 can (12 ounces) lemon-lime soda pop, chilled

1 Mix limeade concentrate and sports drink in large pitcher.

2 Just before serving, add soda pop.

Low fiber

1 SERVING: Calories 110 (Calories from Fat 0); Fat 0g (Saturated 0g); Cholesterol 0mg; Sodium 20mg; Potassium 30mg; Carbohydrate 28g (Dietary Fiber 0g); Protein 0g **% Daily Value:** Vitamin A 0%; Vitamin C 12%; Calcium 0%; Iron 0%; Folic Acid 0%; Magnesium 0%
Diet Exchanges: 2 Fruit

Why is my mouth always dry?

Dr. Ghosh: Dry mouth can be the result of chemotherapy, certain medications or radiation treatment. Neglecting symptoms of dry mouth can lead to developing painful mouth sores, dental problems and changes in taste sensation.

To improve dry mouth:

Drink at least eight to ten glasses of fluid each day.

Avoid citrus fruits and dry foods.

Rinse your mouth every few hours.

Suck on hard candy, especially sour candy.

Keep your lips moist.

Try very sour or very sweet foods and beverages, such as lemonade or cranberry juice; these foods will cause more saliva to flow. (If you have a tender mouth or sore throat, though, sweet or sour foods can make that worse.)

"Try this zesty cranberry ice to whet your whistle and lessen symptoms of dry mouth." —Dr. Ghosh

Cranberry Herbal Tea Granita

8 servings PREP: 15 min · FREEZE: 5 hr · STAND: 20 min

5 whole cloves

1 slice orange

2 cups water

1/2 cup sugar

1 stick cinnamon

3 tea bags red zesty herbal tea flavored with hibiscus, rose hips and lemongrass

1 1/2 cups cranberry juice cocktail

1 1/2 cups pineapple juice

Fresh fruit, if desired

Thin almond wafer cookies, if desired

1 Insert cloves into peel of orange slice. Heat water, sugar, cinnamon and orange slice to boiling in 2-quart saucepan, stirring occasionally; remove from heat. Add tea bags; cover and let steep 5 minutes. Remove tea bags, cinnamon stick and orange slice.

2 Stir cranberry and pineapple juices into tea. Pour into 2-quart nonmetal bowl or square baking dish, 8 × 8 × 2 inches. Cover and freeze about 2 hours or until partially frozen. Stir with fork or wire whisk. Cover and freeze 3 hours or overnight.

3 Remove granita from freezer 20 minutes before serving. Scrape surface with fork and spoon into glasses. Garnish with fruit and cookies.

High in vitamin C; low fiber

1 SERVING: Calories 145 (Calories from Fat 0); Fat 0g (Saturated 0g); Cholesterol 0mg; Sodium 5mg; Potassium 110mg; Carbohydrate 36g (Dietary Fiber 0g); Protein 0g % Daily Value: Vitamin A 0%; Vitamin C 36%; Calcium 2%; Iron 2%; Folic Acid 4%; Magnesium 2% Diet Exchanges: 2 1/2 Fruit

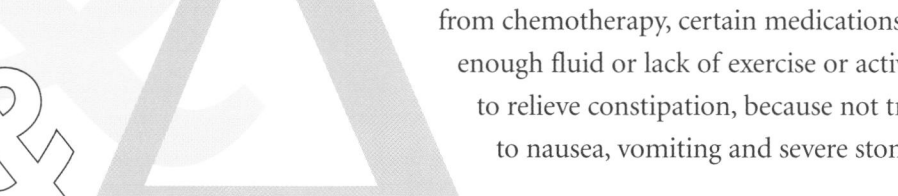

Why am I constipated?

Dr. Ghosh: Constipation can be an unwanted side effect from chemotherapy, certain medications, not drinking enough fluid or lack of exercise or activity. It is crucial to relieve constipation, because not treating it can lead to nausea, vomiting and severe stomach pain.

To avoid or relieve constipation:

Eat plenty of fiber, at least 25 to 35 grams per day. High-fiber choices include whole-grain cereals and breads, fruits (fresh, dried or canned), vegetables (fresh, frozen or cooked) and legumes (dried peas and beans).

Drink eight to ten glasses of water daily.

Exercise.

Drink a hot beverage about half an hour before your usual bowel movement time.

Stool softeners and laxatives are available and sometimes necessary, but it's important to try foods, beverages and exercise first. Save the stool softeners and laxatives to use as a last resort, and take them only with the approval of your doctor.

"Try this high-fiber recipe, along with a glass of water, to help ease constipation. You can make this the day before and simply warm it before serving. It's delicious hot or cold." —Dr. Ghosh

Hot Fruit Compote

10 servings   PREP: 15 min   ·   BAKE: 45 min

1 can (29 ounces) pear halves in heavy syrup

1 can (29 ounces) peach halves in heavy syrup

1 can (20 ounces) pineapple chunks in juice

1/2 cup dried apricots

1/2 cup dried prunes

1/2 cup dried cherries or raisins

2 tablespoons packed brown sugar

1/4 cup brandy, if desired

1/2 teaspoon ground cinnamon

1/4 teaspoon ground nutmeg

1/2 cup slivered almonds, if desired

1 Heat oven to 375°. Drain canned fruits, reserving syrup and juice. Mix syrup and juice; set aside. Cut pears and peaches into bite-size pieces. Layer canned and dried fruits in 3-quart casserole or rectangular baking dish, 13 × 9 × 2 inches.

2 Mix brown sugar and brandy; pour over fruit. (If not using brandy, sprinkle brown sugar over fruit.) Pour juice mixture over fruit just until fruit is covered; discard remaining juice mixture. Sprinkle cinnamon, nutmeg and almonds over fruit.

3 Bake uncovered about 45 minutes or until bubbly. Serve warm or cool.

High in potassium and vitamin A; good source of fiber

1 **SERVING:** Calories 220 (Calories from Fat 0); Fat 0g (Saturated 0g); Cholesterol 0mg; Sodium 15mg; Potassium 410mg; Carbohydrate 58g (Dietary Fiber 4g); Protein 1g % **Daily Value:** Vitamin A 20%; Vitamin C 6%; Calcium 2%; Iron 6%; Folic Acid 2%; Magnesium 6% **Diet Exchanges:** 3 1/2 Fruit

Why do I have diarrhea?

Dr. Ghosh: Radiation and chemotherapy are common causes of diarrhea. And diarrhea causes an excess loss of fluids and nutrients.

There are medications available to treat diarrhea, but here are some things to try on your own:

Try sports drinks, broths or Pedialyte® to replenish lost fluid and electrolytes. Avoid tea, coffee and prune juice.

Take a vitamin and mineral supplement that includes vitamins A, B_{12}, E and K, as well as folic acid.

Eat frequent, small meals that are low in fat and high in carbohydrates and protein.

Avoid milk and milk-based foods because the sugar in milk can stimulate diarrhea.

Eat applesauce.

As diarrhea ends, add these foods to your diet: rice, noodles, potatoes, white bread, yogurt, cottage cheese, hot wheat cereal, eggs, creamy peanut butter, canned peeled fruit, well-cooked vegetables, skinned chicken or turkey, lean beef and fish.

Slowly add small amounts of fiber from fruits and grains.

"This soup is great for breakfast or just about any time. I normally recommend avoiding milk for diarrhea, but in this recipe the milk is added to bananas and rice, which makes it an effective remedy for diarrhea."   —Dr. Ghosh

Milk and Rice "Soup"

4 servings   PREP: 20 min   •   STAND: 10 min

1 cup regular long-grain rice

2 cups water

2 bananas

2 1/2 cups fat-free (skim) milk

2 tablespoons sugar

1 Heat rice and water to boiling in 2-quart saucepan; reduce heat to low. Cover and simmer about 15 minutes or until water is absorbed and rice is tender. Let stand about 10 minutes or until cool enough to eat, or refrigerate.

2 Completely mash bananas in medium bowl. Stir in cooked rice, milk and sugar. Serve immediately. Cover and refrigerate remaining soup.

High in calcium, folic acid and potassium

1 SERVING: Calories 300 (Calories from Fat 10); Fat 1g (Saturated 0g); Cholesterol 5mg; Sodium 80mg; Potassium 540mg; Carbohydrate 64g (Dietary Fiber 2g); Protein 10g % Daily Value: Vitamin A 6%; Vitamin C 10%; Calcium 20%; Iron 10%; Folic Acid 24%; Magnesium 12% Diet Exchanges: 1 Starch, 1 Skim Milk, 2 Fruit

How can I eat with mouth sores?

Dr. Ghosh: Mouth sores can be a troublesome side effect of chemotherapy or radiation therapy and usually occur a few days after treatment. The inside of the mouth can become raw and ulcerated, making eating and swallowing difficult. If pain from mouth sores becomes unbearable, discuss with your doctor because there are medications that may help. You may also try oral topical pain medications such as Orabase®. Rinse your mouth after meals and at bedtime with 8 ounces warm water mixed with 1 teaspoon salt; brush teeth with a soft toothbrush at least twice a day.

Be sure to discuss your mouth sores with your doctor and try the following suggestions:

Omit hard, rough-textured or irritating foods.

Drink nutritional energy beverages, such as Carnation® Instant Breakfast® energy drink, Boost®, or Ensure®.

Avoid spicy or peppery foods.

Avoid citrus foods such as tomatoes, oranges, grapefruit and lemons because of their high acid content.

Eat small, high-calorie, high-protein meals frequently.

Eat only room-temperature foods, not hot or cold foods.

Pour liquids over foods to soften them (milk over toast, for example).

Use buttermilk as a mouthwash to soothe irritations.

Eat soft, easy-to-swallow foods: shakes; bananas; applesauce; watermelon and other soft fruits; yogurt; cottage cheese; mashed potatoes; pasta; noodles; custard; puddings; gelatins; scrambled eggs; oatmeal or other cooked cereals; mashed sweet potatoes, peas or carrots; pureed meats.

Use a straw to drink liquids.

"Try this soft, easy-on-your-mouth risotto. It's an Italian staple and is a great source of many nutrients, like iron, folic acid and potassium." —Dr. Ghosh

Creamy Seafood Risotto

6 servings PREP: 10 min · COOK: 20 min

2 tablespoons olive or
vegetable oil

8 ounces uncooked medium
shrimp (thawed if frozen),
peeled and deveined

1 can (14 1/2 ounces) whole
tomatoes, undrained

1/4 cup whole milk

1/4 cup butter or margarine

1 small onion, chopped
(1/4 cup)

2 cups uncooked Arborio rice

1 cup dry white wine,
water or chicken broth

1/4 teaspoon salt

1/4 teaspoon ground
red pepper (cayenne),
if desired

4 cups chicken broth

2 tablespoons chopped
fresh arugula or spinach

1/2 cup grated Parmesan
cheese

1 Heat oil in 12-inch skillet over medium heat. Cook shrimp in oil 2 to 3 minutes, stirring frequently, until shrimp are pink and firm. Place shrimp, tomatoes, and milk in food processor or blender. Cover and process about 1 minute or until smooth. (If you are up to chewing the shrimp, leave them whole and blend just the tomatoes and milk together in food processor.)

2 Melt butter in 3-quart saucepan over medium heat. Cook onion in butter about 5 minutes, stirring occasionally, until tender. Stir in rice. Cook about 5 minutes, stirring frequently, until edges of rice kernels are translucent.

3 Stir in wine, salt and red pepper. Heat to boiling; reduce heat. Simmer uncovered 10 minutes, stirring occasionally. Stir in broth. Cook over low heat 12 to 14 minutes, stirring occasionally, until liquid is absorbed.

4 Stir in shrimp and tomato mixture and arugula. Cook 3 minutes. Stir in cheese. Serve immediately.

High in iron and folic acid

1 SERVING: Calories 430 (Calories from Fat 135); Fat 15g (Saturated 7g); Cholesterol 80mg; Sodium 1090mg; Potassium 500mg; Carbohydrate 59g (Dietary Fiber 2g); Protein 17g **% Daily Value:** Vitamin A 14%; Vitamin C 10%; Calcium 14%; Iron 22%; Folic Acid 30%; Magnesium 12% **Diet Exchanges:** 4 Starch, 1 Medium-Fat Meat, 1 Fat

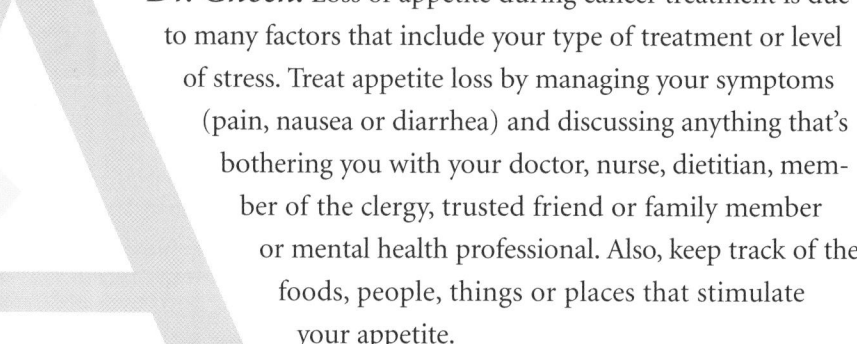

How come I'm not hungry?

Dr. Ghosh: Loss of appetite during cancer treatment is due to many factors that include your type of treatment or level of stress. Treat appetite loss by managing your symptoms (pain, nausea or diarrhea) and discussing anything that's bothering you with your doctor, nurse, dietitian, member of the clergy, trusted friend or family member or mental health professional. Also, keep track of the foods, people, things or places that stimulate your appetite.

Your doctor can prescribe medications that can improve appetite, but try these suggestions to overcome lack of hunger first:

Eat small, frequent meals.

Choose foods high in protein and calories, such as shakes, custards and nutritional beverages (Boost® or Carnation® Instant Breakfast®).

If you crave a particular food, eat it.

Eat whenever you're hungry, no matter what time of day.

Drink plenty of liquids; eight to ten glasses daily are recommended.

Make meals and your eating environment attractive by playing soft music and dimming the lights.

Keep easy snacks on hand to enjoy often, even at bedtime. It's important to eat whenever you feel up to it. Good choices are cheese and crackers, pudding, yogurt, fruit, raisins, muffins and other breads, cereal, nuts and popcorn.

"Keep this easy cereal snack mix that's loaded with nuts and dried fruit on hand. Munch on small amounts often, even if you're not feeling too hungry." —Dr. Ghosh

Crunchy Fruit Snack Mix

14 servings (1/2 cup each)   PREP: 15 min   ·   BAKE: 15 min   ·   COOL: 30 min

4 cups Total® Raisin Bran, Total® Corn Flakes, Whole Grain Total®, or other wheat or corn flake cereal

1/3 cup sliced almonds

1 package (8 ounces) mixed dried fruit (1 1/2 cups), cut into 1/2-inch pieces

1/4 cup packed brown sugar

2 tablespoons butter or margarine

2 teaspoons ground cinnamon

1 teaspoon ground ginger

1 Heat oven to 300°. Place cereal, almonds and fruit in large bowl. Heat brown sugar and butter in 1-quart saucepan over low heat, stirring occasionally, until butter is melted. Stir in cinnamon and ginger.

2 Pour sugar mixture over cereal mixture; toss until evenly coated. Spread in ungreased jelly roll pan, 15 1/2 × 10 1/2 × 1 inch.

3 Bake 15 minutes, stirring twice. Cool 30 minutes. Store in airtight container at room temperature.

High in iron and folic acid; good source of fiber

1 SERVING: Calories 130 (Calories from Fat 25); Fat 3g (Saturated 1g); Cholesterol 5mg; Sodium 85mg; Potassium 240mg; Carbohydrate 27g (Dietary Fiber 3g); Protein 2g **% Daily Value:** Vitamin A 14%; Vitamin C 0%; Calcium 8%; Iron 32%; Folic Acid 28%; Magnesium 6% **Diet Exchanges:** 1 Starch, 1 Fruit

Why do I have so much heartburn?

Dr. Ghosh: Heartburn can be a complication of radiation therapy, surgery, chemotherapy and excessive stress. Heartburn causes symptoms of nausea, vomiting, pain, loss of appetite, bloating, acid reflux and belching. Your doctor can prescribe antibiotics, antacids and medications that may lessen your symptoms.

You can try consuming milk, yogurt or rice for some relief, or follow the list of suggestions below:

Avoid large meals, and refrain from lying down after meals.

Avoid eating within three hours of retiring.

No cigarette smoking or alcoholic beverages.

No caffeine-containing foods or beverages.

No spices, especially black and red peppers.

No citrus fruits, juices or soft drinks.

Avoid peppermint, chocolate and high-fat foods (fried or greasy items).

"The Milk and Rice 'Soup' on page 39 can be helpful for heartburn. Or try this ancient Indian recipe to help lessen stomach discomfort. If spicy foods are bothersome, reduce the amount of onion, allspice and dried chili, or omit them altogether." —Dr. Ghosh

Lentil-Rice Casserole

6 servings PREP: 10 min • COOK: 25 min

1 tablespoon vegetable oil

1 small onion, chopped (1/4 cup)

1 teaspoon grated gingerroot

1 cup regular long-grain rice

1 cup dried red lentils (8 ounces), sorted and rinsed

6 cups boiling water

1 tablespoon ground turmeric

1 teaspoon salt

2 tablespoons safflower or vegetable oil

2 teaspoons whole allspice

1 dried chili

1 dried bay leaf

1 teaspoon sugar

3 tablespoons butter or margarine, cut up

1 Heat vegetable oil in 2-quart saucepan over medium-high heat. Cook onion and gingerroot in oil 2 to 3 minutes, stirring occasionally, until onion is crisp-tender. Stir in rice and lentils. Cook about 3 minutes, stirring frequently, until rice is browned.

2 Reduce heat to medium. Gradually stir in boiling water. Stir in turmeric and salt. Cover and simmer 15 to 20 minutes, stirring occasionally, until rice and lentils are tender.

3 Heat safflower oil in 12-inch skillet over medium-high heat. Heat allspice, chili and bay leaf in oil 1 to 2 minutes, stirring frequently, until allspice pops. Stir in rice and lentil mixture. Stir in sugar. Cook about 5 minutes longer or until heated. Just before serving, stir in butter. Serve casserole with the chili and bay leaf left in, but remember not to eat them.

High in iron; excellent source of fiber

1 **SERVING:** Calories 300 (Calories from Fat 100); Fat 11g (Saturated 3g); Cholesterol 10mg; Sodium 420mg; Potassium 400mg; Carbohydrate 47g (Dietary Fiber 8g); Protein 11g % **Daily Value:** Vitamin A 2%; Vitamin C 2%; Calcium 2%; Iron 24%; Folic Acid 54%; Magnesium 12% **Diet Exchanges:** 3 Starch, 1 1/2 Fat

Why does it hurt when I swallow?

Dr. Ghosh: Having difficulty swallowing foods can sometimes feel like foods are sticking in your throat.

If you experience pain or difficulty swallowing, follow these dietary modifications:

Choose soft or semisolid foods because they are easier to swallow.

Thicken liquids with cornstarch or powdered milk so they go down easier. Eat mashed potatoes or peas.

Eat small, frequent meals at room temperature.

Avoid spicy, acidic or hard, coarse foods.

Sit up and concentrate on coordinating your breathing and swallowing. Allow one to two minutes between each bite.

Avoid talking while chewing and swallowing.

"Easy to eat, these tasty potatoes go down easily, even when chewing and swallowing become a chore. If garlic bothers you, omit it from the recipe." —Dr. Ghosh

Roasted Garlic Mashed Potatoes

5 servings PREP: 10 min • BAKE/COOK: 30 min

1 bulb of garlic

6 medium red or white potatoes (2 pounds)

1 medium sweet potato or yam

1/3 to 1/2 cup milk

1/4 cup butter or margarine, softened

1/2 teaspoon salt

1/4 teaspoon pepper

1 Heat oven to 350°. Peel paperlike skin from garlic bulb, leaving just enough to hold cloves of garlic together. Cut 1/4-inch slice from top of bulb to expose cloves. Place cut side up on 12-inch square of aluminum foil; wrap securely in foil. Place in pie plate or shallow baking pan. Bake about 30 minutes or until garlic is tender when pierced with toothpick or fork. Let stand until cool enough to handle.

2 While garlic is baking, place red or white potatoes and sweet potato in 3-quart saucepan. Add enough water to cover potatoes. Heat to boiling; reduce heat. Cover and simmer 20 to 25 minutes or until tender; drain.

3 Peel sweet potato; leave skins on red or white potatoes if desired. Gently squeeze soft garlic out of cloves into potatoes. Mash potatoes and garlic in pan until no lumps remain. Add milk in small amounts, mashing after each addition.

4 Add butter, salt and pepper. Mash vigorously until light and fluffy. (If running low on energy, blend all ingredients in a food processor.)

High in potassium and good source of fiber

---

1 SERVING: Calories 230 (Calories from Fat 70); Fat 8g (Saturated 5g); Cholesterol 20mg; Sodium 370mg; Potassium 710mg; Carbohydrate 40g (Dietary Fiber 4g); Protein 4g **% Daily Value:** Vitamin A 100%; Vitamin C 24%; Calcium 6%; Iron 8%; Folic Acid 6%; Magnesium 6% **Diet Exchanges:** 1 Starch, 1 Fruit, 1/2 Fat

Key to Common Side Effects

During treatment, the four most common side effects experienced are nausea, mouth sores, constipation and diarrhea. Listed below are the recipes in this cookbook that are most helpful for soothing each of these side effects. If there is a particular ingredient in any of the recipes that is bothersome to you, just leave it out.

n Nausea

Baking Powder Biscuits *(page 68)*

Berry-Banana Smoothie *(page 29)*

Blueberry Brunch Cake *(page 66)*

Cantaloupe and Chicken Salad *(page 120)*

Chicken Soup with Homemade Noodles *(page 152)*

Cinnamon-Raisin Morning Mix *(page 59)*

Citrus-Peach Smoothie *(page 103)*

Cranberry Herbal Tea Granita *(page 35)*

Creamy Caramel Dip with Fruit *(page 100)*

Easy Brown Bread *(page 63)*

Easy Lemon Bars *(page 221)*

Extra-Easy Baked Ziti *(page 162)*

Fresh Salsa *(page 98)*

Fresh Spinach and New Potato Frittata *(page 177)*

Fruit Parfaits *(page 60)*

Grilled Marinated Vegetables *(page 202)*

Layered Chicken Salad *(page 143)*

Macaroni Pasta "Soup" *(page 133)*

Orange-Pineapple Fruit Salad *(page 215)*

Oven-Fried Potato Wedges *(page 82)*

Raspberry-Banana Gelatin Dessert *(page 227)*

Refreshing Lemon-lime Drink *(page 33)*

Roasted Vegetable Dip *(page 80)*

Rosalie's Orange Butter Cookies *(page 224)*

Sugar 'n Spice Green Tea *(page 107)*

m Mouth Sores

Acorn Squash and Apple Soup *(page 175)*

Baked Custard *(page 232)*

Barley-Beef Stew *(page 196)*

Beef-Vegetable Soup *(page 158)*

Berry-Banana Smoothie *(page 29)*

Blueberry Breakfast Bake *(page 56)*

Chai Tea *(page 108)*

Cheesy Vegetable Soup *(page 176)*

Chicken Soup with Homemade Noodles *(page 152)*

Cinnamon Apples *(page 72)*

Cranberry Herbal Tea Granita *(page 35)*

Cream of Broccoli Soup *(page 134)*

Creamy Seafood Risotto *(page 41)*

Easy Creamed Vegetables *(page 203)*

Easy Lemon Bars *(page 221)*

Macaroni Pasta "Soup" *(page 133)*

Mashed Potatoes *(page 205)*

Milk and Rice "Soup" *(page 39)*

Orange-Cream Frosty *(page 226)*

Poached Eggs in Milk *(page 53)*

Raspberry-Banana Gelatin Dessert *(page 227)*

Rice Pudding *(page 233)*

Roasted Garlic Mashed Potatoes *(page 47)*

Sugar 'n Spice Green Tea *(page 107)*

Watermelon-Kiwi-Banana Smoothie *(page 104)*

Diarrhea

Constipation

Country Eggs in Tortilla Cups (Page 52)

Energy-Boosting Breakfasts

2

Country Eggs in Tortilla Cups

4 servings PREP: 10 min • BAKE: 10 min • COOK: 10 min

A NOTE *from* **DR. GHOSH**

The eggs and potatoes are good sources of iron. Try eating an orange, kiwifruit or other food high in vitamin C with this recipe to help you more easily absorb the iron.

4 flour tortillas (6 inches in diameter)

Cooking spray

2 cups frozen Southern-style hash brown potatoes

1/4 cup chopped green bell pepper

3 eggs or 1 cup fat-free, cholesterol-free egg product

1/4 cup milk

1/4 teaspoon salt

3/4 cup shredded Cheddar cheese (3 ounces)

1/4 cup sour cream

Salsa, if desired

1 Heat oven to 400°. Turn four 6-ounce custard cups upside down onto cookie sheet. Spray both sides of each tortilla lightly with cooking spray. Place tortilla over each cup, gently pressing edges toward cup. Bake 8 to 10 minutes or until light golden brown. Remove tortillas from cups; place upright on serving plates.

2 Spray 8- or 10-inch nonstick skillet with cooking spray; heat over medium heat. Cook potatoes and bell pepper in skillet about 5 minutes, stirring occasionally, until potatoes are light brown. Mix eggs, milk and salt; stir into potatoes. Cook about 3 minutes, stirring occasionally, until eggs are almost set.

3 Spoon one-fourth of the egg mixture into each tortilla cup. Top with cheese and sour cream. Serve immediately with salsa.

High in calcium; good source of fiber

1 SERVING: Calories 255 (Calories from Fat 70); Fat 8g (Saturated 4g); Cholesterol 20mg; Sodium 720mg; Potassium 480mg; Carbohydrate 36g (Dietary Fiber 3g); Protein 13g **% Daily Value:** Vitamin A 10%; Vitamin C 12%; Calcium 14%; Iron 12%; Folic Acid 10%; Magnesium 10% **Diet Exchanges:** 2 Starch, 1 Medium-Fat Meat, 1 Vegetable

"When I have mouth sores, I use chopped low-acid tomatoes and no green peppers. When I don't have mouth sores, I eat salsa because that's what makes these eggs taste 'normal.'"

—ANNE R.

Carol N. *Shares* her Recipe

"To keep on keeping on, I had to act like a well person. Even when I didn't feel like it, I got out of bed, showered, got dressed, and smiled. Eating soft foods, like these poached eggs, was a big comfort, and it helped when my mouth was so sore from chemo."

Poached Eggs in Milk

2 servings   PREP: 10 min • COOK: 5 min

1 1/2 cups milk

4 eggs

4 slices bread

1 to 2 tablespoons butter or margarine

1 Heat milk to boiling in 8-inch skillet over medium-high heat; reduce heat so milk is simmering.

2 Break each egg into custard cup or saucer. Carefully slip egg into milk. Cook about 5 minutes or until whites and yolks are firm and not runny.

3 While eggs are cooking, lightly toast bread. Spread butter on toast; break into bite-size pieces into individual bowls. Remove eggs from milk using slotted spoon and place on toast. Pour milk over toast to soften.

FOOD *for* THOUGHT

An important source of calories and protein, eggs and egg yolks are great as sandwich spreads and in salads, dressings and casseroles.

High in calcium, vitamin C and folic acid; low fiber

1 SERVING: Calories 425 (Calories from Fat 200); Fat 22g (Saturated 9g); Cholesterol 450mg; Sodium 520mg; Potassium 470mg; Carbohydrate 35g (Dietary Fiber 1g); Protein 23g % Daily Value: Vitamin A 22%; Vitamin C 0%; Calcium 32%; Iron 16%; Folic Acid 24%; Magnesium 12% Diet Exchanges: 1 1/2 Starch, 1 1/2 High-Fat Meat, 1 Skim Milk, 1 1/2 Fat

Cheesy Ham and Asparagus Bake

8 servings PREP: 20 min • BAKE: 25 min • STAND: 5 min

A NOTE *from*
DR. GHOSH

Loaded with calcium from the cheese and milk, this recipe offers important benefits for cancer healing. Calcium also helps to prevent osteoporosis, the brittle bone disease that often affects us as we age.

1 1/2 cups chopped fully cooked ham

1 medium onion, chopped (1/2 cup)

1/4 cup chopped bell pepper

1 package (10 ounces) frozen asparagus or broccoli cuts

8 eggs or 2 cups fat-free, cholesterol-free egg product

2 cups milk

1 cup all-purpose flour

1/4 cup grated Parmesan cheese

1/2 teaspoon salt

1/2 teaspoon pepper

1/2 teaspoon dried tarragon leaves

1 cup shredded Cheddar cheese (4 ounces)

1 Heat oven to 425°. Generously grease bottom and sides of rectangular baking dish, 13 × 9 × 2 inches, with shortening. Sprinkle ham, onion, bell pepper and asparagus in baking dish.

2 Beat eggs, milk, flour, Parmesan cheese, salt, pepper and tarragon with fork or wire whisk in medium bowl until smooth; pour over ham mixture.

3 Bake uncovered about 20 minutes or until knife inserted in center comes out clean. Sprinkle with Cheddar cheese. Bake 3 to 5 minutes or until cheese is melted. Let stand 5 minutes before cutting.

High in calcium, vitamin A and folic acid; low fiber

1 **SERVING:** Calories 295 (Calories from Fat 135); Fat 15g (Saturated 7g); Cholesterol 250mg; Sodium 780mg; Potassium 390mg; Carbohydrate 19g (Dietary Fiber 1g); Protein 22g % **Daily Value:** Vitamin A 18%; Vitamin C 10%; Calcium 24%; Iron 12%; Folic Acid 22%; Magnesium 8 % **Diet Exchanges:** 1 1/2 Medium-Fat Meat, 1 Vegetable, 1 Skim Milk, 1 Fat

"I sauté green peppers and onions in butter before adding them to recipes. This helps minimize the acid and makes them less bothersome for both mouth sores and gas in the intestine."

—ANNE R.

Cheesy Ham and Asparagus Bake

Blueberry Breakfast Bake

8 servings PREP: 10 min • CHILL: 8 hr • BAKE: 1 hr

8 slices white bread, cut into 1-inch pieces (6 cups)

1 package (8 ounces) reduced-fat cream cheese (Neufchâtel), chilled and cut into 1/2-inch pieces

1 cup fresh or frozen (thawed and drained) blueberries

8 eggs or 2 cups fat-free, cholesterol-free egg product

1 1/2 cups milk

1 cup blueberry syrup

1 Grease bottom and sides of rectangular baking dish, 11 × 7 × 1 1/2 inches, with shortening. Spread half of the bread pieces evenly in baking dish. Top with cream cheese. Sprinkle with blueberries. Spread remaining bread over blueberries.

2 Beat eggs and milk in medium bowl with fork or wire whisk until blended; pour over bread. Cover tightly with aluminum foil and refrigerate at least 8 hours but no longer than 24 hours.

3 Heat oven to 350°. Bake in covered baking dish 30 minutes. Uncover and bake 25 to 30 minutes longer or until top is puffed and center is set. Serve with blueberry syrup.

FOOD *for* THOUGHT

For a tasty source of vitamin A, you can't beat this breakfast. Vitamin A is vital for proper eyesight and healthy hair and skin.

Low fiber

1 **SERVING:** Calories 290 (Calories from Fat 110); Fat 12g (Saturated 5g); Cholesterol 230mg; Sodium 350mg; Potassium 210mg; Carbohydrate 33g (Dietary Fiber 1g); Protein 13g % **Daily Value:** Vitamin A 14%; Vitamin C 2%; Calcium 14%; Iron 8%; Folic Acid 12%; Magnesium 4% **Diet Exchanges:** 1 Starch, 1 1/2 High-Fat Meat, 1 Fruit

"Berries taste 'normal' even with the common metallic taste during many chemotherapy treatments. I love food that I can cook—or have someone else cook for me—and then reheat in the microwave in single servings for quick, low-odor meals . This dish fills the bill perfectly." —ANNE R.

Home-Style Oatmeal with Raisins

1 serving   PREP: 1 min • MICROWAVE: 3 min • STAND: 5 min

3/4 cup milk or water

1/3 cup old-fashioned oats

1/3 cup raisins

1/4 cup milk, if desired

1 Mix 3/4 cup milk and the oats in large microwavable bowl or 4-cup measuring cup. Microwave uncovered on High about 3 minutes or until boiling.

2 Stir in raisins and up to 1/4 cup milk until desired consistency. Let stand about 5 minutes or until cool enough to eat.

"I found oatmeal, in any form, to be so very comforting during my treatment. Sometimes, I ate just plain oatmeal several times a day. When I couldn't have milk, I cooked the oatmeal with water, and the easiest way to cook it was in the microwave."   —SUSAN S.

A NOTE *from* DR. GHOSH

To make this comfort food low residue, prepare oatmeal with water and leave out the raisins. Sprinkling it with a little brown sugar and a dash of ground cinnamon boosts the flavor level.

High in potassium, calcium, and magnesium; good source of fiber

1 SERVING: Calories 340 (Calories from Fat 45); Fat 5g (Saturated 3g); Cholesterol 15mg; Sodium 95mg; Potassium 760mg; Carbohydrate 67g (Dietary Fiber 4g); Protein 12g **% Daily Value:** Vitamin A 8%; Vitamin C 2%; Calcium 26%; Iron 10%; Folic Acid 4%; Magnesium 18% **Diet Exchanges:** 4 Starch

Cheese Grits

8 servings PREP: 20 min • BAKE: 40 min • STAND: 10 min

2 cups milk

2 cups water

1/2 teaspoon salt

1/4 teaspoon pepper

1 cup uncooked white hominy quick grits

1 1/2 cups shredded Cheddar cheese (6 ounces)

2 medium green onions, sliced (2 tablespoons)

2 eggs, slightly beaten

1 tablespoon butter or margarine

1/4 teaspoon paprika

1 Heat oven to 350°. Grease bottom and side of 1 1/2-quart casserole with shortening.

2 Heat milk, water, salt and pepper to boiling in 2-quart saucepan. Gradually add grits, stirring constantly; reduce heat. Simmer uncovered about 5 minutes, stirring frequently, until thickened. Stir in cheese and onions.

3 Stir 1 cup of the grits mixture into eggs, then stir back into remaining grits in saucepan. Pour into casserole. Cut butter into small pieces; sprinkle over grits. Sprinkle with paprika.

4 Bake uncovered 35 to 40 minutes or until set. Let stand 10 minutes before serving.

A NOTE *from* **DR. GHOSH**

Take time to celebrate treatment milestones. Prepare a nice dinner, if you are up to it, meet friends or family at a favorite restaurant or order a cake to celebrate once in a while! This will help lift your spirits.

High in calcium; low fiber

1 SERVING: Calories 220 (Calories from Fat 100); Fat 11g (Saturated 7g); Cholesterol 85mg; Sodium 620mg; Potassium 170mg; Carbohydrate 19g (Dietary Fiber 0g); Protein 11g **% Daily Value:** Vitamin A 10%; Vitamin C 0%; Calcium 20%; Iron 6%; Folic Acid 10%; Magnesium 6% **Diet Exchanges:** 1 Starch, 1 Medium-Fat Meat, 1 Fat

"Flavorful comfort foods like these cheese grits were a lifesaver for me on days when I was feeling awful. When I wanted more flavor, I added a dash of cayenne pepper or red pepper flakes, and served these grits with salsa for a real flavor kick." —SUSAN S.

Cinnamon-Raisin Morning Mix

8 servings PREP: 5 min · MICROWAVE: 4 min

1/4 cup sugar

1 teaspoon ground cinnamon

1/4 cup butter or margarine

1 1/2 cups Corn Chex® cereal

1 1/2 cups Rice Chex® cereal

1 1/2 cups Wheat Chex® cereal

1/2 cup raisins, dried cranberries or dried cherries

1 Mix sugar and cinnamon; set aside.

2 Place butter in large microwavable bowl. Microwave uncovered on High about 40 seconds or until melted. Stir in cereals until evenly coated. Microwave 2 minutes, stirring after 1 minute.

3 Sprinkle half of the sugar mixture evenly over cereal; stir. Sprinkle with remaining sugar mixture. Stir and microwave 1 minute. Stir in raisins. Spread on paper towels to cool.

"This mix was so easy to make in my microwave, and when I used the dried cranberries, the color was pretty. I kept this snack on hand to munch on whenever I felt like having something crunchy."　　　*—SUSAN S.*

A NOTE *from* DR. GHOSH

Fortified ready-to-eat cereal, such as Chex®, provides a good source of folic acid, a nutrient necessary for all cells to function properly. Folic acid also helps to prevent certain birth defects.

High in iron

1/2 CUP: Calories 190 (Calories from Fat 55); Fat 6g (Saturated 4g); Cholesterol 15mg; Sodium 230mg; Potassium 130mg; Carbohydrate 34g (Dietary Fiber 2g); Protein 2g **% Daily Value:** Vitamin A 4%; Vitamin C 2%; Calcium 2%; Iron 40%; Folic Acid 16%; Magnesium 4% **Diet Exchanges:** 1 Starch, 1 Fruit, 1 Fat

Fruit Parfaits

2 servings   PREP: 10 min

FOOD *for* **THOUGHT**

Packed with vitamin C, potassium and calcium, this fruit and yogurt combination can't be beat for nutritional benefits geared toward cancer healing!

1/2 cup chopped cantaloupe

1/2 cup chopped strawberries

1/2 cup chopped honeydew melon or kiwifruit

1/2 banana, sliced

1 cup vanilla low-fat yogurt

2 tablespoons sliced almonds, toasted*

1 Alternate layers of fruit and yogurt in 2 goblets or parfait glasses, beginning and ending with fruit.

2 Top with almonds.

To toast nuts, bake uncovered in ungreased shallow pan in 350° oven about 10 minutes, stirring occasionally, until golden brown. Or cook in ungreased heavy skillet over medium-low heat 5 to 7 minutes, stirring frequently until browning begins, then stirring constantly until golden brown.

High in calcium, potassium, vitamin C and folic acid; good source of fiber

1 SERVING: Calories 230 (Calories from Fat 80); Fat 9g (Saturated 1g); Cholesterol 5mg; Sodium 170mg; Potassium 720mg; Carbohydrate 32g (Dietary Fiber 3g); Protein 8g **% Daily Value:** Vitamin A 16%; Vitamin C 86%; Calcium 22%; Iron 6%; Folic Acid 78%; Magnesium 16% **Diet Exchanges:** 1 Fruit, 1 Skim Milk, 1 Fat

"This 'treat' tastes great and is easy to eat. Even with extremely bad mouth sores, I can eat this by skipping the strawberries and almonds, which don't feel good if your mouth is raw. It is also quick to fix and has very little odor, which is important if you have nausea."

—ANNE R.

"I learned to be careful when I baked wearing my wig! I didn't know that hot air can burn the hair. I found the best thing to do is open the oven door, stand to the side and let out some of the heat first."

A NOTE *from* DR. GHOSH

You may have heard of the BRAT diet. Bananas, the B in BRAT, are a good food source of nutrients when severe diarrhea is a problem. Rice, applesauce and toast make up the rest of the acronym.

Banana Bread

1 loaf (24 slices) PREP: 15 min • BAKE: 1 hr 15 min • COOL: 2 hr

1/2 cup butter or margarine, softened

1 1/3 cups packed brown sugar

2 eggs, well beaten

1 cup very ripe mashed bananas (2 medium)

1/2 cup buttermilk

1 teaspoon vanilla

2 cups all-purpose flour

1 teaspoon baking soda

1/2 teaspoon salt

1 Heat oven to 350°. Grease bottom only of loaf pan, 8 1/2 × 4 1/2 × 2 1/2 or 9 × 5 × 3 inches, with shortening.

2 Mix butter and brown sugar in large bowl. Stir in eggs until well blended. Stir in bananas, buttermilk and vanilla; mix with spoon until smooth. Stir in flour, baking soda and salt just until moistened. Pour into pan.

3 Bake 1 hour to 1 hour 15 minutes or until golden brown and toothpick inserted in center comes out clean. Cool in pan 10 minutes. Loosen sides of loaf from pan; remove from pan to wire rack. Cool completely, about 2 hours, before slicing.

"Save your very ripe bananas in the freezer until you're ready to make this recipe. Thaw and mash, using all the liquid."
— *PATTY N.*

Low fiber; low residue

1 SLICE: Calories 135 (Calories from Fat 45); Fat 5g (Saturated 3g); Cholesterol 30mg; Sodium 140mg; Potassium 100mg; Carbohydrate 22g (Dietary Fiber 1g); Protein 2g **% Daily Value:** Vitamin A 4%; Vitamin C 0%; Calcium 2%; Iron 4%; Folic Acid 4%; Magnesium 2% **Diet Exchanges:** 1/2 Starch, 1 Fruit, 1 Fat

Easy Brown Bread

2 loaves (24 slices each) · PREP: 10 min · BAKE: 35 min · COOL: 2 hr

2 cups graham cracker crumbs (about 26 squares)

1 3/4 cups all-purpose flour

2 teaspoons baking soda

1/2 teaspoon salt

1 cup chopped prunes, dates or raisins

3/4 cup full-flavor molasses

1/3 cup vegetable oil

2 eggs

2 cups buttermilk

1 Heat oven to 375°. Grease bottoms only of 2 loaf pans, 9 × 5 × 3 inches, or 3 loaf pans, 8 1/2 × 4 1/2 × 2 1/2 inches, with shortening.

2 Mix cracker crumbs, flour, baking soda, salt and prunes in large bowl; set aside. Mix molasses, oil and eggs in medium bowl; stir in buttermilk. Stir molasses mixture into cracker mixture until blended. Pour into pans.

3 Bake 30 to 35 minutes or until toothpick inserted in center comes out clean. Cool in pans 5 minutes. Loosen sides of loaves from pans; remove from pans to wire rack. Cool completely, about 2 hours, before slicing.

"I like this recipe because it uses so many of the yummy foods I keep in my kitchen. Once I crushed the graham crackers, it went together in no time. I baked this bread and kept it on hand for any time that I was even a little bit hungry. It freezes very well!"

—THERESA H.

FOOD *for* THOUGHT

Jump-start your day by eating breakfast. Studies show that people who eat breakfast get a head start on their daily nutrition goals and are better prepared to face the challenges of the day.

Low fiber

1 SLICE: Calories 70 (Calories from Fat 20); Fat 2g (Saturated 0g); Cholesterol 10mg; Sodium 110mg; Potassium 130mg; Carbohydrate 12g (Dietary Fiber 0g); Protein 1g **% Daily Value:** Vitamin A 0%; Vitamin C 0%; Calcium 2%; Iron 4%; Folic Acid 2%; Magnesium 2% **Diet Exchanges:** 1 Starch

Rise 'n Shine Muffins with Creamy Orange Glaze

12 muffins PREP: 20 min • BAKE: 20 min

c

A NOTE *from* DR. GHOSH

Grains supply fiber, a nutrient lacking in the diets of most Americans. Daily fiber keeps foods moving through your intestinal tract and can help lessen constipation.

1 cup Fiber One® cereal

2/3 cup calcium-fortified orange juice

1/3 cup honey

2 tablespoons vegetable oil

1 egg

1 1/2 cups Original Bisquick®

1/2 teaspoon baking soda

1/2 cup plus 2 tablespoons salted sunflower nuts, toasted (page 60)

Creamy Orange Glaze (below)

1. Heat oven to 400°. Grease bottoms only of 12 medium muffin cups, 2 1/2 × 1 1/4 inches, with shortening, or line with paper baking cups.

2. Place cereal in plastic bag or between sheets of waxed paper; crush with rolling pin (or crush cereal in blender or food processor); set aside. Mix orange juice, honey, oil and egg; set aside.

3. Mix Bisquick®, cereal, baking soda and 1/2 cup of the nuts in medium bowl. Make a well in center of cereal mixture; stir in orange juice mixture just until moistened. Divide batter evenly among muffin cups. Sprinkle with remaining 2 tablespoons nuts.

4. Bake about 20 minutes or until golden brown. Immediately remove from pan to wire rack (place rack on waxed paper to catch glaze drips). Cool 5 minutes. Drizzle with Creamy Orange Glaze.

Creamy Orange Glaze

1/2 cup powdered sugar

1/2 teaspoon grated orange peel

2 to 3 teaspoons calcium-fortified orange juice

Mix all ingredients until thin enough to drizzle.

"Pain drugs, especially morphine, and some chemos can make a person constipated. These muffins are a really easy way to grab a quick breakfast and help with constipation. The orange glaze makes the muffins taste good even with the metallic taste that's common after some chemotherapy treatments."

—ANNE R.

Good source of fiber

1 MUFFIN WITH GLAZE: Calories 190 (Calories from Fat 70); Fat 8g (Saturated 1g); Cholesterol 15mg; Sodium 350mg; Potassium 140mg; Carbohydrate 29g (Dietary Fiber 3g); Protein 4g **% Daily Value:** Vitamin A 0%; Vitamin C 4%; Calcium 6%; Iron 10%; Folic Acid 8%; Magnesium 12% **Diet Exchanges:** 1 Starch, 1 Fruit, 1 Fat

Streusel-Topped Fruit Brunch Cake

12 servings   PREP: 15 min   •   BAKE: 45 min

2 cups Multi-Bran Chex®
or Wheat Chex® cereal

1 cup calcium-fortified
orange juice

1/4 cup vegetable oil

1 egg, slightly beaten

2 small bananas, thinly sliced

1 1/2 cups all-purpose flour

3/4 cup sugar

1/2 cup raisins, if desired

1 teaspoon baking soda

1 teaspoon ground cinnamon

1/2 teaspoon salt

Streusel Topping (below)

1 Heat oven to 350°. Grease bottom and sides of square pan, 9 × 9 × 2 inches, with shortening. Mix cereal and orange juice in large bowl; let stand about 2 minutes or until cereal is soft. Stir in oil, egg and bananas. Stir in flour, sugar, raisins, baking soda, cinnamon and salt. Spread in pan.

2 Bake about 45 minutes or until top springs back when touched lightly in center. While cake is baking, make Streusel Topping.

3 Set oven control to broil. Sprinkle topping evenly over warm cake. Broil with top about 5 inches from heat about 1 minute or until bubbly (watch carefully to avoid burning).

Streusel Topping

1/2 cup Multi-Bran Chex®
or Wheat Chex® cereal

1/2 cup chopped nuts, if
desired

1/3 cup packed brown sugar

1/4 cup all-purpose flour

2 tablespoons butter or
margarine, softened

1/2 teaspoon ground cinnamon

Coarsely crush cereal. Mix cereal and remaining ingredients until crumbly.

"Close friends make coffee cake and bring it over; it makes all of us feel great. I get to enjoy tasty food, and they really are doing me an important favor. My family loves the treats, too."

—ANNE R.

A NOTE *from* **DR. GHOSH**

Did you know that breakfast cereals, like Chex®, are a great source of iron? We need iron for proper oxygen transfer in our blood to keep us healthy.

High in iron

1 SERVING: Calories 255 (Calories from Fat 65); Fat 7g (Saturated 2g); Cholesterol 25mg; Sodium 270mg; Potassium 180mg; Carbohydrate 46g (Dietary Fiber 2g); Protein 4g % Daily Value: Vitamin A 2%; Vitamin C 8%; Calcium 4%; Iron 20%; Folic Acid 10%; Magnesium 6% Diet Exchanges: 1 1/2 Starch, 1 1/2 Fruit, 1 Fat

"I made it a point to cook and eat foods with happy family memories during treatment. I made this cake and shared the recipe with family and friends during the holidays."

FOOD *for* THOUGHT

Blueberries are a great source of antioxidants. Research shows that these components, found naturally in blueberries, may help with memory and may reduce the risk of certain diseases, such as cancer and heart disease.

Blueberry Brunch Cake

12 servings PREP: 12 min • BAKE: 40 min

2 cups all-purpose flour

2 teaspoons baking powder

1/2 teaspoon salt

1/2 teaspoon ground ginger

1/4 teaspoon baking soda

1 cup sugar

1/2 cup butter or margarine, softened

2 eggs

3/4 cup sour cream or plain fat-free yogurt

1 teaspoon vanilla

2 cups fresh or frozen blueberries

1/4 cup sugar

1 teaspoon ground cinnamon

1 Heat oven to 350°. Grease bottom and sides of rectangular pan, 13 × 9 × 2 inches, with shortening; lightly flour. Mix flour, baking powder, salt, ginger and baking soda in medium bowl; set aside.

2 Mix 1 cup sugar and the butter in large bowl. Stir in eggs, sour cream and vanilla. Stir in flour mixture. Carefully fold in blueberries. Spoon into pan.

3 Mix 1/4 cup sugar and the cinnamon; sprinkle over batter. Bake about 40 minutes or until golden brown.

Low fiber; low residue

1 **SERVING:** Calories 285 (Calories from Fat 110); Fat 12g (Saturated 7g); Cholesterol 65mg; Sodium 300mg; Potassium 80mg; Carbohydrate 41g (Dietary Fiber 1g); Protein 4g **% Daily Value:** Vitamin A 8%; Vitamin C 2%; Calcium 6%; Iron 6%; Folic Acid 6%; Magnesium 2% **Diet Exchanges:** 1 1/2 Starch, 1 Fruit, 2 1/2 Fat

Blueberry Brunch Cake

A NOTE *from*
DR. GHOSH

If you're on a fiber- and residue-restricted diet, these simple biscuits may be just for you. They're both low fiber and low residue, and can be eaten alone or with a meal.

Low fiber; low residue

1 BISCUIT: Calories 160 (Calories from Fat 80); Fat 9g (Saturated 2g); Cholesterol 0mg; Sodium 330mg; Potassium 50mg; Carbohydrate 18g (Dietary Fiber 1g); Protein 3g **% Daily Value:** Vitamin A 0%; Vitamin C 0%; Calcium 8%; Iron 6%; Folic Acid 6%; Magnesium 2% **Diet Exchanges:** 1 Starch, 2 Fat

Baking Powder Biscuits

12 biscuits PREP: 10 min • BAKE: 12 min

2 cups all-purpose flour

1 tablespoon sugar

1 tablespoon baking powder

1 teaspoon salt

1/2 cup shortening

3/4 cup milk

1 Heat oven to 450°.

2 Mix flour, sugar, baking powder and salt in medium bowl. Cut in shortening, using pastry blender or crisscrossing 2 knives, until mixture looks like fine crumbs. Stir in milk until dough leaves side of bowl (dough will be soft and sticky).

3 Place dough on lightly floured surface. Knead lightly 10 times. Roll or pat 1/2 inch thick. Cut with floured 2 to 2 1/4-inch round cutter. Place on ungreased cookie sheet about 1 inch apart for crusty sides, touching for soft sides.

4 Bake 10 to 12 minutes or until golden brown. Immediately remove from cookie sheet. Serve warm.

"To save time, I made drop biscuits with this recipe. I increased the milk to 1 cup and dropped them onto a greased cookie sheet. I liked keeping these on hand and reheating them whenever I needed a little something to eat."

—THERESA H.

Tropical Pancakes

5 servings (two 4-inch pancakes each)   PREP: 10 min   •   COOK: 8 min

1 cup Whole Grain Total®
or Wheaties® cereal

1 egg

1 medium very ripe banana,
mashed (1/2 cup)

1 cup buttermilk

2 tablespoons vegetable oil

1 cup all-purpose flour

1 tablespoon sugar

1 teaspoon baking powder

1/2 teaspoon baking soda

1/2 teaspoon salt

1 Place cereal in plastic bag or between sheets of waxed paper; crush with rolling pin (or crush cereal in blender or food processor); set aside. Beat egg in medium bowl with hand beater or wire whisk until fluffy. Beat in remaining ingredients until well blended. Gently stir in cereal.

2 Heat griddle or skillet over medium heat or to 375°. (To test griddle, sprinkle with a few drops of water. If bubbles jump around, heat is just right.) Grease with butter if necessary.

3 For each pancake, pour slightly less than 1/4 cup batter from cup or pitcher onto hot griddle. Cook until puffed and full of bubbles; turn before bubbles break. Cook other side until golden brown.

A NOTE *from* **DR. GHOSH**

This whole-grain breakfast is a healthy way to begin your day. Whole grains supply fiber and B vitamins and may help to reduce the risk of heart disease and certain types of cancer.

"Serving these pancakes with honey or real maple syrup, whipped cream (I try to add calories whenever I can) and a few slices of banana makes me feel like I am having a real treat. I freeze the pancakes in individual plastic bags (two per bag) and reheat them in the toaster oven. Then I have an instant, low-odor breakfast."   —Anne R.

High in calcium,
iron and folic acid

1 **SERVING:** Calories 230 (Calories from Fat 70); Fat 8g (Saturated 2g); Cholesterol 45mg; Sodium 570mg; Potassium 240mg; Carbohydrate 36g (Dietary Fiber 2g); Protein 7g **% Daily Value:** Vitamin A 8%; Vitamin C 14%; Calcium 18%; Iron 34%; Folic Acid 36%; Magnesium 6% **Diet Exchanges:** 2 Starch, 1 1/2 Fat

Potato Pancakes
with Cinnamon Apples

6 servings (three 4-inch pancakes each)   PREP: 10 min • COOK: 8 min

c

A NOTE *from* DR. GHOSH

Potassium, found in abundance in this recipe, is a nutrient that's helpful in cancer healing. Potassium also helps to maintain the body's natural water balance and aids in nerve and muscle function.

1/2 cup Original Bisquick

1/2 cup milk

1 teaspoon salt

3 eggs

3 cups finely shredded uncooked potatoes

Cinnamon Apples (page 72), if desired

1 Mix Bisquick, milk, salt and eggs in large bowl until blended. Stir in potatoes.

2 Heat griddle or skillet over medium heat or to 375°. (To test griddle, sprinkle with a few drops of water. If bubbles jump around, heat is just right.) Grease with butter if necessary.

3 For each pancake, pour slightly less than 1/4 cup batter from cup or pitcher onto hot griddle, spreading each slightly to make 4-inch pancake. Cook until dry around edges. Turn and cook other side until golden brown. Serve with Cinnamon Apples.

Excellent source of fiber when eaten with Cinnamon Apples

1 SERVING: Calories 145 (Calories from Fat 35); Fat 4g (Saturated 1g); Cholesterol 105mg; Sodium 580mg; Potassium 340mg; Carbohydrate 23g (Dietary Fiber 2g); Protein 6g % Daily Value: Vitamin A 4%; Vitamin C 6%; Calcium 6%; Iron 8%; Folic Acid 4%; Magnesium 4% Diet Exchanges: 1 1/2 Starch, 1/2 Fat

"I add a very good whey protein powder to increase the protein content of breads, pancakes and cakes. I reduce the flour by the amount of powder that I add. This makes every mouthful count. The carbs give me energy, the protein rebuilds damaged tissue and the fat slows down absorption so it lessens the nausea for me. That way, every meal has some fat, carb and good protein."

—ANNE R.

Lois K. Shares *her Recipe*

"These apples are so easy to make and very tasty served with pancakes, waffles or biscuits. I sometimes blend the apples after cooking to make applesauce."

FOOD *for* THOUGHT

A twist on homemade applesauce, these apples offer a big cinnamon taste. If you prefer, remove the peel. For variety, try adding 1/4 teaspoon ground nutmeg and 1/4 teaspoon ground cloves in addition to the cinnamon and enjoy this recipe as a snack or dessert.

Cinnamon Apples

3 or 4 servings   PREP: 10 min

3 medium tart cooking apples (Granny Smith, Greening, Rome, Breaburn), unpeeled and sliced (3 cups)

1/2 cup water

1/3 cup sugar

1 teaspoon ground cinnamon

1 Place apple slices in 2-quart microwavable casserole or large microwavable bowl. Stir in water, sugar and cinnamon.

2 Cover and microwave on High 5 minutes. Uncover and microwave about 5 minutes longer or until apples are tender when pierced with fork.

Good source of fiber

1 SERVING: Calories 160 (Calories from Fat 0); Fat 0g (Saturated 0g); Cholesterol 0mg; Sodium 0mg; Potassium 150mg; Carbohydrate 44g (Dietary Fiber 4g); Protein 0g **% Daily Value:** Vitamin A 2%; Vitamin C 6%; Calcium 2%; Iron 2%; Folic Acid 0%; Magnesium 2% **Diet Exchanges:** 2 1/2 Fruit

Cheesy Pear Oven Pancake

4 servings PREP: 10 min • COOK: 5 min • BAKE: 21 min

1 cup all-purpose flour

1 cup milk

1/4 teaspoon salt

4 eggs

1 tablespoon butter or margarine

2 medium unpeeled pears, thinly sliced (2 cups)

2 tablespoons chopped fresh or 2 teaspoons freeze-dried chives

2 tablespoons sugar

3/4 cup shredded Cheddar cheese (3 ounces)

1 Heat oven to 450°. Grease bottom and sides of rectangular baking dish, 13 × 9 × 2 inches, with shortening. Mix flour, milk, salt and eggs with wire whisk until smooth. Pour into baking dish. Bake 15 to 20 minutes or until puffy and golden brown.

2 While pancake is baking, melt butter in 10-inch nonstick skillet over medium-high heat. Cook pears and chives in butter about 5 minutes, stirring frequently, until pears are slightly softened. Stir in sugar.

3 Spoon pear mixture onto pancake. Sprinkle with cheese. Bake about 1 minute or until cheese is melted.

"After treatment, my energy is really low, so this makes an easy-to-eat breakfast, especially if the pancake-and-pear mixture is already made by my son or husband. If I can't eat it all at once, I can just take it from the refrigerator, reheat and eat."

—ANNE R.

FOOD *for* THOUGHT

Cheese and pears are a wonderful blend of flavors—don't save this oven pancake just for breakfast! The salty richness of the cheese complements the sweetness of the pears.

High in calcium; good source of fiber

1 SERVING: Calories 325 (Calories from Fat 110); Fat 12g (Saturated 7g); Cholesterol 330mg; Sodium 330mg; Potassium 260mg; Carbohydrate 46g (Dietary Fiber 3g); Protein 11g **% Daily Value:** Vitamin A 10%; Vitamin C 4%; Calcium 20%; Iron 10%; Folic Acid 12%; Magnesium 6% **Diet Exchanges:** 2 Starch, 1/2 High-Fat Meat, 1 Fruit, 1 Fat

Baked French Toast with Strawberry-Rhubarb Sauce

6 servings (3 slices each) PREP: 10 min • CHILL: 8 hr • BAKE: 13 min

FOOD *for* THOUGHT

This combination of healthy ingredients is packed with nutritional benefits from vitamin C, calcium, iron, folic acid and magnesium, to name just a few. Magnesium is key to releasing energy from foods, particularly from carbohydrate sources.

1/2 cup all-purpose flour

1 1/2 cups milk

1 tablespoon sugar

1/2 teaspoon vanilla

1/4 teaspoon salt

6 eggs

18 slices French bread, 1 inch thick

Strawberry-Rhubarb Sauce (below)

1 Generously grease bottom and sides of jelly roll pan, 15 1/2 × 10 1/2 × 1 inch, with shortening. Beat flour, milk, sugar, vanilla, salt and eggs with hand beater or wire whisk until smooth.

2 Arrange bread slices to fit in single layer in pan. Pour egg mixture over bread slices; turn to coat both sides. Cover and refrigerate at least 8 hours but no longer than 24 hours.

3 Heat oven to 450°. Uncover and bake 10 to 13 minutes or until golden brown. While French toast is baking, make Strawberry-Rhubarb Sauce. Serve warm sauce with French toast.

Strawberry-Rhubarb Sauce

2 cups medium whole strawberries

2 cups cut-up rhubarb (1 1/3 pounds)

1/3 cup water

1 package (4-serving size) strawberry-flavored gelatin

Heat strawberries, rhubarb and water to boiling in 2-quart saucepan. Boil 5 minutes, stirring occasionally; remove from heat. Stir in gelatin until dissolved. Boil 2 minutes longer, stirring constantly.

High in calcium, iron, vitamin C and folic acid; good source of fiber

1 SERVING: Calories 410 (Calories from Fat 80); Fat 9g (Saturated 3g); Cholesterol 215mg; Sodium 670mg; Potassium 430mg; Carbohydrate 68g (Dietary Fiber 4g); Protein 18g **% Daily Value:** Vitamin A 8%; Vitamin C 26%; Calcium 24%; Iron 20%; Folic Acid 30%; Magnesium 12 % **Diet Exchanges:** 3 Starch, 1 High-Fat Meat, 1 1/2 Fruit

"Strawberry-rhubarb sauce really helps me when I'm mildly constipated and don't want to take another medicine. The strawberry-rhubarb combination works for me, and it tastes great, even after chemo!"
—ANNE R.

Baked French Toast with Strawberry-Rhubarb Sauce

Make-Ahead Waffles with Peanut Butter Spread

6 servings (two 4-inch waffle squares each)   PREP: 10 min • RISE: 1 hr 30 min • CHILL: 8 hr • BAKE: 5 min per waffle

1 package regular active
dry yeast

1/4 cup warm water
(105° to 115°)

1 3/4 cups lukewarm milk
(scalded then cooled)

2 tablespoons sugar

1 teaspoon salt

3 eggs

1/4 cup butter or margarine,
softened

2 cups all-purpose flour

Peanut Butter Spread (below)

1 Dissolve yeast in warm water in large bowl. Add remaining ingredients except Peanut Butter Spread. Beat with electric mixer on medium speed until smooth. Cover and let rise in warm place 1 hour 30 minutes. Stir down batter. Cover and refrigerate at least 8 hours but no longer than 12 hours.

2 Heat waffle iron; grease with shortening if necessary. Stir down batter. Pour about 1/2 cup batter from cup or pitcher onto center of hot waffle iron. (Waffle irons vary in size; check manufacturer's directions for recommended amount of batter.) Close lid of waffle iron.

3 Bake about 5 minutes or until steaming stops. Carefully remove waffle. Repeat with remaining batter. Serve with Peanut Butter Spread.

Peanut Butter Spread

1/2 cup maple-flavored syrup

1/2 cup peanut butter

Mix ingredients until blended.

FOOD *for* THOUGHT

These waffles, made from a blend of peanut butter and flour together, give you plenty of protein, magnesium and iron. Protein supplies needed nitrogen that's vital for life and the growth of new cells in the body. The waffles supply lots of important calories your body needs for healing. If you can eat only one, save the other for later in the day. For a crisp waffle, pop it into the toaster.

High in iron and
folic acid; good source
of fiber

2 WAFFLES: Calories 505 (Calories from Fat 205); Fat 23g (Saturated 9g); Cholesterol 130mg; Sodium 610mg; Potassium 410mg; Carbohydrate 62g (Dietary Fiber 3g); Protein 16g **% Daily Value:** Vitamin A 12%; Vitamin C 0%; Calcium 12%; Iron 18%; Folic Acid 26%; Magnesium 14% **Diet Exchanges:** 4 Starch, 1/2 High-Fat Meat, 3 Fat

"I make these into pancakes by pouring 1/4 cup batter onto a greased hot griddle and cooking until they're puffed and full of bubbles. Then I turn them and cook the other side until golden brown. I freeze them and reheat as needed. Pancakes are so easy to eat; I live on them right after chemo or as soon as I can eat solid food after surgery."

—ANNE R.

Keep a Lemon in Your Kitchen...
and Other Ways to Reduce Nausea

Nausea can be very unpleasant and unsettling. Nausea is a direct side effect for many on chemotherapy or radiation, but there are ways to reduce it. Try these tips:

1. **Take nausea medication.** Only take what your doctor prescribes, and work with him or her to find the most effective medication for you. The right medication will help you eat better, eat more and stay well hydrated.

2. **Keep citrus fruits around.** Keep a lemon in your kitchen or at your desk, and pick it up and sniff it every once in a while. For more citrus power, cut the lemon and squeeze a few drops of juice into your water glass. Add ice and water. Every time you take a sip of water, you will feel refreshed! Don't have a lemon? Try a lime or an orange.

3. **Eat foods that smell good to you.** Aroma is directly linked to taste. If a certain food smells good, it will most likely *taste* good to you, too.

4. **Sip or drink liquids slowly and often throughout the day.** Extra liquids are important, and if you drink them slowly, they can help ease the nausea and relax you.

5. **Eat dry toast or crackers.** Even before getting up, nibble on crackers from your bedside table if you have nausea in the morning.

6. **Wear loose-fitting clothes.** Anything too tight, particularly around your tummy, may worsen or trigger nausea.

7. **Avoid eating for 1 to 2 hours before chemotherapy or radiation.**

8. **Eat small amounts and more frequently.** Eating mini-meals or snacks more often throughout the day instead of three large meals may lessen feelings of nausea.

9. **Eat before you get hungry.** Hunger can actually make the nausea feel much worse. Try to keep something small in your stomach, even if it's just a cracker.

10. **Sit up for about an hour after meals.** Lying down too quickly after a meal can increase nausea or discomfort and interfere with digestion.

Roasted Vegetable Dip (page 80)

Fatigue-Fighting Snacks

3

Judy O. *Shares* her Recipe

"Thinking of things that made me smile really helped. My grandson, Nolan, loves to recite from the book, We're Going on a Bear Hunt, and emphasize 'It's a beauuutiful day!' I often smile and say to myself, 'It's a beauuutiful day!' Serving this dip was fun for both me and Nolan."

A NOTE *from*
DR. GHOSH

Dips, especially healthy ones like this, along with plenty of fun dippers make great excuses for sharing. Surround yourself with family and friends to lift your spirits. Your mental health is as important as your physical health.

Roasted Vegetable Dip

7 servings (1/4 cup each)   PREP: **15** min   ·   BAKE: **30** min

1 medium zucchini, sliced (2 cups)

1 medium yellow summer squash, sliced (1 1/2 cups)

1 medium red bell pepper, sliced

1 medium red onion, thinly sliced

2 cloves garlic, peeled

Cooking spray

1/2 teaspoon salt

1/4 teaspoon ground red pepper (cayenne)

Dippers (baby-cut carrots, cucumber slices, green bell pepper strips, toasted pita bread wedges, baked tortilla chips), if desired

1 Heat oven to 400°. Spread zucchini, yellow squash, bell pepper, onion and garlic in jelly roll pan, 15 1/2 × 10 1/2 × 1 inch. Spray vegetables with cooking spray. Sprinkle with salt and red pepper.

2 Bake about 30 minutes, turning vegetables once, until vegetables are tender and lightly browned.

3 Place vegetables in blender or food processor. Cover and blend on high speed about 1 minute, stopping blender occasionally to scrape sides, until smooth.

4 Serve warm, or refrigerate at least 2 hours until chilled. Serve with dippers.

High in vitamins A and C; low fiber

1/4 CUP: Calories 20 (Calories from Fat 0); Fat 0g (Saturated 0g); Cholesterol 0mg; Sodium 170mg; Potassium 180mg; Carbohydrate 5g (Dietary Fiber 1g); Protein 1g **% Daily Value:** Vitamin A 24%; Vitamin C 32%; Calcium 2%; Iron 2%; Folic Acid 4%; Magnesium 4% **Diet Exchanges:** 1 Serving is free

Zucchini Bites

8 servings (6 bites each)   PREP: 10 min • BAKE: 25 min

1 cup Original Bisquick

1/2 cup grated Parmesan cheese

1/2 cup vegetable oil

2 tablespoons chopped fresh parsley

1/2 teaspoon salt

1/2 teaspoon seasoned salt

1/2 teaspoon dried marjoram or oregano leaves

4 small unpeeled zucchini, thinly sliced (3 cups)

1 medium onion, finely chopped (1/2 cup)

4 eggs, slightly beaten

1 clove garlic, finely chopped

1 Heat oven to 350°. Grease bottom and sides of rectangular pan, 13 × 9 × 2 inches, with shortening.

2 Stir all ingredients until blended. Spread in pan.

3 Bake about 25 minutes or until golden brown. Cut into 2-inch squares; cut squares diagonally in half into triangles.

"Recently I decided to plant a small vegetable and herb garden. It gives me great pleasure to pick something from my garden and then cook with it. I find gardening and enjoying the outdoors very healing."
                                        —JUDY O.

A NOTE *from* DR. GHOSH

A good source of vitamin C, this dish will help you maintain healthy gums, muscles, bones and teeth. A powerful antioxidant, vitamin C is also involved in promoting healing.

Low fiber; low residue

1 SERVING: Calories 260 (Calories from Fat 180); Fat 20g (Saturated 5g); Cholesterol 110mg; Sodium 600mg; Potassium 230mg; Carbohydrate 13g (Dietary Fiber 1g); Protein 8g **% Daily Value:** Vitamin A 14%; Vitamin C 12%; Calcium 14%; Iron 6%; Folic Acid 6%; Magnesium 6% **Diet Exchanges:** 1 Starch, 1 High-Fat Meat, 2 Fat

Oven-Fried Potato Wedges

4 servings   PREP: 10 min   •   BAKE: 30 min

A NOTE *from* **DR. GHOSH**

Some scientific studies suggest that cancer survivors who eat a low-fat diet may live longer. It's important to remember that dieting is not recommended during cancer treatment. Low-fat foods like these potato wedges can be delicious, as well as healthy.

3/4 teaspoon salt

1/2 teaspoon sugar

1/2 teaspoon paprika

1/4 teaspoon ground mustard

1/4 teaspoon garlic powder

3 medium baking potatoes (8 to 10 ounces each)

Cooking spray

1 Heat oven to 425°. Mix salt, sugar, paprika, mustard and garlic powder.

2 Gently scrub potatoes, but do not peel. Cut each potato lengthwise in half; cut each half lengthwise into 4 wedges. Place potato wedges, skin sides down, in ungreased rectangular pan, 13 × 9 × 2 inches.

3 Spray potatoes with cooking spray until lightly coated. Sprinkle with salt mixture.

4 Bake uncovered 25 to 30 minutes or until potatoes are tender when pierced with fork. (Baking time will vary depending on the size and type of the potato used.)

"On days when I am hungry for potatoes, this recipe is a quick and tasty side dish. To make it low residue, peel the skin from the potatoes before cutting. Peeling is a bit of extra work, but doing it makes the recipe better for me."

—THERESA H.

Low residue if skins are removed

1 SERVING: Calories 95 (Calories from Fat 0); Fat 0g (Saturated 0g); Cholesterol 0mg; Sodium 450mg; Potassium 380mg; Carbohydrate 24g (Dietary Fiber 2g); Protein 2g **% Daily Value:** Vitamin A 0%; Vitamin C 10%; Calcium 0%; Iron 6%, Folic Acid 2%; Magnesium 6% **Diet Exchanges:** 1 1/2 Starch

Onion and Rosemary Focaccia Wedges

6 servings (2 wedges each) PREP: 15 min • BAKE: 12 min

Olive oil–flavored cooking spray

1 can (10 ounces) refrigerated pizza crust dough

3 cloves garlic, finely chopped

1/2 teaspoon dried rosemary leaves, crumbled

1 large sweet onion (Bermuda, Maui, Spanish or Vidalia), thinly sliced and separated into rings

3/4 cup grated Parmesan cheese

Cooking spray, if desired

1/4 teaspoon salt, if desired

1 Heat oven 400°. Spray cookie sheet with cooking spray. Roll or pat pizza dough into 13 × 9-inch rectangle on cookie sheet. Sprinkle with garlic and rosemary. Arrange onion rings evenly over dough. Sprinkle with cheese.

2 Bake about 12 minutes or until cheese just begins to brown. Lightly spray focaccia with cooking spray; sprinkle with salt. Cut into 6 wedges. Serve immediately.

FOOD for THOUGHT

If foods taste bland to you and you need a flavor boost, this snack made with garlic and onions just may do the trick. If you're not fond of the flavor of rosemary, substitute fresh or dried basil in its place.

"Remembering the myth about garlic warding off vampires and evil spirits, I figured I had nothing to lose by adding garlic to my diet to ward off the cancer! It made me chuckle when I decided to call in all the help I could get to fight the cancer—even garlic!"

—CATHERINE H.

High in calcium; low fiber

1 WEDGE: Calories 200 (Calories from Fat 55); Fat 6g (Saturated 3g); Cholesterol 10mg; Sodium 440mg; Potassium 100mg; Carbohydrate 28g (Dietary Fiber 1g); Protein 9g **% Daily Value:** Vitamin A 2%; Vitamin C 0%; Calcium 18%; Iron 10%; Folic Acid 12%; Magnesium 4% **Diet Exchanges:** 2 Starch, 1/2 High-Fat Meat

"When I was really fatigued, I turned to the easiest recipes possible, like these tasty bruschetta. Eating small amounts of foods more often throughout the day helped me be able to eat more overall."

A NOTE *from* DR. GHOSH

Skip the feta cheese during neutropenic times when your resistance is down. Try substituting a cooked cheese, such as shredded mozzarella.

Tomato Bruschetta

10 servings (2 slices each)   PREP: 10 min • BAKE: 15 min

1 loaf (1 pound) French or Italian bread

2 tablespoons butter or margarine, softened

4 medium roma (plum) tomatoes, thinly sliced

1/4 cup sliced ripe olives

1/2 teaspoon dried basil leaves

3/4 cup crumbled feta cheese (3 ounces)

2 cloves garlic, finely chopped

1/4 cup olive or vegetable oil

1 Heat oven to 375°. Cut bread loaf horizontally in half. Place halves, cut sides up, on cookie sheet. Brush with butter. Top with tomatoes, olives, basil and cheese.

2 Mix garlic and oil. Drizzle oil mixture over cheese. Bake 12 to 15 minutes or until cheese just begins to brown. Cut into 2-inch slices.

Low fiber

1 SERVING: Calories 220 (Calories from Fat 110); Fat 12g (Saturated 4g); Cholesterol 15mg; Sodium 440mg; Potassium 110mg; Carbohydrate 24g (Dietary Fiber 2g); Protein 6g **% Daily Value:** Vitamin A 6%; Vitamin C 2%; Calcium 10%; Iron 8%; Folic Acid 12%; Magnesium 4% **Diet Exchanges:** 1 Starch, 2 Vegetable, 2 Fat

Tomato Bruschetta

String Cheese Sticks

8 servings (1 cheese stick each) PREP: 10 min • BAKE: 10 min

2 1/4 cups Original Bisquick

2/3 cup milk

1 package (8 ounces) plain or smoked string cheese

1 tablespoon butter or margarine, melted

1/4 teaspoon garlic powder

1 can (8 ounces) pizza sauce, heated

1 Heat oven to 450°. Stir Bisquick and milk until soft dough forms; beat 30 seconds. Place dough on surface sprinkled with Bisquick; gently roll in Bisquick to coat. Shape into a ball; knead 10 times.

2 Roll dough 1/4 inch thick. Cut into eight 6 × 2-inch rectangles. Roll each rectangle around 1 piece of cheese. Pinch edge into roll to seal; seal ends. Roll on surface to completely enclose cheese sticks. Place seam sides down on ungreased cookie sheet.

3 Bake 8 to 10 minutes or until golden brown. Mix butter and garlic powder; brush over warm cheese sticks before removing from cookie sheet. Serve warm with pizza sauce for dipping.

FOOD *for* THOUGHT

There's something about eating with your fingers that brings on a smile. These tasty cheese sticks make a happy snack that's loaded with calcium.

"The smell of bread baking, as in these cheese sticks, reminds me of my mother's kitchen and stimulates my appetite— very therapeutic!"

—JUDY O.

High in calcium, low fiber

1 STICK: Calories 250 (Calories from Fat 115); Fat 13g (Saturated 6g); Cholesterol 20mg; Sodium 780mg; Potassium 190mg; Carbohydrate 24g (Dietary Fiber 1g); Protein 11g **% Daily Value:** Vitamin A 8%; Vitamin C 4%; Calcium 30%; Iron 6%; Folic Acid 2%; Magnesium 6% **Diet Exchanges:** 1 1/2 Starch, 1 Medium-Fat Meat, 1 Fat

Super Grilled Cheese Sandwiches

4 servings   PREP: 5 min · COOK: 8 min

4 slices (1 ounce each) Cheddar, Mozzarella, Colby or Monterey Jack cheese

8 slices Italian sourdough, white or whole wheat bread

2 medium green onions, sliced (2 tablespoons)

1 medium tomato, seeded and chopped (3/4 cup)

8 teaspoons butter or margarine, softened

1 Place cheese slices on 4 slices bread. Top with onions and tomato, then remaining bread. Spread 1 teaspoon butter over each top slice of bread.

2 Place sandwiches, butter sides down, in skillet. Spread remaining butter over top slices of bread. Cook uncovered over medium heat about 5 minutes or until bottoms are golden brown. Turn and cook 2 to 3 minutes or until bottoms are golden brown and cheese is melted. Cut sandwiches into wedges or sticks, using pizza cutter.

"If I cut sandwiches into smaller pieces, like quarters or eighths, I can eat one or two pieces now and one or two later. These are super dunked in tomato soup!"

—*THERESA H.*

FOOD *for* THOUGHT

Read the Nutrition Facts labels on the foods you buy, and check the recipes you make to be sure you're getting enough calcium daily. If you add up all the percentages for the day, you should reach at least 100 percent Daily Value for calcium. This recipe, with 20 percent, is a great start.

High in calcium

1 SERVING: Calories 295 (Calories from Fat 170); Fat 19g (Saturated 11g); Cholesterol 50mg; Sodium 460mg; Potassium 190mg; Carbohydrate 22g (Dietary Fiber 2g); Protein 18g **% Daily Value:** Vitamin A 16%; Vitamin C 6%; Calcium 20%; Iron 8%; Folic Acid 12%; Magnesium 6% **Diet Exchanges:** 1 1/2 Starch, 2 High-Fat Meat, 2 Fat

Veggies and Cheese Mini-Pizzas

4 servings PREP: 10 min • BAKE: 7 min

FOOD *for*
THOUGHT

*Vegetables are loaded
with nutrients you need
each day to be healthy.
The Food Guide Pyramid
recommends three to
five servings of veggies
every day.*

2 pita breads (6 inches in diameter)

4 roma (plum) tomatoes, chopped (1 cup)

2 small zucchini, chopped (2 cups)

1 small onion, chopped (1/4 cup)

2 tablespoons sliced ripe olives

1 teaspoon chopped fresh or 1/4 teaspoon dried basil leaves

1/4 cup spaghetti sauce or pizza sauce

1/2 cup shredded mozzarella cheese (2 ounces)

1 Heat oven to 425°. Split pita breads in half around edge with knife. Place rounds on ungreased cookie sheet. Bake about 5 minutes or just until crisp.

2 Mix tomatoes, zucchini, onion, olives and basil. Spread spaghetti sauce evenly over rounds. Top with vegetable mixture. Sprinkle with cheese. Bake 5 to 7 minutes or until cheese is melted. Cut into wedges.

*"Pizza is a family favorite, and with
this recipe, we are also sure to get our
vegetables."*
—JUDY O.

High in Vitamin A;
low fiber

1 **SERVING:** Calories 130 (Calories from Fat 35); Fat 4g (Saturated 2g); Cholesterol 10mg; Sodium 310mg; Potassium 370mg; Carbohydrate 19g (Dietary Fiber 2g); Protein 7g **% Daily Value:** Vitamin A 20%; Vitamin C 16%; Calcium 14%; Iron 8%; Folic Acid 12%; Magnesium 8% **Diet Exchanges:** 1 Starch, 1 Vegetable, 1/2 Fat

Chicken Salad in Pitas

4 servings   PREP: 15 min

2 pita breads (6 inches in diameter)

2 cups chopped cooked chicken breast

1 cup frozen green peas, thawed and drained

1/2 cup mayonnaise or salad dressing

1/4 teaspoon salt

1/4 teaspoon pepper

1 medium stalk celery, chopped (1/2 cup)

4 medium green onions, sliced (1/4 cup)

1 small mango, peeled, pitted and diced (3/4 cup)

1 Cut pita breads in half; open to form pockets. Mix remaining ingredients.

2 Divide chicken mixture among pita bread halves.

FOOD *for* THOUGHT

Chicken with fruits and vegetables gives you a hefty dose of vitamins, minerals and protein in one tasty combination. The mango adds color, a bit of sweetness and vit-amin A to this dish.

High in vitamin C and good source of fiber

1 **SERVING:** Calories 440 (Calories from Fat 225); Fat 25g (Saturated 4g); Cholesterol 75mg; Sodium 520mg; Carbohydrate 28g (Dietary Fiber 4g); Protein 25g % **Daily Value:** Vitamin A 14%; Vitamin C 34%; Calcium 6%; Iron 12%; Folic Acid 16%; Magnesium 10%
Diet Exchanges: 2 Starch, 2 High-Fat Meat, 2 Fat

"I tried to stimulate my appetite by trying a new twist on an old favorite, which this recipe does in an easy way."

—JUDY O.

Snappy Stuffed Tomatoes

5 servings (4 tomatoes each)   PREP: 25 min • CHILL: 2 hr

FOOD *for*
THOUGHT

When you're tired, any new thing can seem like a daunting task. To make filling the tomatoes easier, fill 5 or 6 roma (plum) tomatoes instead of the cherry tomatoes. No need to scoop out the seeds; just make a hole in the tomato by making a cone-shaped cut near the stem end and removing the stem. Fill the tomatoes with the cheese mixture, and you're all set.

20 cherry tomatoes (1 1/4 to 1 1/2 inches in diameter)

2/3 cup shredded reduced-fat Cheddar cheese

1/2 cup whole kernel corn

6 ounces reduced-fat cream cheese (Neufchâtel), softened

2 medium green onions, sliced (2 tablespoons)

1 teaspoon ground red chilies or chili powder, if desired

1 Cut thin slice from stem ends of tomatoes. Remove pulp and seeds with melon baller or spoon.

2 Mix remaining ingredients. Fill tomatoes with cheese mixture. Sprinkle with additional ground red chilies and sliced green onions if desired. Cover and refrigerate at least 2 hours to blend flavors but no longer than 48 hours.

"Tomatoes make a wonderful snack because they taste the same no matter where I am on my treatment plan."

—ANNE R.

High in vitamins A and C; low fiber

1 SERVING: Calories 125 (Calories from Fat 65); Fat 6g (Saturated 4g); Cholesterol 20mg; Sodium 260mg; Potassium 320mg; Carbohydrate 9g (Dietary Fiber 1g); Protein 8g **% Daily Value:** Vitamin A 22%; Vitamin C 24%; Calcium 10%; Iron 4%; Folic Acid 6%; Magnesium 4% **Diet Exchanges:** 1/2 High-Fat Meat, 2 Vegetable, 1/2 Fat

Mozzarella and Tomatoes

4 servings   PREP: 10 min   •   CHILL: 3 hr

4 medium tomatoes, cut into 1/4-inch slices

1/4 cup olive or vegetable oil

1 tablespoon chopped fresh or 1 teaspoon dried basil leaves

3 tablespoons red wine vinegar

1 tablespoon water

1/8 teaspoon salt

3 drops red pepper sauce

2 large cloves garlic, finely chopped

4 ounces fresh mozzarella cheese, sliced

Salad greens, if desired

1 Place tomatoes in glass or plastic dish.

2 Shake remaining ingredients except cheese and salad greens in tightly covered container. Pour over tomatoes.

3 Cover and refrigerate at least 3 hours, turning occasionally, to blend flavors. Layer tomatoes alternately with cheese on salad greens.

"I love appetizers. And when I didn't feel up to going out, my daughter-in-law would stop over with this tasty dish, made with fresh tomatoes from her garden. So flavorful!" —CATHERINE H.

A NOTE *from* DR. GHOSH

Tomatoes are a good source of lycopene, a phyto-chemical or naturally-occuring plant chemical in foods that may be helpful in reducing the risk of certain types of cancer in some people.

High in calcium and vitamins A and C; low fiber

1 SERVING: Calories 235 (Calories from Fat 170); Fat 19g (Saturated 5g); Cholesterol 15mg; Sodium 240mg; Potassium 320mg; Carbohydrate 8g (Dietary Fiber 1g); Protein 9g % Daily Value: Vitamin A 24%; Vitamin C 20%; Calcium 22%; Iron 4%; Folic Acid 4%; Magnesium 8% Diet Exchanges: 1 1/2 Vegetable, 1 High-Fat Meat, 2 Fat

Theresa SH.ares *her Recipe*

"Though I was told bland foods were better, I preferred stronger seasonings like garlic and herbs. As it turned out, foods with more flavor—like this salsa—worked better for me."

FOOD *for* THOUGHT

For a snack, dip tortilla chips or cut-up veggies into this special salsa. For breakfast, use it to sauce up any kind of eggs. You can even try salsa and eggs in a flour tortilla for a zesty pick-me-up!

Fresh Salsa

20 servings (1/4 cup each)   PREP: **15 min**   •   CHILL: **1 hr**

4 large tomatoes, seeded, chopped and drained (4 cups)

1 medium onion, chopped (1/2 cup)

2 cloves garlic, finely chopped

1 can (4 ounces) chopped green chilies, drained, or 1/2 cup chopped seeded fresh jalapeño chilies

1/2 cup chopped fresh cilantro

2 tablespoons fresh lime juice

1/2 teaspoon salt

1/4 teaspoon pepper

1 Mix all ingredients in glass or plastic bowl.

2 Cover and refrigerate at least 1 hour, but no longer than 1 week, to blend flavors.

Low fiber

1 SERVING: Calories 10 (Calories from Fat 0); Fat 0g (Saturated 0g); Cholesterol 0mg; Sodium 85mg; Potassium 100mg; Carbohydrate 3g (Dietary Fiber 0g); Protein 0g **% Daily Value:** Vitamin A 8%; Vitamin C 16%; Calcium 0%; Iron 2%; Folic Acid 2%; Magnesium 0% **Diet Exchanges:** 1 serving is free

Creamy Caramel Dip with Fruit

4 servings (1/4 cup each) PREP: 10 min • CHILL: 30 min

FOOD *for*
THOUGHT

Experts recommend you eat at least two to four servings of fruits daily to be sure you're getting all the nutrients you need to be healthy. Add this flavorful dip, to make eating fruit even more enjoyable.

4 ounces cream cheese, softened

1/2 cup vanilla low-fat yogurt

1/4 cup plus 1 to 2 teaspoons caramel topping

1 tablespoon chopped crystallized ginger, if desired

1 medium apple, sliced

1 medium pear, sliced

1 medium banana, sliced

1 Beat cream cheese in medium bowl with electric mixer on medium speed until creamy. Beat in yogurt and 1/4 cup of the caramel topping until smooth. Cover and refrigerate at least 30 minutes until chilled.

2 Spoon dip into small serving bowl. Drizzle with 1 to 2 teaspoons caramel topping; swirl with tip of knife. Sprinkle with ginger. Serve with apple, pear and banana slices.

"This recipe has a great 'treat yourself' feel to it. Sometimes it's nice to treat yourself. My kids also love dipping. Having a variety of tasty, healthy dips that are easy for me to make and easy for all of us to eat makes mealtime easier."

—JUDY O.

Good source of fiber

1 SERVING: Calories 270 (Calories from Fat 100); Fat 11g (Saturated 7g); Cholesterol 30mg; Sodium 190mg; Potassium 320mg; Carbohydrate 42g (Dietary Fiber 3g); Protein 4g **% Daily Value:** Vitamin A 10%; Vitamin C 10%; Calcium 8%; Iron 4%; Folic Acid 4%; Magnesium 4% **Diet Exchanges:** 2 Fruit, 1 Skim Milk, 1 1/2 Fat

Spinach Dip in Bread Bowl

8 servings (1/2 cup each) PREP: 15 min • CHILL: 1 hr

1 package (10 ounces) frozen chopped spinach, thawed and squeezed to drain

1 can (4 ounces) sliced water chestnuts, drained and chopped

5 medium green onions, chopped (5 tablespoons)

1 clove garlic, finely chopped

1/2 cup reduced-fat or regular sour cream

1/2 cup plain yogurt

1/4 teaspoon salt

1/4 teaspoon ground mustard

1/8 teaspoon pepper

1-pound unsliced round whole wheat, white or rye bread loaf

1 Mix spinach, water chestnuts, onions and garlic in large bowl. Stir in sour cream, yogurt, salt, mustard and pepper. Cover and refrigerate at least 1 hour to blend flavors.

2 Just before serving, cut 1- to 2-inch slice from top of bread loaf. Hollow out bread loaf by cutting along the edge with a serrated knife, leaving about a 1-inch shell, and pulling out large chunks of bread. Cut or tear the top slice and hollowed-out bread into bite-size pieces.

3 Fill bread loaf with spinach dip, and place on serving plate. Arrange bread pieces around loaf to use for dipping.

"A very easy recipe using two of my favorites: bread and spinach. Besides using the bread as a dipper, I used baby carrots, colorful peppers and any other veggies I had on hand. Eating colorful foods like fresh veggies just made me feel like I was doing something really good for myself." —JUDY O.

FOOD *for* THOUGHT

Spinach is a super source of folic acid. Necessary for all cells to function normally, folic acid is lacking in the diets of many people. Recent studies show that as much as 40 percent of the American population don't meet their folic acid requirement.

High in folic acid and vitamin A; good source of fiber

1 **SERVING:** Calories 190 (Calories from Fat 35); Fat 4g (Saturated 1g); Cholesterol 5mg; Sodium 430mg; Potassium 290mg; Carbohydrate 34g (Dietary Fiber 4g); Protein 8g % **Daily Value:** Vitamin A 44%; Vitamin C 10%; Calcium 14%; Iron 12%; Folic Acid 20%; Magnesium 14% **Diet Exchanges:** 2 Starch, 1 Vegetable

FOOD *for* THOUGHT

Salmon is a fabulous source of the mineral phosphorus. You need phosphorus to build strong bones and help your muscles function properly when they relax and contract. If you crush up and eat the bones in canned salmon, you'll get some extra calcium, too.

Low fiber

1 SERVING: Calories 235 (Calories from Fat 155); Fat 17g (Saturated 8g); Cholesterol 60mg; Sodium 610mg; Potassium 230mg; Carbohydrate 8g (Dietary Fiber 0g); Protein 13g **% Daily Value:** Vitamin A 10%; Vitamin C 0%; Calcium 14%; Iron 6%; Folic Acid 4%; Magnesium 6% **Diet Exchanges:** 1/2 Starch, 2 High-Fat Meat

Easy Salmon Spread

8 servings (1/4 cup each) PREP: 15 min • CHILL: 2 hr

1 package (8 ounces) reduced-fat or fat-free cream cheese, softened

1 can (14 3/4 ounces) red or pink salmon, drained and flaked

3 tablespoons finely chopped red onion

2 tablespoons chopped fresh or 1/4 teaspoon dried dill weed

1 tablespoon Dijon mustard

2 tablespoons capers

Crisp crackers or bagel chips

1 Line 2-cup bowl or mold with plastic wrap. Beat cream cheese in medium bowl with electric mixer on medium speed until smooth. Stir in salmon, 2 tablespoons of the onion, 1 tablespoon of the dill weed and the mustard. Spoon into bowl lined with plastic wrap, pressing firmly. Cover and refrigerate at least 2 hours but no longer than 24 hours.

2 Turn bowl upside down onto serving plate; remove bowl and plastic wrap. Garnish spread with remaining 1 table-spoon onion, 1 tablespoon dill weed and the capers. Serve with crackers.

"I don't eat many meals while I'm on chemo. I usually graze all day long, so a few crackers with salmon spread and two of the Snappy Stuffed Tomatoes (page 96) would make a great snack or mini-meal for me." —ANNE R.

Susan S. Shares her Recipe

"When I was very fatigued, I used any fruit I had on hand to make this quick smoothie. Dropping fresh blueberries into the glass on top of the smoothie adds extra color and flavor that is so good with the lemon and peach."

Citrus-Peach Smoothie

3 servings (1 cup each)   PREP: 5 min

1 container (8 ounces) lemon fat-free yogurt

1 cup unsweetened frozen, fresh or canned (drained) sliced peaches

3/4 cup calcium-fortified orange juice

3 tablespoons blueberries, if desired

1 Place yogurt, peaches and orange juice in blender. Cover and blend on high speed about 30 seconds or until smooth.

2 Pour mixture into glasses. Garnish with blueberries.

A NOTE *from* DR. GHOSH

Orange juice is a well-known source of vitamin C. When eaten with a food containing iron, the vitamin C in foods can improve iron absorption to help prevent anemia. Having a diet high in vitamin C also decreases the risk of infections and helps heal wounds.

High in calcium and vitamin C

1 SERVING: Calories 100 (Calories from Fat 0); Fat 0g (Saturated 0g); Cholesterol 0mg; Sodium 40mg; Potassium 350mg; Carbohydrate 22g (Dietary Fiber 1g); Protein 4g **% Daily Value:** Vitamin A 12%; Vitamin C 100%; Calcium 20%; Iron 6%; Folic Acid 4%; Magnesium 6% **Diet Exchanges:** 1 1/2 Fruit

Judy O. Shares *her Recipe*

"When I didn't feel like eating a meal, smoothies were quick, easy to swallow and nutritious. I keep ripe bananas in the freezer—then they're always ready for this refreshing shake."

A NOTE *from* **DR. GHOSH**

Smoothies make a great solution for mouth sores, as they are soothing. Because citrus foods can make the discomfort worse, kiwifruit, watermelon and bananas are good choices.

Watermelon-Kiwi-Banana Smoothie

2 servings (1 cup each)   PREP: 10 min

1 cup coarsely chopped seeded watermelon

1 kiwifruit, peeled and cut into pieces

2 ice cubes

1 ripe banana, frozen, peeled and cut into chunks

1/4 cup chilled apple juice

1 Place all ingredients in blender. Cover and blend on high speed about 30 seconds or until smooth.

2 Pour mixture into glasses.

High in vitamin C; good source of fiber

1 SERVING: Calories 115 (Calories from Fat 10); Fat 1g (Saturated 0g); Cholesterol 0mg; Sodium 5mg; Potassium 480mg; Carbohydrate 29g (Dietary Fiber 3g); Protein 1g % **Daily Value:** Vitamin A 10%; Vitamin C 84%; Calcium 2%; Iron 2%; Folic Acid 6%; Magnesium 8% **Diet Exchanges:** 2 Fruit

Citrus-Peach Smoothie (page 103), Orange-Pineapple Smoothie (page 106), and Watermelon-Kiwi-Banana Smoothie

Judy O. Shares *her Recipe*

"The two changes I've made to my diet are drinking more water and eating more fruits and vegetables. Now I never get in my car without my water bottle, and this smoothie is an easy way to load up on fruit."

A NOTE *from* DR. GHOSH

This smoothie is a great choice during chemotherapy when you may be experiencing nausea, vomiting or diarrhea or having difficulty chewing. Staying well-hydrated can be half the battle.

Orange-Pineapple Smoothie

3 servings (1 cup each)   PREP: 10 min

1 1/2 cups calcium-fortified orange juice

1/2 cup fresh or canned pineapple chunks

1 ripe banana, frozen and cut into chunks

2 tablespoons vanilla-protein powder or 1/4 cup orange yogurt

3 ice cubes

1 Place all ingredients in blender. Cover and blend on high speed about 30 seconds or until smooth.

2 Pour mixture into glasses.

High in calcium and vitamin C

1 SERVING: Calories 120 (Calories from Fat 10); Fat 1g (Saturated 1g); Cholesterol 0mg; Sodium 15mg; Potassium 440mg; Carbohydrate 28g (Dietary Fiber 2g); Protein 2g % **Daily Value:** Vitamin A 2%; Vitamin C 84%; Calcium 20%; Iron 4%; Folic Acid 8%; Magnesium 8% **Diet Exchanges:** 2 Fruit

Sugar 'n Spice Green Tea

4 servings PREP: 10 min

4 cups boiling water

4 tea bags green tea

6 whole cloves, broken into pieces

1/4 teaspoon ground cinnamon

1/4 cup sugar

1/4 cup fresh orange juice

2 tablespoons fresh lemon juice

2 orange slices, cut in half

1 Pour boiling water over tea in heatproof container. Add cloves and cinnamon. Cover and let steep 3 to 5 minutes.

2 Remove tea bags; strain tea to remove cloves. Stir sugar, orange juice and lemon juice into tea. Serve hot with orange slice half in each cup.

A NOTE *from* **DR. GHOSH**

This fruity tea is helpful if you have a metallic taste in your mouth. The combination of citrus and spices can help to disguise an off taste. Don't forget that green tea is not an herbal tea; like black tea, it contains caffeine.

"I have always enjoyed coffee, but now I'm trying to drink more tea—green tea especially. This spicy, sweet tea is a great alternative to plain green tea, and it's good when served chilled. Sometimes, I'd make it up hot and refrigerate the rest to drink later as iced tea, especially in the summer." —JUDY O.

Low fiber

1 SERVING: Calories 60 (Calories from Fat 0); Fat 0g (Saturated 0g); Cholesterol 0mg; Sodium 10mg; Potassium 120mg; Carbohydrate 15g (Dietary Fiber 0g); Protein 0g **% Daily Value:** Vitamin A 0%; Vitamin C 6%; Calcium 0%; Iron 0%; Folic Acid 4%; Magnesium 2% **Diet Exchanges:** 1 Fruit

Chai Tea

4 servings (1 cup each)   PREP: 6 min   •   COOK: 4 min

2 cups water

4 tea bags black tea

2 1/2 cups milk

2 tablespoons honey

1/2 teaspoon ground ginger

1/2 teaspoon ground nutmeg

1/4 teaspoon ground cinnamon

1 Heat water to boiling in 2-quart saucepan. Add tea bags; reduce heat. Simmer 2 minutes. Remove tea bags.

2 Stir remaining ingredients into tea. Heat to boiling. Stir with wire whisk to foam milk. Pour into cups.

A NOTE *from* DR. GHOSH

Tea has long been linked to relaxation. Chai, popular in India, is black tea mixed with fragrant spices such as nutmeg and cinnamon, milk and a sweetener. This warming tea is especially comforting on cool mornings. It's also good served iced on warm days.

"I found hot tea to be a lifesaver during treatment; it went down very easily. The honey and spices in this tea are very soothing. If black tea doesn't sound good to you right now, use any herbal tea."

—LOIS K.

High in calcium

1 SERVING: Calories 120 (Calories from Fat 25); Fat 3g (Saturated 2g); Cholesterol 10mg; Sodium 8omg; Potassium 290mg; Carbohydrate 17g (Dietary Fiber og); Protein 5g **% Daily Value:** Vitamin A 6%; Vitamin C 0%; Calcium 18%; Iron 2%; Folic Acid 4%; Magnesium 6% **Diet Exchanges:** 1/2 Skim Milk; 1 Fruit

Snack Busters

At times, you may not feel up to eating a full meal and instead may find that eating more often throughout the day is better. If a regular-sized meal is too much for you, try eating mini-meals or snacks instead of large meals. For good snack choices, check out the list below:

- **Fresh fruits and vegetables** provide many needed nutrients. Keep baby carrots, celery sticks, fresh or frozen grapes, bananas and apples on hand.

- **String cheese, cheese chunks and cottage cheese,** eaten with or without fresh fruit, provide much-needed calcium.

- **Graham and saltine crackers** are easy to digest and are low in residue. Eat them plain, or spread them with peanut butter, cheese or jam.

- **Cereal with or without milk** contains many nutrients from fortification. Cereal is very convenient to snack on right from the box or to add to salted peanuts or pretzels, as well as to eat with milk.

- **Nuts, snack mixes, popcorn and granola bars** work well for those not needing to follow a low-residue diet. Quick energy and convenience are key to these tasty snacks.

- **Canned and dried fruits.** Mandarin oranges, applesauce, dried plums or apricots and dates are great snacks on their own, or team them up with nuts, popcorn or cheese crackers.

- **Small sandwiches,** such as grilled cheese or turkey, cut into fourths, work well as mini-meals. Eat one piece now, then if you're up to it, eat another; otherwise save the rest for later.

- **Soup and crackers.** For convenience, use canned soup and serve yourself a small bowl. Miniature crackers, such as oyster crackers or fish-shaped cheese crackers, may not seem as overwhelming as larger crackers, so start with them first.

- **Shakes and smoothies containing milk or yogurt** can be a source of extra calcium and other important nutrients. Because no chewing is required, beverages are particularly soothing if you have mouth sores.

- **Make the most of leftovers.** Reheat mashed potatoes, pizza or pasta. Turn yesterday's salad into a filling for sandwiches. For flavor boosters, see page 125.

- **Something sweet.** Small cookies or cakes may provide necessary carbohydrates to boost your energy in a pinch, but save room for more sustaining foods, too.

Fettuccine with Asparagus and Mushrooms (page 112)

20-Minute Main Dishes

4

"A good friend, well known for her healthy eating habits, shared this recipe with me. I found it to be very soothing, tasty and colorful."

A NOTE *from* **DR. GHOSH**

The pasta (grain), pinenuts and cheese make this recipe a good choice for vegetarians with cancer.

Fettuccine with Asparagus and Mushrooms

6 servings (1 1/3 cup each) PREP: 10 min • COOK: 10 min

1/4 cup sun-dried tomatoes (not oil-packed)

8 ounces uncooked fettuccine

1 teaspoon olive or vegetable oil

1 pound thin asparagus, broken into 2-inch pieces

1 pound mushrooms, sliced (6 cups)

2 cloves garlic, finely chopped

3 tablespoons chopped fresh parsley

2 tablespoons chopped fresh basil leaves

2 tablespoons cornstarch

1/2 teaspoon salt

1/4 teaspoon pepper

1 cup dry white wine or chicken broth

1 cup chicken broth

2 tablespoons pine nuts

1/4 cup freshly grated Parmesan cheese

1 Cover dried tomatoes with boiling water. Let stand 10 minutes; drain. Chop tomatoes.

2 Cook and drain fettuccine as directed on package.

3 While fettuccine is cooking, heat oil in 12-inch skillet over medium heat. Cook asparagus, mushrooms, garlic, parsley and basil in oil 5 minutes, stirring occasionally. Stir in tomatoes. Simmer 2 to 3 minutes, until tomatoes are heated.

4 Beat cornstarch, salt and pepper into wine and broth in small bowl with wire whisk; stir into vegetable mixture. Heat to boiling over medium heat, stirring constantly, until mixture is smooth and bubbly; boil and stir 1 minute. Serve over fettuccine. Sprinkle with nuts and cheese.

High in folic acid; good source of fiber

1 SERVING: Calories 225 (Calories from Fat 55); Fat 2g (Saturated 1g); Cholesterol 35mg; Sodium 680mg; Potassium 570mg; Carbohydrate 31g (Dietary Fiber 3g); Protein 11g **% Daily Value:** Vitamin A 14%; Vitamin C 12%; Calcium 8%; Iron 18%; Folic Acid 34%; Magnesium 12% **Diet Exchanges:** 1 Starch, 3 Vegetable, 1 Fat

Mediterranean Couscous and Beans

4 servings PREP: 10 min • COOK: 3 min • STAND: 5 min

3 cups chicken broth

2 cups uncooked couscous

1/2 cup raisins or currants

1/4 teaspoon pepper

1/8 teaspoon ground red pepper (cayenne)

1 small tomato, chopped (1/2 cup)

1 can (15 to 16 ounces) garbanzo beans, rinsed and drained

1/3 cup crumbled feta cheese

1 Heat broth to boiling in 3-quart saucepan. Stir in remaining ingredients except cheese; remove from heat.

2 Cover and let stand about 5 minutes or until liquid is absorbed; stir gently. Sprinkle each serving with cheese.

"This great main dish has the added benefit of containing fruit and vegetables and is quick to cook. Best of all, my family loves couscous!" —JUDY O.

A NOTE *from* **DR. GHOSH**

Legumes, such as dried beans, peas and garbanzo beans, are a great source of fiber. Eating plenty of fiber helps keep the digestive tract moving. This, in turn, lessens the amount of time the intestinal tract is exposed to foods and breakdown products of foods, some of which may contain toxins.

High in potassium, iron, magnesium and folic acid; excellent source of fiber

1 **SERVING:** Calories 575 (Calories from Fat 65); Fat 7g (Saturated 3g); Cholesterol 10mg; Sodium 1070mg; Potassium 800mg; Carbohydrate 114g (Dietary Fiber 13g); Protein 27g % **Daily Value:** Vitamin A 4%; Vitamin C 4%; Calcium 14%; Iron 28%; Folic Acid 52%; Magnesium 26% **Diet Exchanges:** 6 starch, 1 Very-Lean Meat, 1 Fruit, 1 Vegetable

Susan S. *Shares* her Recipe

"There is something so appealing about the flavor combination of tomato, avocado and basil with pasta that was very comforting to me and satisfied my cravings."

A NOTE *from* DR. GHOSH

Coconut oil can be substituted for soy, corn, olive or safflower oil. Coconut oil is a source of medium-chain fatty acids, which for some, may be more easily digested.

Angel Hair Pasta with Avocado and Tomatoes

6 servings (1 1/3 cups each) PREP: 15 min • COOK: 5 min

8 ounces uncooked angel hair pasta

2 tablespoons olive or vegetable oil

2 cloves garlic, finely chopped

3/4 cup chopped fresh basil leaves

1/2 to 3/4 large avocado, peeled and cut into small cubes

4 medium tomatoes, cut into small cubes

1/2 teaspoon salt

1/4 teaspoon pepper

1 Cook and drain pasta as directed on package.

2 While pasta is cooking, heat oil in 3-quart saucepan over medium heat; add garlic. Cook 1 to 2 minutes, stirring occasionally, until garlic is tender but not brown; remove from heat.

3 Stir basil, avocado and tomatoes into garlic in saucepan. Toss vegetable mixture and pasta. Sprinkle with salt and pepper.

High in vitamin A and folic acid; good source of fiber

1 SERVING: Calories 220 (Calories from Fat 90); Fat 10g (Saturated 1g); Cholesterol 30mg; Sodium 210mg; Potassium 370mg; Carbohydrate 30g (Dietary Fiber 3g); Protein 6g **% Daily Value:** Vitamin A 22%; Vitamin C 14%; Calcium 2%; Iron 12%; Folic Acid 22%; Magnesium 10% **Diet Exchanges:** 1 1/2 Starch, 2 Vegetable, 1 Fat

Creamy Quinoa Primavera

6 servings   PREP: 10 min   •   COOK: 18 min

1 1/2 cups uncooked quinoa

3 cups chicken broth

1 package (3 ounces) cream cheese

1 tablespoon chopped fresh or 1 teaspoon dried basil leaves

2 teaspoons butter or margarine

2 cloves garlic, finely chopped

5 cups thinly sliced or bite-size pieces assorted uncooked vegetables (asparagus, broccoli, carrot or zucchini)

2 tablespoons grated Romano cheese

1 Rinse quinoa thoroughly; drain. Heat quinoa and broth to boiling in 2-quart saucepan; reduce heat. Cover and simmer 10 to 15 minutes or until all broth is absorbed. Stir in cream cheese and basil.

2 Melt butter in 10-inch nonstick skillet over medium-high heat. Cook garlic in butter about 30 seconds, stirring frequently, until golden. Stir in vegetables. Cook about 2 minutes, stirring frequently, until vegetables are crisp-tender.

3 Toss vegetables and quinoa mixture. Sprinkle with Romano cheese.

FOOD for THOUGHT

Quinoa, pronounced "keen-wa," was a staple grain of the Incas of Peru. Loaded with nutrients, quinoa has a sweet, slightly nutty flavor. Be sure to rinse quinoa to remove the natural bitter coating of the grain.

High in potassium, vitamins A and C, iron, folic acid and magnesium; excellent source of fiber

1 SERVING: Calories 265 (Calories from Fat 90); Fat 10g (Saturated 5g); Cholesterol 20mg; Sodium 630mg; Potassium 710mg; Carbohydrate 37g (Dietary Fiber 5g); Protein 12g % **Daily Value:** Vitamin A 100%; Vitamin C 22%; Calcium 10%; Iron 28%; Folic Acid 22%; Magnesium 26% **Diet Exchanges:** 1 Starch, 4 Vegetable, 2 Fat

"Quinoa is such a great source of protein and tastes great! I cooked quinoa for my kids when they were 8 and 11 and for my nieces and nephews (now ages 4 through 9), and they loved it! They didn't even know they were eating something healthy!"   —ANNE R.

"I needed to eat low-residue foods, so having this simple recipe really helped me!"

Pasta with Chicken in Chili Sauce

4 servings PREP: 5 min • COOK: 15 min

4 ounces uncooked spinach fettuccine, vermicelli or other pasta

2 tablespoons vegetable oil

4 boneless, skinless chicken breast halves (about 1 1/4 pounds)

1 medium onion, sliced

1 cup chicken broth

1/2 cup chili sauce

Grated Parmesan cheese, if desired

1 Cook and drain fettuccine as directed on package.

2 While fettuccine is cooking, heat oil in 10-inch skillet over medium-high heat. Cook chicken and onion in oil 10 to 12 minutes, turning chicken once and stirring onions occasionally, until brown.

3 Stir broth and chili sauce into chicken and onion. Cook about 5 minutes or until sauce is thickened and juice of chicken is no longer pink when centers of thickest pieces are cut.

4 Place fettuccine on serving platter. Top with chicken and sauce. Sprinkle with cheese.

FOOD *for* **THOUGHT**

This recipe supplies a good source of potassium, a nutrient needed to help the body maintain its fluid balance. Potassium also helps with nerve and muscle function.

Low residue

1 SERVING: Calories 380 (Calories from Fat 125); Fat 14g (Saturated 4g); Cholesterol 100mg; Sodium 850mg; Potassium 500mg; Carbohydrate 31g (Dietary Fiber 2g); Protein 35g **% Daily Value:** Vitamin A 10%; Vitamin C 6%; Calcium 12%; Iron 14%; Folic Acid 16%; Magnesium 12% **Diet Exchanges:** 2 Starch, 4 Lean Meat

Honey-Mustard Turkey with Snap Peas

4 servings   PREP: 5 min   •   MARINATE: 20 min   •   COOK: 15 min

FOOD *for* **THOUGHT**

This zesty turkey recipe cooks in a flash. Just marinate the turkey as described above, throw in some carrots and pea pods for vitamins A and C and you're ready to go.

1 pound uncooked turkey breast slices, about 1/4 inch thick

1/2 cup Dijon and honey poultry and meat marinade

1 cup baby-cut carrots, cut lengthwise in half

2 cups frozen snap pea pods

1 Place turkey in shallow glass or plastic dish. Pour marinade over turkey; turn slices to coat evenly. Cover dish and let stand at room temperature 20 minutes.

2 Spray 10-inch skillet with cooking spray; heat over medium heat. Drain most of marinade from turkey. Cook turkey in skillet about 5 minutes, turning once, until brown.

3 Add carrots, lifting turkey to place carrots on bottom of skillet. Top turkey and carrots with pea pods. Cover and cook about 7 minutes or until carrots are crisp-tender and turkey is no longer pink in center.

"The thin slices of turkey make it easy to eat a small portion and still get a well-balanced and pretty-looking plate. It is very important for food to be appetizing and yet served in small enough quantities so I am not overwhelmed."

—ANNE R.

High in iron and vitamins A and C; good source of fiber

1 SERVING: Calories 145 (Calories from Fat 10); Fat 1g (Saturated 0g); Cholesterol 75mg; Sodium 500mg; Potassium 530mg; Carbohydrate 10g (Dietary Fiber 3g); Protein 29g **% Daily Value:** Vitamin A 100%; Vitamin C 28%; Calcium 6%; Iron 18%; Folic Acid 8%; Magnesium 12% **Diet Exchanges:** 3 Very-Lean Meat, 2 Vegetable

Caribbean Chicken Salad

4 servings PREP: 10 min • COOK: 12 min

1 pound boneless, skinless chicken breasts, cut into 1/2-inch strips

2 tablespoons blackened seasoning blend

1 tablespoon vegetable oil

1 package (5 ounces) mixed baby salad greens (4 cups)

1 medium mango, peeled, pitted and diced (1 cup)

1/2 medium red onion, sliced (3/4 cup)

1 small red bell pepper, chopped (1/2 cup)

2/3 cup fruit-flavored vinaigrette

1 Place chicken in heavy-duty resealable plastic food-storage bag. Sprinkle seasoning blend over chicken; seal bag and shake until chicken is evenly coated.

2 Heat oil in 10-inch nonstick skillet over medium-high heat. Cook chicken in oil 10 to 12 minutes, stirring frequently, until no longer pink in center. Remove chicken from skillet; drain on paper towels.

3 Toss salad greens, mango, onion and bell pepper in large bowl; divide among 4 plates. Top with chicken. Drizzle with vinaigrette.

"I always have boneless, skinless chicken breasts on hand, ready for an easy, quick meal." —JUDY O.

n

FOOD *for* THOUGHT

Loaded with mango and bell pepper, this salad is a tasty source of vitamins A and C. Vitamin C helps promote healthy gums, blood vessels, bones and teeth and can also help us to absorb iron better.

High in vitamins A and C; good source of fiber

1 **SERVING:** Calories 240 (Calories from Fat 70); Fat 8g (Saturated 2g); Cholesterol 70mg; Sodium 550mg; Potassium 490mg; Carbohydrate 19g (Dietary Fiber 3g); Protein 26g % **Daily Value:** Vitamin A 52%; Vitamin C 94%; Calcium 6%; Iron 12%; Folic Acid 16%; Magnesium 10% **Diet Exchanges:** 3 Lean Meat, 1 Vegetable, 1 Fruit.

Marie E. *Shares* her Recipe

"A very easy chicken and fruit salad, this recipe has always been a hit for me and with family and friends."

A NOTE *from* **DR. GHOSH**

Cantaloupe and grapes are moist, tasty fruits that blend well with this tangy dressing. Sometimes eating fruits that contain a lot of water can help soothe dry mouth. The vitamin C helps boost the immune system and fight infection.

Cantaloupe and Chicken Salad

6 servings (1 1/2 cups each)   PREP: 20 min

1/4 cup plain yogurt

1/4 cup mayonnaise or salad dressing

1 tablespoon fresh lemon juice

1 tablespoon chopped fresh chives

1/4 teaspoon salt

5 cups 1 1/2-inch pieces cantaloupe

2 1/2 cups cut-up cooked chicken

1 cup red or green grapes, cut in half

1 medium cucumber, cut into strips

1 Mix yogurt and mayonnaise in large bowl. Stir in lemon juice, chives and salt.

2 Stir in remaining ingredients. Serve immediately, or refrigerate until chilled, at least 2 hours but no longer than 24 hours.

High in potassium and vitamins A and C

1 SERVING: Calories 250 (Calories from Fat 110); Fat 12g (Saturated 2g); Cholesterol 5mg; Sodium 220mg; Potassium 680mg; Carbohydrate 18g (Dietary Fiber 2g); Protein 19g **% Daily Value:** Vitamin A 74%; Vitamin C 100%; Calcium 4%; Iron 6%; Folic Acid 8%; Magnesium 8% **Diet Exchanges:** 2 1/2 Lean Meat, 1 Vegetable, 1 Fruit, 1/2 Fat

Cantaloupe and Chicken Salad

Spinach-Shrimp Salad with Hot Bacon Dressing

4 servings   PREP: 10 min • COOK: 10 min

4 slices bacon, cut into 1-inch pieces

1/4 cup white vinegar

1 tablespoon sugar

1/4 teaspoon ground mustard

4 cups lightly packed bite-size pieces spinach leaves

1 cup sliced mushrooms (3 ounces)

1 cup crumbled feta cheese (4 ounces)

1/2 pound cooked, peeled, deveined medium shrimp

1 Cook bacon in 10-inch skillet over medium-high heat, stirring occasionally, until crisp. Stir in vinegar, sugar and mustard; continue stirring until sugar is dissolved.

2 Toss spinach, mushrooms, cheese and shrimp in large bowl. Drizzle hot bacon dressing over spinach mixture; toss to coat. Serve immediately.

FOOD for THOUGHT

Shrimp provides the body with a source of vitamin D, which is crucial for helping the body build calcium and phosphorus into strong bones and teeth. Drinking milk and exposure to sunlight are other ways in which the body receives vitamin D.

"I'm trying to eat more spinach, and this recipe makes it easy as it uses three of my favorite foods: mushrooms, cheese and shrimp."   —JUDY O.

High in calcium, iron, vitamin A and folic acid; low fiber

1 **SERVING:** Calories 210 (Calories from Fat 110); Fat 12g (Saturated 7g); Cholesterol 150mg; Sodium 670mg; Potassium 400mg; Carbohydrate 7g (Dietary Fiber 1g); Protein 20g % **Daily Value:** Vitamin A 62%; Vitamin C 16%; Calcium 24%; Iron 18%; Folic Acid 18%; Magnesium 14% **Diet Exchanges:** 2 1/2 Lean Meat, 1 Vegetable, 1 Fat

Chutney-Salmon Salad

4 servings PREP: 10 min

2 cans (6 ounces each)
skinless boneless salmon,
drained and flaked

3 cups broccoli slaw

2/3 cup mayonnaise or
salad dressing

1/3 cup chutney

1/4 cup dry-roasted peanuts,
chopped

1 Mix salmon, broccoli slaw, mayonnaise and chutney in glass or plastic bowl.

2 Stir in peanuts just before serving.

*"When I'm tired, I like to use shortcuts.
Broccoli slaw is one of my favorites."*

—JUDY O.

FOOD *for* THOUGHT

Salmon is a super source of vitamin B_{12}. We need vitamin B_{12} for all body cells to function properly. Other sources of vitamin B_{12} include lean cuts of beef and pork loin.

High in calcium, potassium, vitamin C and folic acid; good source of fiber

1 SERVING: Calories 480 (Calories from Fat 350); Fat 39g (Saturated 6g); Cholesterol 70mg; Sodium 750mg; Potassium 600mg; Carbohydrate 14g (Dietary Fiber 3g); Protein 22g % Daily Value: Vitamin A 20%; Vitamin C 100%; Calcium 22%; Iron 10%; Folic Acid 18%; Magnesium 16% Diet Exchanges: 2 High-Fat Meat, 3 Vegetable, 4 1/2 Fat

Savory Scallops and Shrimp

4 servings PREP: 10 min • COOK: 10 min

2 tablespoons olive or vegetable oil

1 clove garlic, finely chopped

1 medium green onion, chopped (1 tablespoon)

1 medium green bell pepper, diced (1 cup)

1 tablespoon chopped fresh parsley or 1 teaspoon parsley flakes

1 pound sea scallops, cut in half

1 pound uncooked medium shrimp (thawed if frozen), peeled and deveined

1/2 cup dry white wine or chicken broth

1 tablespoon lemon juice

1/4 to 1/2 teaspoon crushed red pepper

1 Heat oil in 10-inch skillet over medium heat. Cook garlic, onion, bell pepper and parsley in oil about 5 minutes, stirring occasionally, until bell pepper is crisp-tender.

2 Stir in remaining ingredients. Cook 4 to 5 minutes, stirring frequently, until shrimp are pink and firm and scallops are white.

A NOTE *from* DR. GHOSH

Broth or apple juice can often be substituted for the wine used to flavor a recipe. Use your judgment to determine which flavor would work best with the recipe. Some studies have shown that small amounts of alcohol, such as wine, may lessen the risk of developing coronary heart disease in middle-aged men and women.

"I'm using more fresh herbs in my cooking, which enhances the aroma and flavor of foods. This makes me feel more like eating."
—JUDY O.

High in iron and vitamin C; low fiber

1 SERVING: Calories 190 (Calories from Fat 70); Fat 8g (Saturated 1g); Cholesterol 125mg; Sodium 400mg; Potassium 470mg; Carbohydrate 5g (Dietary Fiber 1g); Protein 25g % Daily Value: Vitamin A 10%; Vitamin C 26%; Calcium 10%; Iron 20%; Folic Acid 6%; Magnesium 16% Diet Exchanges: 3 Lean Meat, 1 Vegetable

Flavor Boosters

"Food just tastes different during chemotherapy, not like it used to." Sound familiar? Due to chemotherapy or radiation and the effect these treatments have on the way food tastes, finding ways to enjoy your food can be a real challenge.

What works for one person may not work for another; some patients find that eating bland or plain foods is best, and some find they tolerate highly seasoned or spicy foods and even crave them. Try a few of these ideas to boost the flavor of your foods.

1. Add grated lemon, lime or orange, or the juice from these fruits, to cookies, cakes, chicken and fish.

2. Marinate chicken breasts or turkey breast slices in soy sauce, teriyaki sauce or sauté sauce (such as Dijon chicken sauté sauce) for 30 minutes before cooking.

3. Add pesto or salsa to pasta, fish and main dishes.

4. Use fresh herbs when cooking chicken and fish.

5. Use small amounts of foods that pack a lot of flavor: Kalamata olives, anchovies, capers, roasted garlic, blue cheese, feta cheese, Dijon mustard, toasted walnuts, crushed red pepper.

6. Use garlic to boost the flavor of meats, side dishes, pilafs, salads and soups.

7. Cook rice in broth or apple juice instead of water.

8. Sprinkle toasted nuts over fish, salads and main and side dishes.

9. Caramelize meat by sprinkling brown sugar, drizzling with orange juice or molasses and cooking until the mixture thickens and coats the meat.

10. Experiment with balsamic, raspberry, tarragon, white wine and seasoned rice vinegars to add zing to cooked vegetables, pasta, soups, salads and cooked meats.

11. Use curry powder and coriander in chicken salads and casseroles and to add a jolt of exotic flavor to soups and stews.

FOOD *for* THOUGHT

This salad is a great source of the mineral magnesium. Considered one of the healing nutrients, magnesium is important in helping to release carbohydrate energy from foods. Magnesium also works to transmit nerve impulses through muscles.

High in potassium, magnesium, folic acid and vitamin C; excellent source of fiber

1 **SERVING:** Calories 430 (Calories from Fat 215); Fat 24g (Saturated 3g); Cholesterol 75mg; Sodium 520mg; Potassium 1040mg; Carbohydrate 37g (Dietary Fiber 9g); Protein 25g % **Daily Value:** Vitamin A 41%; Vitamin C 100%; Calcium 14%; Iron 12%; Folic Acid 40%; Magnesium 24% **Diet Exchanges:** 3 High-Fat Meat, 1 Vegetable, 2 Fruit

Chopped Vegetable and Crabmeat Salad

4 servings PREP: 20 min

Lime Dressing (below)

2 cups torn escarole

2 cans (6 ounces each) crabmeat, drained and flaked, or 2 cups chopped cooked turkey or chicken

1 small jicama, peeled and chopped (1 cup)

1 large papaya, peeled, seeded and chopped (1 cup)

1 large yellow or red bell pepper, chopped (1 cup)

1/2 cup dry-roasted peanuts

1/4 cup chopped fresh cilantro

Lime Dressing

1/3 cup frozen (thawed) limeade concentrate

1/4 cup vegetable oil

1 tablespoon rice or white vinegar

1 teaspoon grated gingerroot

1/4 teaspoon salt

1 Make Lime Dressing.

2 Place remaining ingredients except peanuts and cilantro in large bowl. Pour dressing over salad; toss to coat.

3 Top with peanuts and cilantro.

Shake all ingredients in tightly covered container.

"Me first—that's my new motto. Most of my life I have been caring for other people. During chemo, I allowed myself and my family to put me first on the care list."
—JUDY O.

Chopped Vegetable and Crabmeat Salad

"It was important to me to keep things on a routine and prepare foods that my family would eat, like this easy salad."

FOOD *for* **THOUGHT**

Carrots are a great source of beta-carotene, a form of vitamin A. You need vitamin A daily for proper vision in dim light and for healthy hair and skin.

Carrot-Tuna Salad

6 servings (1 cup each)   PREP: 20 min • CHILL: 1 hr

1/2 cup mayonnaise or salad dressing

1/4 teaspoon salt

1/4 teaspoon pepper

2 medium carrots, shredded (1 cup)

2 medium stalks celery, diced (1 cup)

1 small onion, chopped (1/4 cup)

2 hard-cooked eggs, sliced

2 cans (6 ounces each) tuna in water, drained

1 can (4 ounces) shoestring potatoes

1 Mix all ingredients except tuna and potatoes in large bowl. Stir in tuna. Cover and refrigerate about 1 hour or until chilled.

2 Stir in potatoes just before serving.

High in vitamins A and C

1 SERVING: Calories 360 (Calories from Fat 55); Fat 23g (Saturated 5g); Cholesterol 100mg; Sodium 490mg; Potassium 580mg; Carbohydrate 16g (Dietary Fiber 2g); Protein 19g **% Daily Value:** Vitamin A 100%; Vitamin C 24%; Calcium 4%; Iron 10%; Folic Acid 6%; Magnesium 8% **Diet Exchanges:** 1/2 Starch, 2 Lean Meat, 2 Vegetable, 3 Fat

Fiesta Taco Salad

5 servings   PREP: 15 min   •   COOK: 10 min

1 can (15 ounces) black beans,
rinsed and drained

1/2 cup taco sauce

6 cups bite-size pieces lettuce

1 medium green bell pepper,
cut into strips

2 medium tomatoes,
cut into wedges

1/2 cup pitted ripe olives,
drained

1 cup corn chips

1 cup shredded Cheddar
cheese (4 ounces)

1/2 cup Thousand Island
dressing

1 Heat beans and taco sauce in 2-quart saucepan over medium
heat 2 to 3 minutes, stirring occasionally, until heated.

2 Toss lettuce, bell pepper, tomatoes, olives and corn chips in
large bowl. Spoon bean mixture over lettuce mixture; toss.
Sprinkle with cheese. Serve immediately with dressing.

*"The beans replace the hamburger in
this taco salad. It's a great 'new' way
to serve a family favorite."*   —JUDY O.

FOOD *for* THOUGHT

*This nutrient-dense recipe
is a powerhouse! That
means for the amount of
calories it provides, it's
loaded with vitamins and
minerals such as fiber, calcium, iron, magnesium
and vitamin C—key nutri-
ents important to the
healing process.*

High in calcium, iron,
magnesium and vita-
min C; excellent source
of fiber

1 **SERVING:** Calories 270 (Calories
from Fat 215); Fat 12g (Saturated 5g);
Cholesterol 25mg; Sodium 730mg;
Potassium 540mg; Carbohydrate 31g
(Dietary Fiber 8g); Protein 18g % **Daily
Value:** Vitamin A 14%; Vitamin C 46%;
Calcium 20%; Iron 20%; Folic Acid 14%;
Magnesium 18% **Diet Exchanges:** 2 Starch,
2 Lean Meat

Potato-Tomato-Tofu Dinner

5 servings PREP: 5 min • COOK: 15 min

A NOTE *from* DR. GHOSH

Tofu is a great alternative to meat. Made from soybeans, it provides protein, iron and calcium. Tofu can be comforting when mouth sores or dry mouth are a bother, because it's so very easy to chew!

2 tablespoons olive or vegetable oil

1/2 cup coarsely chopped red onion

5 small red potatoes, sliced (2 1/2 cups)

2 cups frozen cut green beans

1/2 teaspoon Italian seasoning

1/2 teaspoon garlic salt

1 package (14-ounce size) firm tofu, cut into 1/2-inch cubes

2 roma (plum) tomatoes, thinly sliced

1 hard-cooked egg, chopped

1 Heat oil in 12-inch skillet over medium-high heat. Cook onion in oil 2 minutes, stirring frequently. Stir in potatoes; reduce heat to medium-low. Cover and cook about 8 minutes, stirring occasionally, until potatoes are tender.

2 Stir in green beans, Italian seasoning and garlic salt. Cover and cook about 5 minutes, stirring occasionally, until beans are tender and potatoes are light golden brown.

3 Stir in tofu and tomatoes. Cook 2 to 3 minutes, stirring occasionally and gently, just until hot. Sprinkle each serving with egg.

Good source of fiber

1 SERVING: Calories 205 (Calories from Fat 100); Fat 11g (Saturated 2g); Cholesterol 85mg; Sodium 140mg; Potassium 460mg; Carbohydrate 20g (Dietary Fiber 3g); Protein 10g % Daily Value: Vitamin A 12%; Vitamin C 10%; Calcium 12%; Iron 12%; Folic Acid 16%; Magnesium 12% Diet Exchanges: 1 Starch, 1 Very-Lean Meat, 1 Vegetable, 1 1/2 Fat

"I love tofu when I'm on chemo because it doesn't have the metallic taste that meat has. I used it in mock chicken enchiladas and three-color lasagna, and even my dad didn't notice that he wasn't eating meat!"

—ANNE R.

Loaded Potatoes

4 servings PREP: 15 min • COOK: 5 min • STAND: 5 min

**4 medium unpeeled
red potatoes**

**1 package (8 ounces)
sliced mushrooms (3 cups)**

**3/4 cup chopped fully cooked
ham**

**8 medium green onions,
sliced (1/2 cup)**

**1/8 teaspoon ground
red pepper (cayenne)**

**1/2 cup reduced-fat
sour cream**

**1/2 cup shredded reduced-fat
sharp Cheddar cheese
(2 ounces)**

1 Pierce potatoes with fork. Arrange potatoes about 1 inch apart in circle on microwavable paper towel in microwave oven. Microwave uncovered on High 8 to 10 minutes or until tender. (Or bake potatoes in 375° oven 1 to 1 1/2 hours.) Let potatoes stand until cool enough to handle.

2 Spray 4-quart Dutch oven with cooking spray; heat over medium-high heat. Cook mushrooms in Dutch oven 1 minute, stirring frequently; reduce heat to medium. Cover and cook 3 minutes; remove from heat. Stir in ham, onions and red pepper. Cover and let stand 5 minutes.

3 Split baked potatoes lengthwise in half; fluff with fork. Spread 1 tablespoon of the sour cream over each potato half. Top with ham mixture and cheese.

FOOD *for* THOUGHT

These loaded potatoes are a tasty comfort food. If you don't like the taste of green onions or ham, leave them out for a creamy-textured topping that may help soothe mouth sores. If you find sharp Cheddar is too strong right now, try ricotta or mozarella.

High in potassium,
iron and vitamin C;
good source of fiber

1 SERVING: Calories 250 (Calories from Fat 55); Fat 6g (Saturated 3g); Cholesterol 25mg; Sodium 510mg; Potassium 980mg; Carbohydrate 40g (Dietary Fiber 4g); Protein 16g **% Daily Value:** Vitamin A 10%; Vitamin C 18%; Calcium 14%; Iron 18%; Folic Acid 12%; Magnesium 16% **Diet Exchanges:** 2 Starch, 1 Lean Meat, 1 Vegetable

"Baked potatoes are a major comfort food, so doctoring them up to make a meal really helps keep my appetite up. Plus, I can add as much butter and cheese and sour cream as I want without any guilt because I need the calories."

—ANNE R.

Lois K. *Shares* her Recipe

"I had this soup often when I was a kid, and it is still a comfort food for my four grown children and grandchildren. I made it when other food didn't appeal and many times during and after radiation treatments when my digestive tract was in turmoil."

Macaroni Pasta "Soup"

4 servings (1 cup each)   PREP: **5** min   •   COOK: **10** min

1 package (7 ounces) elbow macaroni (2 cups)

1 1/2 cups whole milk

1/2 teaspoon salt

1/4 teaspoon pepper

1/4 cup butter or margarine, softened

1/2 cup shredded Cheddar cheese (2 ounces)

1 Cook macaroni in 2-quart saucepan as directed on package—except cook 2 minutes less than recommended time; drain.

2 Return macaroni to saucepan. Stir in milk, salt and pepper. Heat just until mixture begins to simmer; do not boil. Remove from pan. Pour into heatproof bowl. Stir in butter until melted.

3 Sprinkle cheese over top just before serving.

A NOTE *from* **DR. GHOSH**

Macaroni soup helps to relieve digestive discomfort and dry mouth. Mashed potatoes, noodles and cooked cereals are other choices that may help, as well. When suffering from dry mouth, try making your food moist by adding sauces or soaking dry, crisp foods like cereal until they get soggy.

High in calcium and folic acid; low fiber

1 **SERVING:** Calories 360 (Calories from Fat 155); Fat 17g (Saturated 10g); Cholesterol 50mg; Sodium 460mg; Potassium 180mg; Carbohydrate 43g (Dietary Fiber 2g); Protein 11g % **Daily Value:** Vitamin A 12%; Vitamin C 0%; Calcium 20%; Iron 10%; Folic Acid 24%; Magnesium 8% **Diet Exchanges:** 2 Starch, 1 Skim Milk, 3 Fat

"I like this recipe because it's another way to use broccoli and it satisfies my desire for cream soups without all the fat. I use fat-free sour cream for a low-fat soup."

FOOD *for* THOUGHT

Broccoli, in the cruciferous family of vegetables along with Brussels sprouts, cabbage and kale, is a nutrition powerhouse. Broccoli provides a source of vitamin K, a nutrient that assists the body with blood clotting, particularly important after surgery.

Cream of Broccoli Soup

4 servings (1 cup each)   PREP: 10 min • COOK: 15 min

2 tablespoons butter or margarine

1 medium onion, chopped (1/2 cup)

2 medium carrots, thinly sliced (1 cup)

2 teaspoons mustard seed

1/2 teaspoon salt

1/4 teaspoon pepper

3/4 pound broccoli, coarsely chopped (3 1/2 cups) or 2 10 ounce packages frozen, chopped broccoli

1 can (14 1/2 ounces) chicken broth

1 cup water

2 teaspoons lemon juice

1/4 cup sour cream

1 Melt butter in 3-quart saucepan over medium heat. Cook onion and carrots in butter about 5 minutes, stirring occasionally, until onion is tender. Stir in mustard seed, salt and pepper. Stir in broccoli, broth and water. Heat to boiling; reduce heat. Cover and simmer about 10 minutes or until broccoli is tender.

2 Place one-third of the broccoli mixture in blender. Cover and blend on high speed until smooth; pour into bowl. Continue to blend in small batches until all soup is pureed.

3 Return blended mixture to saucepan. Stir in lemon juice. Heat over low heat just until hot. Stir in sour cream.

High in vitamins A and C and folic acid; good source of fiber

1 **SERVING:** Calories 140 (Calories from Fat 90); Fat 10g (Saturated 6g); Cholesterol 25mg; Sodium 840mg; Potassium 550mg; Carbohydrate 11g (Dietary Fiber 4g); Protein 6g **% Daily Value:** Vitamin A 100%; Vitamin C 70%; Calcium 8%; Iron 6%; Folic Acid 18%; Magnesium 8% **Diet Exchanges:** 2 Vegetable, 2 Fat

Onion and Rosemary Foccacia Wedges (page 85) and Cream of Broccoli Soup

"Eating my main meal at noon was a good solution for me because my food settled better when I had more energy; in the evening I was too tired for a big meal. This recipe was one of my favorites."

FOOD *for* THOUGHT

This easy recipe is a good choice because of the high iron and folic acid nutrients it provides. Both folic acid and iron are nutrients that are necessary for good health.

Easy Beef Stroganoff

4 servings PREP: **10 min** • COOK: **20 min**

1 pound beef sirloin or round steak

2 tablespoons butter or margarine

2/3 cup water

1 can (4 ounces) sliced mushrooms, drained

1/2 package (2-ounce size) onion soup mix (1 envelope)

1 cup sour cream

4 cups hot cooked rice or noodles

Chopped fresh parsley, if desired

1 Remove fat from beef. Cut beef across grain into about 1 1/2 × 1/2-inch strips. (Beef is easier to cut if partially frozen, 30 to 60 minutes.)

2 Melt butter in 10-inch skillet over medium-high heat. Cook beef in butter about 10 minutes, stirring occasionally, until brown. Stir in water, mushrooms and soup mix. Cook about 10 minutes, stirring occasionally, until beef is tender.

3 Stir in sour cream; heat until hot. Serve over rice. Sprinkle with parsley.

High in iron and folic acid

1 SERVING: Calories 515 (Calories from Fat 190); Fat 21g (Saturated 10g); Cholesterol 110mg; Sodium 810mg; Potassium 540mg; Carbohydrate 52g (Dietary Fiber 2g); Protein 29g **% Daily Value:** Vitamin A 12%; Vitamin C 2%; Calcium 8%; Iron 24%; Folic Acid 28%; Magnesium 12% **Diet Exchanges:** 3 Starch, 3 Medium-Fat Meat, 1 Vegetable

Caramelized Pork Slices

4 servings PREP: 10 min • COOK: 10 min

1 pound pork tenderloin

2 cloves garlic, finely chopped

2 tablespoons packed
brown sugar

1 tablespoon orange juice

1 tablespoon molasses or
maple-flavored syrup

1/2 teaspoon salt

1/4 teaspoon pepper

4 cups hot cooked rice

1 Trim fat from pork. Cut pork into 1/2-inch slices. (Pork is easier to cut if partially frozen, 30 to 60 minutes.)

2 Spray 10-inch nonstick skillet with cooking spray; heat over medium-high heat. Cook pork and garlic in skillet 6 to 8 minutes, turning pork occasionally, until pork is light brown on outside and no longer pink in center. Drain if necessary.

3 Stir in remaining ingredients except rice. Cook, stirring occasionally, until mixture thickens and coats pork. Serve with rice.

"Pork tenderloin is lean, cooks quickly and is becoming a family favorite. The fact that it is low residue, which works for me, makes it even more appealing."

—THERESA H.

A NOTE *from* DR. GHOSH

Pork is a good source of iron. Helping with proper oxygen transfer in the bloodstream, iron is crucial for life. Iron also helps prevent anemia and is helpful with immune functions.

High in iron and folic acid; low fiber; low residue

1 **SERVING:** Calories 385 (Calories from Fat 45); Fat 5g (Saturated 2g); Cholesterol 70mg; Sodium 350mg; Potassium 560mg; Carbohydrate 56g (Dietary Fiber 1g); Protein 30g **% Daily Value:** Vitamin A 0%; Vitamin C 2%; Calcium 4%; Iron 20%; Folic Acid 24%; Magnesium 14% **Diet Exchanges:** 3 Starch, 3 Very Lean Meat, 1/2 Fruit

Sausage, Vegetable and Cheese Strata (page 166)

Make-Ahead Meals

5

Theresa *Shares* *her Recipe*

"Because of my fatigue, I sometimes made dinner in steps. I could make this salad ahead of time and chill it while I was making the rest of the meal."

A NOTE *from* **DR. GHOSH**

A great source of protein, this recipe delivers some of the necessities for rebuilding strength. However, legumes, beans and other gas-producing foods such as broccoli and cabbage should be avoided after surgery, especially surgery involving the intestines.

Corn and Black Bean Salad

6 servings (1/2 cup each) PREP: **5** min • CHILL: **2** hr

1 can (15 ounces) black beans, rinsed and drained

1 can (about 8 ounces) whole kernel corn, drained

1 can (4 ounces) chopped green chilies, drained

1/2 cup medium salsa

1/4 cup chopped onion

2 tablespoons chopped fresh cilantro

1 Mix all ingredients in medium bowl.

2 Cover and refrigerate at least 2 hours but no longer than 24 hours.

High in vitamin C and folic acid; excellent source of fiber

1 SERVING: Calories 135 (Calories from Fat 10); Fat 1g (Saturated 0g); Cholesterol 0mg; Sodium 760mg; Potassium 440mg; Carbohydrate 29g (Dietary Fiber 6g); Protein 8g **% Daily Value:** Vitamin A 8%; Vitamin C 16%; Calcium 6%; Iron 14%; Folic Acid 30%; Magnesium 14% **Diet Exchanges:** 2 Starch

Corn and Black Bean Salad

Seven-Layer Pasta Salad

8 servings (1 cup each)   PREP: 30 min • COOK: 15 min • CHILL: 8 hr

FOOD *for* **THOUGHT**

You can get quite an assortment of phytochemicals, which are naturally-occurring plant chemicals, by eating the whole food. It's also important to eat a variety of different foods, especially fruits and vegetables.

2 cups uncooked farfalle (bow-tie) pasta (4 ounces)

2 cups broccoli flowerets

2 medium tomatoes, chopped (1 1/2 cups)

1 medium yellow bell pepper, chopped (1 cup)

1/3 cup diced red onion

3/4 cup mayonnaise or salad dressing

3/4 cup plain yogurt

2 tablespoons sugar

1/2 teaspoon curry powder

1 1/2 cups shredded Cheddar cheese (6 ounces)

1 tablespoon bacon flavor bits or chips

2 tablespoons finely chopped fresh parsley

1 Cook and drain pasta as directed on package. While pasta is cooking, place broccoli in boiling water. Cover and cook 1 minute; drain. Immediately rinse with cold water; drain.

2 Layer tomatoes, broccoli, bell pepper and onion in 2-quart glass serving bowl.

3 Mix mayonnaise, yogurt, sugar and curry powder in medium bowl. Stir in pasta. Layer pasta evenly over onion in serving bowl.

4 Sprinkle with cheese. Top with bacon bits and parsley. Cover and refrigerate at least 8 hours but no longer than 24 hours.

"This is a really tasty and colorful salad. I made it in the morning when I had more energy. Then I could take a nap during the day and serve it for an easy dinner when I felt a little more rested."

—SUSAN S.

High in calcium and vitamins A and C

1 SERVING: Calories 330 (Calories from Fat 215); Fat 24g (Saturated 7g); Cholesterol 35mg; Sodium 290mg; Potassium 290mg; Carbohydrate 21g (Dietary Fiber 2g); Protein 10g **% Daily Value:** Vitamin A 18%; Vitamin C 92%; Calcium 18%; Iron 6%; Folic Acid 16%; Magnesium 8% **Diet Exchanges:** 1 Starch, 1 High-Fat Meat, 1 Vegetable, 3 Fat

Layered Chicken Salad

5 servings   PREP: 15 min • CHILL: 2 hr

1 bag (10 ounces) salad mix
(about 8 cups)

1 small zucchini, thinly sliced

1 can (10 ounces) chunk
chicken, drained

1/4 cup chopped red onion

1/2 cup pimiento-stuffed
salad olives

1/2 cup mayonnaise or
salad dressing

3/4 cup shredded reduced-fat
Cheddar cheese (3 ounces)

1 cup frozen green peas,
rinsed and drained

1 medium tomato,
cut into wedges

1 Layer salad mix, zucchini, chicken, onion and olives in large bowl.

2 Spread mayonnaise over olives, sealing to edge of bowl. Sprinkle with cheese and peas. Cover and refrigerate at least 2 hours but no longer than 24 hours.

3 Just before serving, add tomato and toss salad.

"When I needed to reduce the fat in this or any recipe, I used less mayonnaise and cheese than was called for. Though I know some fat in our diets is important, I felt better during treatments when I knew my diet was not high in fat."

—MARY W.

A NOTE *from* DR. GHOSH

This recipe is higher in fat than most in this cookbook. But not all fat is bad! We need fat to provide energy, insulation and protection for the body. For some cancer patients, though, high-fat foods may cause intestinal distress or nausea and should be avoided.

High in vitamins A and C and folic acid; good source of fiber

1 **SERVING:** Calories 285 (Calories from Fat 200); Fat 22g (Saturated 4g); Cholesterol 40mg; Sodium 810mg; Potassium 380mg; Carbohydrate 9g (Dietary Fiber 3g); Protein 16g % **Daily Value:** Vitamin A 48%; Vitamin C 32%; Calcium 12%; Iron 12%; Folic Acid 26%; Magnesium 10% **Diet Exchanges:** 2 High-Fat Meat, 1 Vegetable, 3 Fat

Southwestern Pork Salad

4 servings   PREP: 15 min   •   BAKE: 40 min

c

A NOTE *from* **DR. GHOSH**

This recipe is loaded with plenty of vitamins and minerals. One of them, magnesium, is a healing nutrient that is important for releasing energy from food so the body can use it properly.

High in potassium, iron, calcium, magnesium, vitamins A and C and folic acid; excellent source of fiber

1 SERVING: Calories 305 (Calories from Fat 100); Fat 11g (Saturated 2g); Cholesterol 55mg; Sodium 400mg; Potassium 1470mg; Carbohydrate 32g (Dietary Fiber 9g); Protein 28g **% Daily Value:** Vitamin A 90%; Vitamin C 100%; Calcium 26%; Iron 24%; Folic Acid 76%; Magnesium 28% **Diet Exchanges:** 1 Starch, 3 Lean Meat, 3 Vegetable

---

3/4 pound pork tenderloin

1/4 teaspoon salt

1/4 teaspoon pepper

Creamy Lime Dressing (below)

8 cups bite-size pieces mixed salad greens or 1 package (4 ounces) mixed salad greens

1 medium yellow bell pepper, sliced

1/2 pound mushrooms, sliced (3 cups)

1 can (15 to 16 ounces) black-eyed peas, rinsed and drained

Creamy Lime Dressing

1/2 cup fat-free sour cream or plain yogurt

1/4 cup chopped fresh cilantro

2 tablespoons lime juice

2 tablespoons vegetable oil

1/4 teaspoon salt

---

1 Heat oven to 350°. Place pork on rack in shallow roasting pan. Sprinkle with salt and pepper. Insert meat thermometer so tip is in thickest part of pork.

2 Bake uncovered 30 to 40 minutes or until thermometer reads 160° (medium doneness) and pork is slightly pink in center. Meanwhile, make Creamy Lime Dressing. Cool pork; cut into slices.

3 Arrange greens, bell pepper, mushrooms and peas on large serving plate. Top with pork. Serve with dressing.

TO MAKE AHEAD: Cook pork and cool. Make Creamy Lime Dressing. Prepare vegetables. Refrigerate all ingredients no longer than 48 hours. Just before serving, continue as directed in Step 3.

Mix all ingredients.

"Lime juice really helps meat taste great. It covers up the metallic taste that I get from chemotherapy. I've found that ethnic foods, especially Southwestern, Mexican and Italian are often so flavorful that I don't notice the metallic taste." —ANNE R.

Southwestern Pork Salad

"Using crushed dried tarragon instead of rosemary is also good in this mustardy chicken. Whenever I made this dish, I made two batches, and kept one on hand in the freezer for another meal."

d

A NOTE *from* DR. GHOSH

Low in fiber and residue, this recipe is a great choice among survivors who have had intestinal trouble. All ingredients are easy to digest. For a different spin, substitute mashed potatoes or yams for the pasta or rice.

Dijon Chicken

4 servings   PREP: 5 min   •   BAKE: 30 min

4 boneless, skinless chicken breast halves (about 1 1/4 pounds)

1/4 cup Dijon mustard

1 tablespoon olive or vegetable oil

1 tablespoon lemon juice

1/2 teaspoon dried rosemary leaves, crumbled

1/4 teaspoon pepper

Chopped fresh parsley, if desired

4 cups hot cooked rosamarina (orzo) pasta or rice

1 Heat oven to 375°. Spray rectangular baking dish, 11 × 7 × 1 1/2 inches, with cooking spray. Place chicken in baking dish.

2 Mix remaining ingredients except parsley and pasta. Spread mustard mixture over chicken to coat thoroughly.

3 Bake uncovered 25 to 30 minutes or until juice of chicken is no longer pink when centers of thickest pieces are cut. Garnish with parsley. Serve with pasta.

TO MAKE AHEAD: Mix all ingredients except chicken, parsley and pasta in heavy-duty plastic food-storage bag. Add chicken, turning to coat. Freeze no longer than 2 months. At least 12 hours before serving, place frozen chicken in refrigerator to thaw. Heat oven to 375°. Place chicken in rectangular baking dish and continue as directed in Step 3.

Low fiber; low residue

1 SERVING: Calories 190 (Calories from Fat 70); Fat 8g (Saturated 2g); Cholesterol 75mg; Sodium 440mg; Potassium 230mg; Carbohydrate 2g (Dietary Fiber 0g); Protein 27g % Daily Value: Vitamin A 0%; Vitamin C 0%; Calcium 2%; Iron 6%; Folic Acid 0%; Magnesium 6% Diet Exchanges: 4 Very Lean Meat, 1 Fat

Italian Chicken Rolls

4 servings   PREP: 20 min • BAKE: 30 min

4 boneless, skinless
chicken breast halves
(about 1 1/4 pounds)

2 slices (1/2 ounce each)
provolone cheese, cut in half

4 thin slices pastrami

1/3 cup seasoned dry
bread crumbs

1/4 cup grated Romano
or Parmesan cheese

2 tablespoons finely chopped
fresh parsley

1/4 cup milk

1 Heat oven to 425°. Grease square pan, 8 × 8 × 2 inches. Flatten each chicken breast half to 1/4-inch thickness between sheets of plastic wrap or waxed paper.

2 Place piece of provolone cheese and slice of pastrami on each chicken piece. Fold long sides of each chicken piece over pastrami. Roll up chicken from short side; secure with toothpick.

3 Mix bread crumbs, Romano cheese and parsley. Dip chicken rolls into milk, then coat evenly with bread crumb mixture. Place seam sides down in pan.

4 Bake uncovered about 30 minutes or until chicken is no longer pink in center.

TO MAKE AHEAD: Freeze unbaked chicken rolls uncovered about 1 hour or until firm. Wrap tightly and label. Freeze no longer than 2 months. About 1 1/4 hours before serving, heat oven to 375°. Bake uncovered about 50 minutes or until chicken is no longer pink in center.

"A meal that I can serve to my family or company and eat with them helps me feel like I am still able to be a normal mom. This meal doesn't take a lot of energy to prepare, which is important when you get fatigued from cancer treatments." —ANNE R.

FOOD *for* THOUGHT

Chicken is a good source of vitamin B$_6$, pyridoxine. Vitamin B$_6$ is important for helping the body break down proteins to free the smaller protein components, called amino acids, that the body needs.

High in calcium;
low fiber

1 SERVING: Calories 330 (Calories from fat 135); Fat 15g (Saturated 8g); Cholesterol 110mg; Sodium 780mg; Potassium 360mg; Carbohydrate 8g (Dietary Fiber 0g); Protein 41g **% Daily Value:** Vitamin A 10%; Vitamin C 2%; Calcium 34%; Iron 10%; Folic Acid 6%; Magnesium 10% **Diet Exchanges:** 1/2 Starch, 6 Very Lean Meat, 2 Fat

"This is a marvelous comfort food, and I ate it many times while I was on chemo. I often take this casserole to potluck dinners, and everybody loves it!"

A NOTE *from* DR. GHOSH

Recipes that are high in fiber, such as this one, can help with constipation. Increase fluid intake and activity level, if you can tolerate it, to help relieve severe constipation. At times, you may need a stool softener or laxative—consult your doctor.

High in iron and folic acid; good source of fiber

1 SERVING: Calories 280 (Calories from Fat 100); Fat 11g (Saturated 3g); Cholesterol 75mg; Sodium 910mg; Potassium 390mg; Carbohydrate 27g (Dietary Fiber 4g); Protein 25g **% Daily Value:** Vitamin A 10%; Vitamin C 4%; Calcium 4%; Iron 20%; Folic Acid 18%; Magnesium 10% **Diet Exchanges:** 2 Starch, 3 Very Lean Meat, 1 Fat

Chicken Noodle Casserole

6 servings (1 1/2 cups each) PREP: 15 min • BAKE: 45 min

4 cups uncooked egg noodles (8 ounces)

1 tablespoon vegetable oil

1 medium onion, chopped (1/2 cup)

2 medium stalks celery, sliced (1 cup)

3 cups cut-up cooked chicken

1/2 teaspoon salt

1/4 teaspoon pepper

1 can (14 1/2 ounces) chicken broth

1 can (10 3/4 ounces) condensed cream of chicken soup

1 package (10 ounces) frozen green peas

1 can (4 ounces) sliced mushrooms, drained

1 Heat oven to 350°. Butter 3-quart casserole. Cook noodles as directed on package—except cook 2 minutes less than package directions.

2 While noodles are cooking, heat oil in 10-inch skillet over medium-high heat. Cook onion and celery in oil about 5 minutes, stirring occasionally, until tender. Stir in remaining ingredients.

3 Drain noodles; place in casserole. Top with chicken mixture. Cover and bake 30 minutes; stir. Bake uncovered about 15 minutes longer or until liquid is absorbed.

TO MAKE AHEAD: Cover baked casserole with aluminum foil. Freeze no longer than 2 months. About 1 hour before serving, heat oven to 350°. Bake in covered casserole 45 minutes. Uncover and bake 10 to 15 minutes longer or until hot.

Humor and Healing

Think back to a time when you were really uptight or worried about something. Then remember when someone made a joke—after a hearty laugh, you instantly felt much better.

This is no accident. Studies show that laughter, particularly the kind that makes your whole body shake, promotes better blood circulation and lowers blood pressure. It also releases endorphins, the chemicals in the brain that relieve pain and have a calming effect. Keeping your spirits up and having a smile on your face make it easier to deal with the stresses and strains of the world around you. Laughter has been called an inexpensive and effective wonder drug and a universal medicine.

Let your family know how important humor is to you. They may be hesitant, so you may have to take the first step and crack the first jokes. Because laughter is contagious, once people get the message, they will start to lighten up and share funny stories with you. If you have trouble getting going, try a few humor starters that have worked for others:

Laugh at yourself. Lots of funny things occur to all of us on any given day. Choosing to laugh rather than get upset will brighten your day and make you and others less tense.

Schedule a laughter break. Everyone who attends must bring a funny story or something humorous to share.

Request a cartoon or humorous book as a gift. The giver will also enjoy the hunt for the humor.

Rent videos that tickle your funny bone and have a laugh fest with friends.

Start a humor basket. Anyone who visits adds a funny saying, a funny story or a joke contribution to the basket.

"When I don't feel well, I don't like fussing in the kitchen. This was such an easy recipe, I was up to preparing it even when I was very tired. It's also great for entertaining."

A NOTE *from* DR. GHOSH

This recipe is a great source of many essential minerals. Lack of magnesium, one of the minerals here, can become a problem if malnutrition occurs, as it can during cisplatin chemotherapy. Magnesium deficiencies can lead to weakness, lethargy, nausea and vomiting.

High in vitamins A and C; good source of fiber

1 SERVING: Calories 380 (Calories from Fat 170); Fat 19g (Saturated 4g); Cholesterol 75mg; Sodium 660mg; Potassium 470mg; Carbohydrate 22g (Dietary Fiber 3g); Protein 33g % Daily Value: Vitamin A 26%; Vitamin C 22%; Calcium 12%; Iron 12%; Folic Acid 14%; Magnesium 14% Diet Exchanges: 1 Starch, 4 Lean Meat, 1 Vegetable, 1 Fat

The Ultimate Chicken Casserole

8 to 10 servings PREP: 30 min · BAKE: 45 min

1 tablespoon vegetable oil

2 pounds chicken breast tenders (not breaded)

2 packages (10 ounces each) frozen broccoli spears, thawed and drained

1 can (8 ounces) sliced water chestnuts, drained

1 can (10 3/4 ounces) condensed cream of chicken soup

1/2 cup reduced-fat mayonnaise

1 teaspoon lemon juice

1/2 cup milk

1/2 teaspoon curry powder, if desired

1/2 cup shredded reduced-fat Cheddar cheese (2 ounces)

1/2 cup dry bread crumbs

1 can (2.8 ounces) French-fried onions

1/4 cup slivered almonds

1 Heat oven to 350°. Heat oil in 12-inch skillet over medium-high heat. Cook chicken in oil 5 to 6 minutes, stirring occasionally, until chicken is no longer pink in center. Layer broccoli spears, water chestnuts and chicken in ungreased rectangular baking dish, 13 × 9 × 2 inches.

2 Mix soup, mayonnaise, lemon juice, milk and curry powder; pour over chicken and broccoli. Sprinkle with cheese, bread crumbs, onions and almonds.

3 Cover and bake 30 minutes. Uncover and bake about 15 minutes longer or until broccoli is tender.

TO MAKE AHEAD: Cover baked casserole with aluminum foil. Freeze no longer than 2 months. About 1 hour before serving, heat oven to 350°. Bake in covered baking dish 45 minutes. Uncover and bake 10 to 15 minutes longer or until hot.

Joan K. *Shares* her Recipe

"When I was growing up, my mother always served chicken soup when I was sick. It is still a comforting food for me today, and I make it often for my family. I made this a make-ahead recipe by cooking the chicken and stock one day, then finishing the rest the next day."

A NOTE *from* **DR. GHOSH**

Iron is an important mineral needed to help fight fatigue and is especially key during chemotherapy and radiation.

High in vitamin A; good source of fiber

1 SERVING: Calories 270 (Calories from Fat 70); Fat 8g (Saturated 2g); Cholesterol 140mg; Sodium 620mg; Potassium 420mg; Carbohydrate 24g (Dietary Fiber 3g); Protein 29g **% Daily Value:** Vitamin A 80%; Vitamin C 4%; Calcium 6%; Iron 14%; Folic Acid 14%; Magnesium 10% **Diet Exchanges:** 1 Starch, 3 Very Lean Meat, 2 Vegetable, 1 Fat

Chicken Soup with Homemade Noodles

6 servings PREP: 1 hr • COOK: 1 hr 15 min

3- to 3 1/2-pound cut-up broiler-fryer chicken

4 1/2 cups cold water

1 teaspoon salt

1/2 teaspoon pepper

1 medium stalk celery with leaves, cut up

1 medium onion, cut up

1 medium carrot, cut up

4 cups water

1 teaspoon chicken bouillon granules

1 cup frozen green peas

2 medium stalks celery, sliced (1 cup)

1 medium onion, sliced

2 medium carrots, sliced (1 cup) or 1 bag (8 ounces) baby-cut carrots

Noodles (right) or 1 package (14 ounces) frozen noodles (2 cups)

1 Remove excess fat from chicken. Place chicken in 4-quart Dutch oven. Add 4 1/2 cups cold water, salt, pepper, cut-up celery, onion and carrot. Heat to boiling; reduce heat. Cover and simmer about 45 minutes or until juice of chicken is no longer pink when centers of thickest pieces are cut.

2 Remove chicken from broth. Cool chicken about 10 minutes or just until cool enough to handle. Skim fat from broth. Strain broth; discard vegetables. Remove skin and bones from chicken. Cut chicken into 1/2-inch pieces.

3 Return chicken and broth to Dutch oven. Stir in 4 cups water and the bouillon. Heat to boiling; reduce heat. Stir in peas and sliced celery, onion and carrots. Simmer uncovered 15 minutes.

4 Make Noodles; press a few tablespoons of the batter at a time through colander (preferably one with large holes) into boiling soup. Stir once or twice to prevent sticking. Cook about 5 minutes or until noodles rise to the surface and are tender.

Noodles

2 eggs, beaten

1/4 cup milk or water

1 cup all-purpose flour

1/4 teaspoon salt

Dash of pepper

Mix all ingredients (batter will be thick).

TO MAKE AHEAD: Cook chicken and broth one day. Refrigerate separately. The next day, skim fat from broth, and continue with Step 2.

To freeze after preparing entire recipe, cool soup 30 minutes. Place in 2-quart airtight freezer container and label. Freeze no longer than 2 months. About 35 minutes before serving, remove lid from freezer container; place container upside down in 2-quart microwavable casserole. Cover and microwave on Medium (50%) 25 minutes; remove container. Break up and stir. Cover and microwave on Medium about 20 minutes longer, stirring 2 or 3 times, until hot.

"This is such an easy recipe to put together. I soak the beans overnight, drain them in the morning and finish the rest of the cooking just in time for lunch. Eating my main meal of the day at lunch worked better for me; I just felt more like eating then."

FOOD *for* THOUGHT

Brimming with beans—navy beans, that is—this recipe is rich in fiber. Typically Americans don't eat enough fiber. Experts recommend we eat 25 to 30 grams of fiber daily for good health and to prevent constipation.

High in magnesium, potassium, iron and folic acid; excellent source of fiber

---

1 SERVING: Calories 245 (Calories from Fat 25); Fat 3g (Saturated 1g); Cholesterol 40mg; Sodium 1490mg; Potassium 670mg; Carbohydrate 36g (Dietary Fiber 9g); Protein 27g **% Daily Value:** Vitamin A 8%; Vitamin C 4%; Calcium 16%; Iron 24%; Folic Acid 44%; Magnesium 22% **Diet Exchanges:** 2 Starch, 2 Very Lean Meat, 1 Vegetable

White Turkey Chili

8 servings   PREP: 15 min • STAND: 8 hr • COOK: 1 hr 15 min

2 cups dried navy beans (1 pound), sorted and rinsed

8 cups water

2 tablespoons chicken bouillon granules

2 tablespoons chopped fresh cilantro or parsley

2 teaspoons ground cumin

1 1/2 teaspoons dried basil leaves

1/4 teaspoon ground cloves

1/8 teaspoon ground red pepper (cayenne)

1 medium onion, chopped (1/2 cup)

4 cloves garlic, finely chopped

2 cans (4 ounces each) chopped green chilies, undrained

6 cups water

1 pound turkey breast tenderloins, cut into 1/2-inch pieces

1/2 cup shredded reduced-fat mozzarella or Cheddar cheese

1 Place beans and water in 4-quart Dutch oven. Soak at least 8 hours but no longer than 10 hours; drain.

2 Stir in remaining ingredients except turkey and cheese. Heat to boiling; reduce heat. Cover and simmer about 1 hour or until beans are tender.

3 Stir in turkey. Simmer uncovered about 15 minutes or until turkey is no longer pink in center. Sprinkle with cheese.

TO MAKE AHEAD: Divide chili among 3 airtight 2-quart freezer containers and label. Cool quickly and freeze no longer than 2 months. Remove lid from 1 freezer container; place upside down in 1-quart microwavable casserole. Microwave on High 5 minutes; remove container. Cover and microwave on High 20 to 25 minutes, breaking up and stirring every 5 minutes, until hot.

White Turkey Chili

Crowd-Size Minestrone

10 servings PREP: 25 min • COOK: 1 hr 15 min

FOOD *for* THOUGHT

Packed with vegetables and legumes, this is a tasty vegetarian delight. The Food Guide Pyramid recommends a plant-based diet, loaded with fiber, vitamins and minerals, and this soup fills the bill.

1 tablespoon vegetable oil

2 cloves garlic, finely chopped

1 medium onion, chopped (1/2 cup)

4 cups chicken broth or water

4 cups tomato juice

1 cup dry red wine or water

1 tablespoon dried basil leaves

1 teaspoon salt

1/2 teaspoon dried oregano leaves

1/4 teaspoon pepper

1/2 medium head green cabbage, chopped (3 cups)

2 small zucchini, chopped (2 cups)

2 medium carrots, sliced (1 cup)

2 medium stalks celery, chopped (1 cup)

1 can (28 ounces) diced tomatoes, undrained

2 cans (15 to 16 ounces each) kidney, garbanzo or great northern beans, rinsed and drained

1 package (10 ounces) frozen chopped spinach, thawed and squeezed to drain

Grated Parmesan cheese

1 Heat oil in 8-quart Dutch oven over medium heat. Cook garlic and onion in oil about 2 minutes, stirring occasionally, until onion is tender.

2 Stir in remaining ingredients except cheese. Heat to boiling; reduce heat. Cover and simmer 1 hour. Serve with cheese.

TO MAKE AHEAD: Tightly cover soup and refrigerate no longer than 48 hours. To reheat, cover and heat to boiling over medium heat, stirring occasionally. Serve with cheese.

"Soup is healing to the soul as well as the body. Though this recipe looks long, it serves many and keeps a long time in the freezer. Just store in individual containers and heat when ready to serve."

—JUDY O.

High in vitamins A and C, iron, folic acid, magnesium and potassium; excellent source of fiber

1 SERVING: Calories 190 (Calories from fat 35); Fat 4g (Saturated 1g); Cholesterol 0mg; Sodium 1310mg; Potassium 1080mg; Carbohydrate 36g (Dietary Fiber 10g); Protein 13g **% Daily Value:** Vitamin A 100%; Vitamin C 42%; Calcium 12%; Iron 24%; Folic Acid 52%; Magnesium 22% **Diet Exchanges:** 2 Starch, 1/2 Very Lean Meat, 1 Vegetable

"I found that sometimes only stubbornness and sheer will are what allow you to eat. However, the right recipes— like this easy dinner, help as well."

Layered Beef and Vegetable Dinner

4 servings PREP: 15 min • BAKE: 1 hr

1 pound lean ground beef

1 teaspoon salt

1/2 teaspoon pepper

2 medium potatoes, peeled and sliced (2 cups)

6 medium carrots (1 pound), sliced (3 cups)

1 medium onion, sliced

2 medium stalks celery, sliced (1 cup)

1 can (10 3/4 ounces) condensed cream of chicken soup

1 Heat oven to 375°. Grease 3-quart casserole. Crumble beef in bottom of casserole. Sprinkle with half of the salt and pepper.

2 Layer potatoes, carrots, onion and celery on beef. Sprinkle with remaining salt and pepper. Spread soup over top.

3 Cover and bake about 1 hour or until beef is brown and vegetables are tender.

TO MAKE AHEAD: Cover baked casserole with aluminum foil. Freeze no longer than 2 months. About 1 hour before serving, heat oven to 375°. Bake in covered pan 45 minutes. Uncover and bake 15 to 20 minutes longer or until hot.

A NOTE *from* DR. GHOSH

Because of the high iron content, this recipe is a good choice for cancer patients with neutropenia, a time when white blood cell count is low and risk of infection is high. Just omit the pepper.

High in potassium, iron and vitamin A; excellent source of fiber

1 SERVING: Calories 405 (Calories from Fat 190); Fat 21g (Saturated 8g); Cholesterol 70mg; Sodium 1240mg; Potassium 980mg; Carbohydrate 33g (Dietary Fiber 5g); Protein 26g **% Daily Value:** Vitamin A 100%; Vitamin C 16%; Calcium 6%; Iron 20%; Folic Acid 10%; Magnesium 14% **Diet Exchanges:** 1 1/2 Starch, 2 Medium-Fat Meat, 2 Vegetable

MaryElaine W. Shares *her Recipe*

"Soups, like this one, became one of my favorite foods because it went down so easily. Other favorites: fruit cocktail, grapes, plums, watermelon, frozen pops and gelatin."

FOOD *for* THOUGHT

If your body weight is getting too low, you probably need more calories. One way to increase the calorie content of a recipe is by adding heavy cream. Cream, butter and margarine are easy high-calorie additions for soups, stews, sauces and gravies.

High in iron, potassium and vitamins A and C; good source of fiber

1 **SERVING:** Calories 330 (Calories from Fat 155); Fat 17g (Saturated 7g); Cholesterol 75mg; Sodium 1090mg; Potassium 860mg; Carbohydrate 26g (Dietary Fiber 4g); Protein 22g **% Daily Value:** Vitamin A 88%; Vitamin C 18%; Calcium 6%; Iron 20%; Folic Acid 14%; Magnesium 12% **Diet Exchanges:** 1 Starch, 2 High-Fat Meat, 2 Vegetable

Beef-Vegetable Soup

6 servings (1 1/2 cups)   PREP: 20 min   •   COOK: 3 hr 30 min

2 tablespoons vegetable oil

2 pounds beef shank cross-cuts or soup bones

1 medium onion, sliced (1 cup)

6 cups cold water

1 teaspoon salt

1 dried bay leaf

1 tablespoon pickling spice

1 can (10 1/2 ounces) condensed beef broth

2 medium potatoes, cubed (2 cups)

2 medium carrots, sliced (1 cup)

2 medium stalks celery, sliced (1 cup)

2 cups shredded cabbage

1/2 cup ketchup

1 can (15 ounces) sliced beets, drained, cut in half

3/4 cup whipping (heavy) cream

1 Heat oil in 4-quart Dutch oven over medium heat. Cook beef and onion in oil until beef is brown on both sides. Add water; heat to boiling. Skim foam from broth. Stir in salt, bay leaf and pickling spice; reduce heat. Cover and simmer 3 hours.

2 Remove beef from broth. Cool beef about 10 minutes or just until cool enough to handle. Strain broth; discard vegetables and seasonings. Remove beef from bones. Cut beef into 1/2-inch pieces. Skim fat from broth.

3 Add enough canned broth to broth from beef to measure 5 cups. Return broth and beef to Dutch oven. Stir in potatoes, carrots, celery, cabbage, ketchup and beets. Heat to boiling; reduce heat. Cover and simmer about 30 minutes or until vegetables are tender. Cool 10 minutes. Stir in whipping cream.

TO MAKE AHEAD: Cook beef bones and water one day. Refrigerate separately. The next day, skim fat from broth, and continue with Step 2.

To freeze, cool soup 30 minutes. Place in 2-quart freezer container. Freeze no longer than 2 months. About 35 minutes before serving, remove lid from freezer container; place container upside down in 2-quart microwavable casserole. Cover and microwave on Medium (50%) 25 minutes; remove container. Break up and stir. Cover and microwave on Medium about 20 minutes longer, stirring 2 or 3 times, until hot.

Beef-Vegetable Soup

FOOD *for* THOUGHT

Having beef for dinner? Beef provides a super source of the mineral zinc, which is important for growth, wound healing and your ability to taste foods.

Spaghetti and Meat Squares

6 servings   PREP: 10 min   •   BAKE: 15 min

1 pound lean ground beef or ground turkey

1/2 cup dry bread crumbs

1/2 cup applesauce

1 tablespoon instant minced onion

3/4 teaspoon garlic salt

1/4 teaspoon pepper

1 jar (26 to 28 ounces) tomato pasta sauce (any variety)

3 cups hot cooked spaghetti

1 Heat oven to 400°. Mix all ingredients except pasta sauce and spaghetti. Press mixture evenly in ungreased rectangular pan, 11 × 7 × 1 1/2 inches. Cut into 1 1/4-inch squares.

2 Bake uncovered about 15 minutes or until no longer pink in center and juice is clear; drain. Separate meat squares.

3 Mix meat squares and pasta sauce in 3-quart saucepan. Heat to boiling; reduce heat. Simmer uncovered about 15 minutes, stirring occasionally, until hot. Serve over spaghetti.

TO MAKE AHEAD: Cool meat squares 5 minutes. Place on cookie sheet; freeze uncovered 15 minutes. Place meat squares in airtight 1 1/2-quart freezer container and label. Freeze no longer than 2 months. About 45 minutes before serving, heat meat squares and pasta sauce to boiling in 3-quart saucepan; reduce heat. Simmer uncovered about 25 minutes, stirring occasionally, until hot. Serve over spaghetti.

High in iron, potassium, folic acid and vitamin A; good source of fiber

1 **SERVING:** Calories 435 (Calories from Fat 145); Fat 16g (Saturated 5g); Cholesterol 45mg; Sodium 900mg; Potassium 690; Carbohydrate 56g (Dietary Fiber 3g); Protein 20g **% Daily Value:** Vitamin A 18%; Vitamin C 16%; Calcium 6%; Iron 20%; Folic Acid 18%; Magnesium 14% **Diet Exchanges:** 3 Starch, 1 High-Fat Meat, 2 Vegetable, 1 Fat

"During my good week when I'm on chemo, I cook make-ahead foods and freeze them so that on the days when I have less energy and can't cook, I can just put something in the oven and still have a great meal to eat with my family. It's important to use your energy wisely when you have it because it comes and goes during treatment."

—ANNE R.

Almond-Stuffed Pork Chops

4 servings PREP: 15 min • BROIL: 25 min

1/2 cup chicken broth

1/4 cup uncooked
quick-cooking brown rice

2 tablespoons finely chopped
dried apricots

2 tablespoons slivered
almonds, toasted*

2 teaspoons chopped fresh
or 3/4 teaspoon dried
marjoram leaves

2 tablespoons chopped
fresh parsley

4 pork loin chops, 1 inch thick
(about 2 pounds)

1/4 cup apricot preserves

1 Mix broth, rice, apricots, almonds and marjoram in 1 1/2-quart saucepan. Heat to boiling; reduce heat to low. Cover and simmer about 10 minutes or until rice is tender. Stir in parsley.

2 Cut 3-inch pocket in each pork chop, cutting from fat side almost to bone. Spoon about 2 tablespoons rice mixture into each pocket. Secure pockets with toothpicks.

3 Set oven control to broil. Place pork on rack in broiler pan. Broil with tops 5 to 6 inches from heat 10 minutes; turn. Broil 10 to 15 minutes longer or until thermometer reads 160° (medium doneness) and pork is slightly pink when cut near bone.

4 Heat preserves; brush over pork.

TO MAKE AHEAD: Place broiled pork in square baking dish, 8 × 8 × 2 inches. Wrap tightly with aluminum foil and label. Freeze no longer than 2 months. About 1 1/4 hours before serving, heat oven to 375°. Bake in covered baking dish about 1 hour or until stuffing is hot in center and meat thermometer in stuffing reads 160°. Heat preserves; brush over pork.

*To toast nuts, bake uncovered in ungreased shallow pan in 350° oven about 10 minutes, stirring occasionally, until golden brown. Or cook in ungreased heavy skillet over medium-low heat 5 to 7 minutes, stirring frequently until browning begins, then stirring constantly until golden brown.

"Pork with fruit and rice tastes great even on chemo. I didn't even know I liked apricots until they were one of about five fruits still left on my food list after surgery! Now I love them."
—ANNE R.

d

A NOTE *from*
DR. GHOSH

Pork is a tasty source of thiamin, or vitamin B$_1$. Thiamin is vitally important for energy release from foods, plus it helps keep your nervous system healthy, too.

Low fiber; low residue

1 SERVING: Calories 280 (Calories from Fat 90); Fat 10g (Saturated 3g); Cholesterol 65mg; Sodium 180mg; Potassium 440mg; Carbohydrate 25g (Dietary Fiber 1g); Protein 25g **% Daily Value:** Vitamin A 8%; Vitamin C 4%; Calcium 2%; Iron 8%; Folic Acid 4%; Magnesium 12% **Diet Exchanges:** 1 1/2 Starch, 3 Lean Meat

Extra-Easy Baked Ziti

10 to 12 servings   PREP: 20 min   •   BAKE: 40 min

1 package (16 ounces)
ziti pasta

4 cups (1/4 recipe) Italian
Spaghetti Sauce (page 164)
or purchased spaghetti sauce

1 1/2 cups freshly shredded
Parmesan cheese (6 ounces)

1 Heat oven to 350°. Cook and drain pasta as directed on package.

2 Mix pasta, Italian Spaghetti Sauce and 3/4 cup of the cheese in ungreased 3-quart casserole.

3 Cover and bake 30 minutes. Sprinkle with remaining 3/4 cup cheese. Bake uncovered 5 to 10 minutes or until cheese is melted.

TO MAKE AHEAD: Cover unbaked casserole tightly and refrigerate no longer than 24 hours. About 50 minutes before serving, heat oven to 350°. Continue as directed in Step 3.

FOOD *for* THOUGHT

Pasta, derived from wheat, is an easy carbohydrate source of energy. You begin breaking down carbohydrates to extract the energy they provide as soon as they enter your mouth. That's why we call carbohydrates a fast energy source.

High in calcium and folic acid; good source of fiber

1 SERVING: Calories 340 (Calories from fat 80); Fat 9g (Saturated 4g); Cholesterol 10mg; Sodium 770mg; Potassium 370mg; Carbohydrate 54g (Dietary Fiber 3g); Protein 14g **% Daily Value:** Vitamin A 14%; Vitamin C 12%; Calcium 24%; Iron 14%; Folic Acid 24%; Magnesium 12% **Diet Exchanges:** 3 1/2 Starch, 1/2 High Fat Meat

"This is a great comfort food, and easy enough for my daughter to prepare when she got home from school, especially if it was ready to pop into the oven. She would add soft bread (I couldn't get hard bread down), and a salad, and our meal was complete."

—ANNE R.

Easy Lasagna

12 servings   PREP: 20 min • BAKE: 1 hr • STAND: 15 min

2 cups ricotta cheese

3/4 cup grated Parmesan cheese

2 tablespoons chopped fresh parsley

1 tablespoon chopped fresh or 1 1/2 teaspoons dried oregano leaves

8 cups (1/2 recipe) Italian Spaghetti Sauce (page 164) or purchased spaghetti sauce

12 uncooked lasagna noodles

2 cups shredded mozzarella cheese (8 ounces)

1 Heat oven to 350°. Mix ricotta cheese, 1/2 cup of the Parmesan cheese, the parsley and oregano.

2 Spread 2 cups of the Italian Spaghetti Sauce in ungreased rectangular pan, 13 × 9 × 2 inches; top with 4 of the noodles. Spread cheese mixture over noodles. Spread with 2 cups spaghetti sauce and top with 4 noodles; repeat with 2 cups spaghetti sauce and 4 noodles.

3 Sprinkle with 1 1/2 cups of the mozzarella cheese. Spread with remaining 2 cups spaghetti sauce. Sprinkle with remaining 1/4 cup Parmesan cheese.

4 Cover and bake 30 minutes. Uncover and bake about 30 minutes longer or until hot and bubbly. Sprinkle with remaining 1/2 cup mozzarella cheese. Let stand 15 minutes before cutting.

TO MAKE AHEAD: Wrap unbaked lasagna tightly with aluminum foil and label. Freeze no longer than 2 months. About 2 hours before serving, heat oven to 350°. Bake in covered pan 45 minutes. Uncover and bake 15 to 20 minutes longer or until hot and bubbly. Sprinkle with mozzarella cheese. Let stand 15 minutes before cutting.

"I used to make all my spaghetti sauce from scratch. Now I purchase it. That way, I have more time to rest."

—JUDY O.

A NOTE *from* DR. GHOSH

Ricotta, Parmesan and mozzarella cheeses are delicious sources of calcium. Vital for strong bones and teeth, calcium also helps with proper nerve and muscle function—even for the heart.

High in calcium and vitamins A and C; good source of fiber

1 SERVING: Calories 395 (Calories from fat 160); Fat 18g (Saturated 9g); Cholesterol 40mg; Sodium 940mg; Potassium 510mg; Carbohydrate 37g (Dietary Fiber 3g); Protein 24g % Daily Value: Vitamin A 24%; Vitamin C 22%; Calcium 54%; Iron 14%; Folic Acid 8%; Magnesium 14% Diet Exchanges: 1 Starch, 2 High-Fat Meat, 1 Vegetable, 1 Milk

Italian Spaghetti Sauce

16 cups sauce   PREP: 15 min   •   COOK: 2 hr 15 min

A NOTE *from*
DR. GHOSH

Popping with bell peppers and tomatoes, this recipe is loaded with vitamin C, a nutrient key to bolstering the immune system.

4 pounds bulk Italian sausage

2 tablespoons olive or vegetable oil

6 medium onions, finely chopped (3 cups)

1 large bell pepper, finely chopped (1 1/2 cups)

12 cloves garlic, finely chopped

4 cans (14 1/2 ounces each) diced tomatoes, undrained

3 cans (15 ounces each) tomato sauce

1/4 cup chopped fresh or 2 tablespoons dried basil leaves

1/4 cup chopped fresh or 2 tablespoons dried oregano leaves

2 tablespoons sugar

2 teaspoons salt

1/2 teaspoon pepper

1 cup dry red wine or beef broth

1. Cook sausage in 6-quart Dutch oven over medium-high heat about 15 minutes, stirring occasionally, until no longer pink. Remove from Dutch oven; drain.

2. Heat oil in same Dutch oven over medium heat. Cook onions, bell pepper and garlic in oil, stirring occasionally, until onions are tender. Stir in sausage and remaining ingredients except wine.

3. Heat to boiling, stirring occasionally; reduce heat. Simmer uncovered 1 hour, stirring occasionally.

4. Stir in wine. Simmer uncovered 1 hour longer, stirring occasionally.

TO MAKE AHEAD: Place sauce in 4 upright, airtight 1-quart freezer containers and label. Cool quickly and freeze no longer than 2 months. About 10 minutes before serving, place in 1 1/2-quart microwavable casserole. Cover tightly and microwave on High 6 to 8 minutes, stirring after 3 minutes, until hot.

High in potassium and vitamins A and C; good source of fiber

1 CUP: Calories 345 (Calories from Fat 205); Fat 23g (Saturated 8g); Cholesterol 65mg; Sodium 1800mg; Potassium 900mg; Carbohydrate 18g (Dietary Fiber 3g); Protein 20g % **Daily Value:** Vitamin A 20%; Vitamin C 32%; Calcium 8%;Iron 14%; Folic Acid 8%; Magnesium 12% **Diet Exchanges:** 2 High-Fat Meat, 4 Vegetable, 1 Fat

"My neighbor makes me homemade spaghetti sauce and spaghetti, that way the smells don't upset my stomach and I still get to eat some really great food. She also feels like she is really helping me out, and she is!"   —ANNE R.

"Soaking the rice cuts down on the cooking time. I would make this the day before my chemo, refrigerate and bake it that evening. It helped to know that I had my family's favorite casserole in the refrigerator and all I had to do was heat it."

Wild Rice, Sausage and Mushroom Casserole

6 servings (1 cup each)   PREP: 15 min · STAND: 2 hr · COOK: 30 min · BAKE: 1 hr

1 cup uncooked wild rice

2 cups water

1 pound bulk pork sausage

1 medium onion, chopped (1/2 cup)

2 medium stalks celery, sliced (1 cup)

1 can (10 3/4 ounces) condensed cream of mushroom soup

1 can (6 ounces) sliced mushrooms, drained

1 package (2 ounces) slivered almonds (1/4 cup)

1 Place wild rice and water in 2-quart saucepan. Soak 2 hours or overnight; do not drain. Heat to boiling; reduce heat. Cover and simmer 20 minutes while continuing with recipe.

2 Heat oven to 350°. Grease bottom and side of 2-quart casserole with shortening. Cook sausage, onion and celery in 10-inch skillet over medium heat 8 to 10 minutes, stirring occasionally, until sausage is no longer pink; drain.

3 Mix sausage mixture, soup, mushrooms and cooked wild rice in casserole. Sprinkle with almonds. Cover and bake about 1 hour or until hot and bubbly.

TO MAKE AHEAD: Cover unbaked casserole tightly and refrigerate no longer than 24 hours. About 1 hour before serving, heat oven to 350°. Bake uncovered 45 to 50 minutes or until center is hot.

A NOTE *from* **DR. GHOSH**

You can reduce the residue of this recipe by omitting the almonds and using white rice instead of wild rice. (If using white rice, remember to omit the soaking step and reduce the cooking time.) Avoid high-residue diets when having intestinal problems.

High in magnesium; good source of fiber

---

1 SERVING: Calories 350 (Calories from Fat 180); Fat 20g (Saturated 5g); Cholesterol 30mg; Sodium 970mg; Potassium 450mg; Carbohydrate 32g (Dietary Fiber 4g); Protein 14g **% Daily Value:** Vitamin A 0%; Vitamin C 2%; Calcium 6%; Iron 10%; Folic Acid 12%; Magnesium 30% **Diet Exchanges:** 2 Starch, 1 High-Fat Meat, 2 Fat

"I served this at brunch the day after my daughter Amy's wedding, and it was a real hit! It was convenient for me because the assembly is done the day before; all I had to do the day of serving was bake it."

A NOTE *from* DR. GHOSH

Green leafy vegetables such as spinach are a good source of vitamin K, essential for normal blood clotting. If taking a blood thinner such as Coumadin®, however, avoid excessive intake of dietary vitamin K because it may interfere with the medication.

High in calcium, folic acid and vitamins A and C

1 **SERVING:** Calories 335 (Calories from Fat 190); Fat 21g (Saturated 10g); Cholesterol 175mg; Sodium 830mg; Potassium 400mg; Carbohydrate 17g (Dietary Fiber 2g); Protein 21g **% Daily Value:** Vitamin A 46%; Vitamin C 20%; Calcium 34%; Iron 10%; Folic Acid 18%; Magnesium 12% **Diet Exchanges:** 1 Starch, 2 1/2 High-Fat Meat

Sausage, Vegetable and Cheese Strata

12 servings PREP: 25 min • COOK: 15 min • CHILL: 4 hr • BAKE: 1 hr 15 min

1/2 pound bulk mild pork sausage

1/2 pound bulk hot pork sausage

1 tablespoon butter or margarine

1 package (10 ounces) frozen chopped spinach, thawed and squeezed to drain, or 1/2 pound leaf spinach

4 small zucchini (1 pound), sliced

2 medium green bell peppers, sliced

1 medium onion, sliced

10 slices white bread

7 eggs

1 1/2 cups low-fat milk

1 teaspoon ground mustard

1 teaspoon salt

1/2 teaspoon pepper

2 cups shredded reduced-fat Cheddar cheese (8 ounces)

2 cups shredded mozzarella cheese (8 ounces)

1 Grease rectangular pan, 13 × 9 × 2 inches. Cook sausage in 12-inch skillet over medium heat 7 to 8 minutes, stirring occasionally, until no longer pink; drain. Melt butter in same skillet over medium-high heat. Cook spinach, zucchini, bell peppers and onion in butter about 5 minutes, stirring frequently, until zucchini is crisp-tender.

2 Break each bread slice into 4 pieces. Layer sausage, vegetables and bread in pan. Beat eggs, milk, mustard, salt and pepper with hand beater or wire whisk until blended; pour over bread. Sprinkle cheeses over top. Cover and refrigerate at least 4 hours but no longer than 24 hours.

3 Heat oven to 325°. Cover and bake 30 minutes. Uncover and bake about 45 minutes longer or until top is golden brown and knife inserted in center comes out clean.

Crab Scramble Casserole

8 servings   PREP: 10 min   •   CHILL: 4 hr   •   BAKE: 50 min

1 tablespoon butter
or margarine, melted

12 eggs

1/2 cup milk

1 teaspoon salt

1/2 teaspoon white pepper

1 1/2 teaspoons chopped
fresh or 1/2 teaspoon dried
dill weed

1 cup chopped cooked
crabmeat or imitation
crabmeat

1 package (8 ounces)
reduced-fat cream cheese
(Neufchâtel), cut into
1/2-inch cubes

2 medium green onions,
sliced (2 tablespoons)

Paprika

1 Pour butter into square baking dish, 8 × 8 × 2 inches; tilt dish to coat bottom. Beat eggs, milk, salt, white pepper and dill weed in large bowl with fork or wire whisk. Stir in crabmeat, cream cheese and onions. Pour into baking dish. Cover and refrigerate at least 4 hours but no longer than 24 hours.

2 Heat oven to 350°. Sprinkle paprika over egg mixture. Bake uncovered 45 to 50 minutes or until center is set.

"So quick to put together, refrigerate and bake later. I liked having this easy recipe for times when I needed to bring something to a potluck but didn't want to spend much time putting it together or baking it."   —MARY W.

A NOTE *from* DR. GHOSH

This tasty low-fiber egg dish is great for anyone who needs to restrict fiber, particularly those who have had stomach or intestinal surgery. To eat well, try adding a colorful napkin or a small centerpiece or light a candle to put yourself in an eating mood.

High in vitamin A;
low fiber

1 SERVING: Calories 205 (Calories from Fat 125); Fat 14g (Saturated 6g); Cholesterol 350mg; Sodium 590mg; Potassium 210mg; Carbohydrate 4g (Dietary Fiber 0g); Protein 16g % **Daily Value:** Vitamin A 18%; Vitamin C 0%; Calcium 10%; Iron 6%; Folic Acid 12%; Magnesium 4% **Diet Exchanges:** 2 Lean Meat, 2 Fat

Chicken and Green Beans with Rice (page 187)

Family-Pleasing Main Dishes

Creamy Corn and Garlic Risotto

4 servings   PREP: 5 min   •   COOK: 27 min

3 3/4 cups chicken broth

4 cloves garlic, finely chopped

1 cup uncooked Arborio or regular medium-grain white rice

3 cups frozen whole kernel corn

1/2 cup grated Parmesan cheese

1/3 cup shredded mozzarella cheese

1/4 cup chopped fresh parsley

1. Heat 1/3 cup of the broth to boiling in 10-inch skillet. Cook garlic in broth 1 minute, stirring occasionally. Stir in rice and corn. Cook 1 minute, stirring occasionally.

2. Stir in remaining broth. Heat to boiling; reduce heat to medium. Continue cooking uncovered 15 to 20 minutes, stirring occasionally, until rice is tender and creamy; remove from heat. Stir in cheeses and parsley.

FOOD *for* **THOUGHT**

Though the calories in this dish are high, the fat amount is low. This risotto also contains a very high amount of your body's favorite fuel source, carbohydrates.

"This is a very tasty main dish, one that my whole family just loves! When my 14-year-old daughter was doing the cooking, this was one of her favorites! We used chopped garlic from a jar, which made the preparation even easier."

—ANNE R.

High in calcium and folic acid; good source of fiber

1 **SERVING:** Calories 400 (Calories from Fat 70); Fat 8g (Saturated 4g); Cholesterol 15mg; Sodium 1250mg; Potassium 470mg; Carbohydrate 66g (Dietary Fiber 4g); Protein 20g **% Daily Value:** Vitamin A 14%; Vitamin C 8%; Calcium 28%; Iron 16%; Folic Acid 32%; Magnesium 12% **Diet Exchanges:** 4 1/2 Starch, 1 Lean Meat

Spaghetti and "Meatballs"

6 servings   PREP: 12 min • COOK: 15 min

1 package (7 ounces) spaghetti

2 cups cold cooked white rice

1/2 cup quick-cooking oats

1 medium onion, chopped (1/2 cup)

1/4 cup dry bread crumbs

1/4 cup milk

1 tablespoon chopped fresh or 1 teaspoon dried basil leaves

2 teaspoons chopped fresh or 1/2 teaspoon dried oregano leaves

1 egg, beaten

1/2 cup wheat germ

1 tablespoon vegetable oil

2 cups spaghetti sauce

Shredded Parmesan cheese, if desired

1 Cook and drain spaghetti as directed on package.

2 While spaghetti is cooking, mix rice, oats, onion, bread crumbs, milk, basil, oregano and egg. Shape into 12 balls. Roll balls in wheat germ.

3 Heat oil in 10-inch skillet over medium heat. Cook balls in oil about 10 minutes, turning occasionally, until golden brown.

4 Heat spaghetti sauce until hot. Serve sauce and rice balls over spaghetti. Sprinkle with cheese.

"This is a vegetarian spaghetti and meatballs, but my family didn't notice the difference, and they're pretty determined meat eaters. Spaghetti tastes great after chemo, and it is easy to reheat in single servings in the microwave. However, the real meatballs taste like aluminum foil and these don't, so they are a great alternative."

—ANNE R.

FOOD *for* THOUGHT

These "meatballs" are rolled in a small amount of wheat germ, which gives them a golden brown color and just a bit of crunch. Wheat germ has a nutty flavor and provides vitamin E, an antioxidant that helps protect cells from damaging substances.

High in iron, folic acid and magnesium; excellent source of fiber

1 SERVING: Calories 390 (Calories from Fat 70); Fat 8g (Saturated 1g); Cholesterol 35mg; Sodium 470mg; Potassium 460mg; Carbohydrate 74g (Dietary Fiber 6g); Protein 12g % Daily Value: Vitamin A 12%; Vitamin C 10%; Calcium 6%; Iron 22%; Folic Acid 32%; Magnesium 22% Diet Exchanges: 5 Starch

Ravioli with Tomato-Alfredo Sauce

6 servings PREP: 10 min • COOK: 10 min

FOOD *for* THOUGHT

This heavenly combo of tomato and cheese is brimming with calcium, an important healing nutrient. Calcium is key to strong bones and teeth and helps prevent osteoporosis. For women in menopause, maintaining strong bones can be a challenge, so sufficient calcium and vitamin D are necessary to prevent bone fractures. Regular health maintenance is very important during cancer treatment.

2 packages (9 ounces each) refrigerated cheese-filled ravioli

1 package (8 ounces) sliced mushrooms (3 cups)

1 large onion, coarsely chopped (1 cup)

1 jar (24 to 28 ounces) tomato pasta sauce

1/2 cup half-and-half or refrigerated nondairy creamer

1/4 cup grated Parmesan cheese

1/4 cup chopped fresh parsley

1 Cook and drain ravioli as directed on package; keep warm.

2 Spray same saucepan with cooking spray; heat over medium heat. Cook mushrooms and onion in saucepan about 5 minutes, stirring frequently, until onion is crisp-tender.

3 Stir in pasta sauce and half-and-half. Heat to boiling; reduce heat to low. Stir in ravioli, cheese and parsley.

High in potassium, calcium and vitamins A and C; good source of fiber

1 SERVING: Calories 345 (Calories from Fat 135); Fat 15g (Saturated 6g); Cholesterol 95mg; Sodium 1400mg; Potassium 680mg; Carbohydrate 42g (Dietary Fiber 3g); Protein 14g % **Daily Value:** Vitamin A 28%; Vitamin C 20%; Calcium 28%; Iron 14%; Folic Acid 14%; Magnesium 10% **Diet Exchanges:** 2 Starch, 1/2 High-Fat Meat, 2 Vegetable, 2 Fat

"I love pasta because it is easy to make and then reheat in small portions. It is also so satisfying. I really feel like I've eaten good-for-me food, even if I eat only five or six ravioli squares at a serving."

—ANNE R.

Ravioli with Tomato-Alfredo Sauce

Potato and Tomato Pizza

6 servings PREP: 15 min • BAKE: 25 min

FOOD *for*
THOUGHT

This is a fun twist on a traditional Italian pizza. For variety, try adding mushrooms, artichoke hearts or any leftover cooked vegetable.

1 can (10 ounces) refrigerated pizza crust dough

2 cups frozen potato wedges with skins, thawed (about 32 pieces)

1 tablespoon Dijon mustard

1 medium zucchini, cut lengthwise in half, then cut crosswise into slices

3 medium roma (plum) tomatoes, coarsely chopped (1 1/2 cups)

1/2 teaspoon dried basil leaves

1/4 teaspoon coarsely ground pepper

1 cup shredded mozzarella cheese (4 ounces)

1 Heat oven to 425°. Spray 14-inch pizza pan with cooking spray. Press pizza crust dough in pan.

2 Toss potatoes and mustard until potatoes are coated; arrange on crust. Top with zucchini, tomatoes, basil, pepper and cheese.

3 Bake 20 to 25 minutes or until cheese is melted and crust is golden brown.

"In between treatments, I went to Italy with my daughter and the Latin Club. We couldn't believe the first time we were served 'American pizza,' which was cheese pizza covered with French fries. This recipe reminds me of that, and is a quick and easy meal for the entire family."
—ANNE R.

High in magnesium; good source of fiber

1 **SERVING:** Calories 225 (Calories from Fat 55); Fat 6g (Saturated 3g); Cholesterol 10mg; Sodium 520mg; Potassium 380mg; Carbohydrate 36g (Dietary Fiber 3g); Protein 10g **% Daily Value:** Vitamin A 10%; Vitamin C 10%; Calcium 14%; Iron 12%; Folic Acid 16%; Magnesium 18% **Diet Exchanges:** 2 Starch, 1 Vegetable, 1 Fat

Mary W. Shares *her Recipe*

"I found ways to make meals a time of enjoyment. Candles, music, a glass of wine and good company do wonders for the appetite. Great recipes, such as this soup, also boost my spirit."

Acorn Squash and Apple Soup

6 servings (1 cup each)   PREP: 20 min • BAKE: 1 hr • COOK: 35 min

1 medium acorn or butternut squash (1 1/2 to 2 pounds)

2 tablespoons butter or margarine

1 medium yellow onion, sliced (1/2 cup)

2 medium tart cooking apples (Granny Smith, Greening or Haralson), peeled and sliced

1 teaspoon dried thyme leaves

1/4 teaspoon dried basil leaves

2 cans (14 1/2 ounces each) chicken broth (4 cups)

1/2 cup half-and-half

1 teaspoon ground nutmeg

1/2 teaspoon salt

1/4 teaspoon white or black pepper

1 Heat oven to 350°. Cut squash in half; remove seeds and fibers. Place cut sides up in rectangular pan, 13 × 9 × 2 inches. Pour 1/4 inch water into pan. Bake uncovered about 40 minutes or until tender. Cool; remove pulp from rind and set aside.

2 Melt butter in heavy 3-quart saucepan over medium heat. Cook onion in butter 2 to 3 minutes, stirring occasionally, until crisp-tender. Stir in apples, thyme and basil. Cook 2 minutes, stirring constantly. Stir in broth. Heat to boiling; reduce heat. Simmer uncovered 30 minutes.

3 Remove 1 cup apples with slotted spoon; set aside. Place one third of the remaining apple mixture and squash in blender or food processor. Cover and blend on medium speed about 1 minute or until smooth; pour into bowl. Continue to blend in small batches until all soup is pureed.

4 Return blended mixture and 1 cup reserved apples to saucepan. Stir in half-and-half, nutmeg, salt and pepper; heat through.

A NOTE *from* DR. GHOSH

Fruits and vegetables are important sources of fiber, vitamins and minerals. Hundreds of studies have shown there may be a protective effect against certain types of cancers when plant foods, such as fruits and vegetables, are consumed in quantity.

High in potassium

1 SERVING: Calories 155 (Calories from Fat 65); Fat 7g (Saturated 4g); Cholesterol 15mg; Sodium 910mg; Potassium 560mg; Carbohydrate 20g (Dietary Fiber 2g); Protein 5g **% Daily Value:** Vitamin A 10%; Vitamin C 8%; Calcium 6%; Iron 6%; Folic Acid 4%; Magnesium 8% **Diet Exchanges:** 2 Vegetable, 1/2 Fruit, 1 1/2 Fat

Cheesy Vegetable Soup

8 servings PREP: 5 min • COOK: 10 min

4 ounces reduced-fat process cheese spread loaf, cubed

3 1/2 cups fat-free (skim) milk

1/2 teaspoon chili powder

2 cups cooked brown or white rice

1 bag (1 pound) frozen cauliflower, carrots and asparagus (or other combination), thawed and drained

1 Heat cheese and milk in 3-quart saucepan over low heat until cheese is melted.

2 Stir in chili powder. Stir in rice and vegetables; cook until hot.

A NOTE *from* DR. GHOSH

Soothing to a sore mouth, this creamy soup can really bring comfort. If the larger pieces of veggies are difficult to swallow, try pureeing the cooked veggies in the blender or food processor to smooth out the texture of the soup.

"Soup is a comfort food, and since the whole family loves it, we eat soup often at our house. This is one of my favorite recipes because I can use whatever combination of vegetables I want, and if I cook the rice ahead of time, it comes together in just a few minutes."

—MARY W.

High in calcium and vitamin A

1 SERVING: Calories 130 (Calories from Fat 20); Fat 2g (Saturated 1g); Cholesterol 5mg; Sodium 290mg; Potassium 360mg; Carbohydrate 22g (Dietary Fiber 2g); Protein 8g % Daily Value: Vitamin A 82%; Vitamin C 10%; Calcium 20%; Iron 2%; Folic Acid 10%; Magnesium 10% Diet Exchanges: 1 Starch, 2 Vegetable

Fresh Spinach and New Potato Frittata

4 servings   PREP: 15 min   •   COOK: 20 min

6 eggs

2 tablespoons milk

1/4 teaspoon dried marjoram leaves

1/4 teaspoon salt

2 tablespoons butter or margarine

6 or 7 small red potatoes, thinly sliced (2 cups)

1/4 teaspoon salt

1 cup firmly packed bite-size pieces spinach

1/4 cup oil-packed sun-dried tomatoes, drained and sliced

3 medium green onions, cut into 1/4-inch pieces

1/2 cup shredded Swiss cheese (2 ounces)

1 Beat eggs, milk, marjoram and 1/4 teaspoon salt; set aside.

2 Melt butter in 10-inch nonstick skillet over medium heat. Add potatoes to skillet; sprinkle with 1/4 teaspoon salt. Cover and cook 8 to 10 minutes, stirring occasionally, until potatoes are tender.

3 Stir in spinach, tomatoes and onions. Cook, stirring occasionally, just until spinach is wilted; reduce heat to low.

4 Carefully pour egg mixture over potato mixture. Cover and cook 6 to 8 minutes or just until top is set. Sprinkle with cheese. Cover and cook about 1 minute or until cheese is melted.

"After surgery, I was put on a low-residue diet. All of a sudden, green beans and spinach were my only choices for green leafy vegetables. This recipe tastes great even without the onions and tomatoes, which aren't on my low-residue list. I used onion salt to get the onion flavor I like. Frittatas, easy to make and reheat in small slices, are great for grazing!"   —ANNE R.

A NOTE *from* **DR. GHOSH**

Spinach is a wonderful source of so many nutrients, including folic acid. We need folic acid for all cells to operate properly and to prevent birth defects to the brain and spinal cord of developing unborn babies.

High in calcium, iron, folic acid, vitamins A and C and potassium; good source of fiber

1 SERVING: Calories 370 (Calories from Fat 170); Fat 19g (Saturated 9g); Cholesterol 345mg; Sodium 500mg; Potassium 840mg; Carbohydrate 37g (Dietary Fiber 4g); Protein 17g % **Daily Value:** Vitamin A 32%; Vitamin C 22%; Calcium 20%; Iron 18%; Folic Acid 18%; Magnesium 16% **Diet Exchanges:** 2 Starch, 1 1/2 High-Fat Meat, 1 Vegetable, 1 Fat

Hash Brown Frittata

4 servings PREP: 10 min • COOK: 25 min

FOOD *for* **THOUGHT**

Offering a great source of potassium, potatoes can help maintain the body's fluid balance. Potassium is also key for proper nerve and muscle function.

2 cups refrigerated shredded hash brown potatoes

1 can (11 ounces) whole kernel corn with red and green peppers, drained

1 teaspoon onion salt

5 eggs or 1 cup fat-free, cholesterol-free egg product

1/3 cup milk

1 1/2 teaspoons chopped fresh or 1/2 teaspoon dried marjoram leaves

1/2 teaspoon red pepper sauce

2/3 cup shredded Cheddar cheese

1 Mix potatoes, corn and onion salt. Spray 10-inch nonstick skillet with cooking spray; heat over medium heat. Pack potato mixture firmly into skillet, leaving 1/2-inch space around edge. Reduce heat to medium-low. Cook uncovered about 10 minutes or until bottom starts to brown.

2 While potato mixture is cooking, mix eggs, milk, marjoram and pepper sauce. Pour egg mixture over potato mixture. Cook uncovered over medium-low heat. As mixture begins to set on bottom and side, gently lift cooked portions with spatula so that thin, uncooked portion can flow to bottom. Avoid constant stirring. Cook about 5 minutes or until eggs are thickened throughout but still moist.

3 Sprinkle with cheese. Reduce heat to low. Cover and cook about 10 minutes or until center is set and cheese is bubbly. Loosen bottom of frittata with spatula. Cut frittata into 4 wedges.

High in calcium, potassium and folic acid; good source of fiber

1 **SERVING:** Calories 360 (Calories from Fat 135); Fat 15g (Saturated 7g); Cholesterol 290mg; Sodium 1130mg; Potassium 700mg; Carbohydrate 42g (Dietary Fiber 4g); Protein 18g **% Daily Value:** Vitamin A 14%; Vitamin C 14%; Calcium 18%; Iron 10%; Folic Acid 20%; Magnesium 14% **Diet Exchanges:** 2 1/2 Starch, 1 1/2 High Fat Meat

"For a couple of days after my chemotherapy treatments, I lived on refrigerated potatoes. Not only were they easy to get down and soothing to my mouth, I could keep them on hand and put them in tasty recipes like this."

—SUSAN S.

Hash Brown Frittata

Salmon Burgers

5 servings PREP: 10 min • COOK: 10 min

Cucumber Sauce (below)

1 can (14 3/4 ounces) salmon, drained and flaked

1/2 cup crushed round buttery crackers

2 tablespoons chopped fresh parsley

1/2 teaspoon grated lemon peel

1 tablespoon lemon juice

2 medium green onions, sliced (2 tablespoons)

1 egg

2 tablespoons vegetable oil

5 English muffins, split and toasted

1 Make Cucumber Sauce. Mix salmon, crackers, parsley, lemon peel, lemon juice, onions and egg. Shape mixture into 5 patties.

2 Heat oil in 10-inch skillet over medium heat. Cook patties in oil 8 to 10 minutes, turning once, until golden brown. Serve patties on muffins with sauce.

Cucumber Sauce

1/3 cup finely chopped seeded peeled cucumber

1/4 cup plain yogurt

1/4 cup mayonnaise or salad dressing

1 teaspoon chopped fresh or 1/4 teaspoon dried tarragon leaves

Mix all ingredients.

A NOTE *from* **DR. GHOSH**

Salmon contains a vitamin called pantothenic acid, which we don't often hear about. Pantothenic acid helps release energy from carbohydrate-containing foods, plus it helps manufacture certain body hormones.

High in calcium and folic acid

1 SERVING: Calories 410 (Calories from Fat 190); Fat 21g (Saturated 4g); Cholesterol 95mg; Sodium 870mg; Potassium 440mg; Carbohydrate 33g (Dietary Fiber 2g); Protein 24g **% Daily Value:** Vitamin A 6%; Vitamin C 2%; Calcium 30%; Iron 14%; Folic Acid 20%; Magnesium 12% **Diet Exchanges:** 2 Starch, 2 1/2 Medium-Fat Meat, 1 Vegetable, 1 Fat

"Salmon is great-tasting, even during chemo, and the cool taste of the cucumbers is super. Quick and easy is good! This recipe makes me think spring."

—ANNE R.

"Stress can affect digestion, so relax and breathe deeply when you are eating. And remember, you have all the time in the world, so enjoy your food. Foods like this casserole are too good to hurry through — enjoy it."

Layered Tuna Casserole

4 servings (1 1/2 cups each)   PREP: 10 min   •   BAKE: 35 min

1 package (6 ounces) chow mein noodles (3 cups)

1 can (10 3/4 ounces) condensed cream of celery soup

1 can (5 ounces) evaporated milk (2/3 cup)

1 can (6 ounces) tuna packed in water or 1 can (5 ounces) chunk chicken, drained

1 can (10 3/4 ounces) condensed chicken rice soup

1/4 to 1/2 cup dry bread crumbs or crushed potato chips

1 Heat oven to 350°. Spray 3-quart casserole with cooking spray. Layer all ingredients except bread crumbs in casserole in order listed. Sprinkle with bread crumbs.

2 Bake uncovered 30 to 35 minutes or until bread crumbs are brown and tuna mixture is hot and bubbly in center.

FOOD *for* THOUGHT

This recipe supplies many essential nutrients, such as niacin, that are key to the release of energy from foods. Niacin is important for healthy skin, mouth and nervous system.

High in calcium, iron, folic acid and vitamin A; good source of fiber

1 SERVING: Calories 445 (Calories from Fat 190); Fat 21g (Saturated 5g); Cholesterol 25mg; Sodium 1480mg; Potassium 480mg; Carbohydrate 45g (Dietary Fiber 3g); Protein 22g **% Daily Value:** Vitamin A 26%; Vitamin C 2%; Calcium 20%; Iron 22%; Folic Acid 18%; Magnesium 14% **Diet Exchanges:** 3 Starch, 2 High-Fat Meat

Crispy Baked Fish with Tropical Fruit Salsa

4 servings   PREP: 10 min   •   CHILL: 1 hr   •   BAKE: 25 min

A NOTE *from*
DR. GHOSH

Potassium is a mineral essential for muscle function. Additional sources of potassium are needed during times of prolonged vomiting, diarrhea or diuretic use or when taking certain antibiotics.

Tropical Fruit Salsa (below) or 2 cups purchased peach, mango or pineapple salsa

3 tablespoons butter or margarine

2/3 cup Original Bisquick

1/4 cup yellow cornmeal

1 teaspoon chili powder

1 teaspoon salt

1 pound orange roughy or other mild-flavored fish fillets

1 egg, beaten

1. Make Tropical Fruit Salsa. Heat oven to 425°. Melt butter in rectangular pan, 13 × 9 × 2 inches, in oven.

2. Mix Bisquick, cornmeal, chili powder and salt. Dip fish into egg, then coat with Bisquick mixture. Place in pan.

3. Bake uncovered 10 minutes; turn fish. Bake about 15 minutes longer or until fish flakes easily with fork. Serve with salsa.

Tropical Fruit Salsa

1 cup pineapple chunks

1 tablespoon finely chopped red onion

1 tablespoon chopped fresh cilantro

2 tablespoons lime juice

2 kiwifruit, peeled and chopped

1 medium mango, peeled, pitted and chopped (1 cup)

1 medium papaya, peeled, seeded and chopped (1 cup)

1 jalapeño chili, seeded and finely chopped

Mix all ingredients in glass or plastic bowl. Cover and refrigerate at least 1 hour to blend flavors.

High in potassium, magnesium, folic acid and vitamins A and C; excellent source of fiber

1 **SERVING:** Calories 400 (Calories from Fat 110); Fat 12g (Saturated 2g); Cholesterol 130mg; Sodium 1030mg; Potassium 870mg; Carbohydrate 52g (Dietary Fiber 5g); Protein 27g % **Daily Value:** Vitamin A 34%; Vitamin C 90%; Calcium 10%; Iron 10%; Folic Acid 20%; Magnesium 24% **Diet Exchanges:** 1 1/2 Starch, 3 Lean Meat, 2 Fruit

"Food is always more appetizing when beautifully presented. The bright colors of the fruit in the salsa make this a very pretty dish—so refreshing and healthy, too."
—MARY W.

Crispy Baked Fish with Tropical Fruit Salsa

FOOD *for* THOUGHT

This simple recipe is a huge help when you need to prepare dinner in a flash. If you don't like the frozen vegetable combination, select one you prefer and prepare the dish the same way.

Lemony Fish over Vegetables and Rice

4 servings   PREP: 10 min • COOK: 23 min

1 package (about 6.2 ounces) fried rice (rice and vermicelli mix with almonds and oriental seasonings)

2 tablespoons butter or margarine

2 cups water

1/2 teaspoon grated lemon peel

1 bag (1 pound) frozen corn, broccoli and red peppers

1 pound cod, haddock or other mild-flavored fish fillets, about 1/2 inch thick

1/2 teaspoon lemon pepper or 1/8 teaspoon pepper

1 tablespoon lemon juice

2 tablespoons chopped fresh parsley

1 Cook rice and butter in 12-inch nonstick skillet over medium heat 2 to 3 minutes, stirring occasionally, until rice is golden brown. Stir in water, seasoning packet from rice mix and lemon peel. Heat to boiling; reduce heat. Cover and simmer 10 minutes.

2 Stir in vegetables. Heat to boiling, stirring occasionally. Cut fish into 4 serving pieces; arrange on rice mixture. Sprinkle fish with lemon pepper; drizzle with lemon juice.

3 Reduce heat. Cover and simmer 8 to 10 minutes or until fish flakes easily with fork and vegetables are tender. Sprinkle with parsley.

High in magnesium, vitamins A and C and folic acid; good source of fiber

1 SERVING: Calories 255 (Calories from Fat 70); Fat 8g (Saturated 4g); Cholesterol 75mg; Sodium 330mg; Potassium 530mg; Carbohydrate 23g (Dietary Fiber 3g); Protein 26g **% Daily Value:** Vitamin A 64%; Vitamin C 72%; Calcium 4%; Iron 8%; Folic Acid 18%; Magnesium 18% **Diet Exchanges:** 1 1/2 Starch, 3 Very Lean Meat, 1 Fat

"This tastes great on the post-chemo days after a bout with diarrhea. I eat this with a large strawberry smoothie made with strawberries, frozen daiquiri mix and ice cubes in the blender. It's a great potassium booster that tastes sensational, too."   —ANNE R.

Chicken and Vegetable Stir-Fry

4 servings PREP: 10 min • COOK: 15 min

1 cup uncooked regular long-grain rice

1 pound boneless, skinless chicken breast halves

1/4 teaspoon salt

1 bag (1 pound) fresh (refrigerated) stir-fry vegetables (4 cups)

1/2 cup water

1/2 cup classic-style stir-fry sauce

1 tablespoon honey

2 cups chow mein noodles

1/4 cup cashew pieces

1 Cook rice as directed on package. While rice is cooking, cut chicken into 1/2-inch pieces.

2 Spray 12-inch nonstick skillet with cooking spray; heat over medium-high heat. Add chicken; sprinkle with salt. Stir-fry 4 to 6 minutes or until brown.

3 Add vegetables and water to skillet. Heat to boiling; reduce heat to medium. Cover and cook 5 to 7 minutes, stirring occasionally, until vegetables are crisp-tender. Stir in stir-fry sauce and honey; heat through.

4 Divide rice and noodles among bowls. Top with chicken mixture. Sprinkle with cashews.

FOOD *for* THOUGHT

Loaded with nutrients, this chicken and veggie dish is outstanding. If you need a bit of extra flavor, add a dash or two of red pepper flakes to bring on the heat.

"A satisfying meal with family and friends is a large part of a renewed emphasis on quality of life. This quick recipe, because it can easily be doubled and cooked in batches, lends itself to sharing with others." —MARY W.

High in potassium, iron, magnesium, folic acid and vitamins A and C; good source of fiber

1 **SERVING:** Calories 550 (Calories from Fat 135); Fat 15g (Saturated 3g); Cholesterol 70mg; Sodium 1060mg; Potassium 670mg; Carbohydrate 72g (Dietary Fiber 4g); Protein 36g **% Daily Value:** Vitamin A 100%; Vitamin C 30%; Calcium 8%; Iron 30%; Folic Acid 38%; Magnesium 28% **Diet Exchanges:** 4 Starch, 3 Lean Meat, 2 Vegetable

Cheesy Chicken and Vegetable Dinner

5 servings   PREP: 10 min   •   COOK: 10 min

A NOTE *from* DR. GHOSH

Reduce the amount of cheese in this recipe if foods containing fat bother you. Sprinkling just a bit of Parmesan cheese on top of the chicken gives it a little extra zing, but not a lot of fat.

1 teaspoon vegetable oil

1 1/4 pounds boneless, skinless chicken breasts, cut into 3/4-inch pieces

2 large carrots, cut into 1/8-inch slices (2 cups)

1 medium zucchini, cut into 1/8-inch slices (2 cups)

2 tablespoons soy sauce

16 medium green onions, sliced (1 cup)

1 1/2 cups shredded sharp Cheddar cheese (6 ounces)

1 Heat 12-inch nonstick skillet over medium-high heat. Add oil; rotate to coat bottom. Cook chicken in oil 4 to 5 minutes, stirring frequently, until no longer pink in center. Remove from skillet.

2 Cook carrots and zucchini in skillet 4 to 5 minutes, stirring frequently, until crisp-tender. Add chicken and soy sauce; toss until chicken and vegetables are coated with soy sauce.

3 Sprinkle with onions and cheese. Cover skillet until cheese is melted.

"I do the cooking and food preparation as I feel up to it; otherwise, I let my husband take over." —MARY W.

High in calcium and vitamin A; good source of fiber

1 **SERVING:** Calories 310 (Calories from Fat 145); Fat 16g (Saturated 8g); Cholesterol 105mg; Sodium 660mg; Potassium 570mg; Carbohydrate 9g (Dietary Fiber 3g); Protein 35g % **Daily Value:** Vitamin A 100%; Vitamin C 12%; Calcium 24%; Iron 12%; Folic Acid 12%; Magnesium 14% **Diet Exchanges:** 5 Lean Meat, 2 Vegetable

Pat Y. *Shares* *her Recipe*

"I was told that drinking water with your meal will help settle your food, and it worked for me! Reliable recipes such as this one also helped me."

Chicken and Green Beans with Rice

6 servings (1 cup each)   PREP: 10 min · BAKE: 50 min

2 cups cut-up cooked chicken

2 cups cooked rice

1/2 teaspoon salt

1/4 teaspoon pepper

2 medium stalks celery, sliced (1 cup)

1 medium onion, chopped (1/2 cup)

1 can (14 1/2 ounces) chicken broth

1 package (9 or 10 ounces) frozen cut green or yellow wax beans, thawed

1 Heat oven to 350°. Butter 2-quart casserole. Mix all ingredients in casserole.

2 Cover and bake 45 to 50 minutes or until beans are tender.

A NOTE *from* **DR. GHOSH**

If you're looking for low-fiber, low-residue options after surgery, omit the celery and onion and cut the green bean amount in half for a simple casserole that can bring you comfort.

High in vitamin A; low fiber

1 **SERVING:** Calories 175 (Calories from Fat 35); Fat 4g (Saturated 1g); Cholesterol 40mg; Sodium 560mg; Potassium 310mg; Carbohydrate 20g (Dietary Fiber 2g); Protein 17g **% Daily Value:** Vitamin A 34%; Vitamin C 2%; Calcium 4%; Iron 10%; Folic Acid 12%; Magnesium 8% **Diet Exchanges:** 1 Starch, 2 Very Lean Meat, 1 Vegetable

Mary W. *Shares* her Recipe

"During my chemotherapy, this is the one dish everyone in my family could sit down to and enjoy. It freezes well, so it can be frozen and reheated when you need it."

FOOD *for* THOUGHT

Poultry, such as turkey and chicken, is a good source of zinc, a mineral needed in very small amounts. Deficiencies of zinc can lead to decreased appetite and a reduced ability to taste and smell.

Turkey Tetrazzini

5 servings (1 cup each)   PREP: 15 min   •   COOK: 10 min   •   BAKE: 30 min

1 package (7 ounces) spaghetti, broken into thirds

1/4 cup butter or margarine

1/4 cup all-purpose flour

1/2 teaspoon salt

1/4 teaspoon pepper

3/4 cup chicken broth

1 1/4 cups milk

2 cups cubed cooked turkey or chicken

1 can (4 ounces) sliced mushrooms, drained

1/2 cup grated Parmesan cheese

1 Heat oven to 350°. Cook spaghetti as directed on package.

2 While spaghetti is cooking, melt butter in 3-quart saucepan over medium heat. Stir in flour, salt and pepper. Cook, stirring constantly, until mixture is bubbly; remove from heat.

3 Stir in broth and milk. Heat to boiling, stirring constantly. Boil and stir 1 minute. Stir in turkey and mushrooms.

4 Drain spaghetti; place in ungreased 2-quart casserole. Stir in turkey mixture. Sprinkle with cheese. Bake uncovered about 30 minutes or until hot and bubbly.

High in calcium and folic acid; low fiber

1 SERVING: Calories 435 (Calories from Fat 160); Fat 18g (Saturated 10g); Cholesterol 85mg; Sodium 810mg; Potassium 340mg; Carbohydrate 41g (Dietary Fiber 2g); Protein 29g **% Daily Value:** Vitamin A 10%; Vitamin C 0%; Calcium 24%; Iron 16%; Folic Acid 24%; Magnesium 12% **Diet Exchanges:** 3 Starch, 3 Medium-Fat Meat

Turkey Tetrazzini

Turkey Club Squares

6 servings PREP: 10 min • BAKE: 16 min

2 cups Original Bisquick

1/3 cup mayonnaise or salad dressing

1/3 cup milk

2 cups cubed cooked turkey

2 medium green onions, sliced (2 tablespoons)

4 slices bacon, crisply cooked and crumbled

1/4 cup mayonnaise or salad dressing

1 large tomato, chopped (1 cup)

1 cup shredded reduced-fat mozzarella cheese (4 ounces)

1 Heat oven to 450°. Grease cookie sheet. Mix Bisquick, 1/3 cup mayonnaise and the milk until soft dough forms. Roll or pat dough into 12 × 8-inch rectangle on cookie sheet. Bake 8 to 10 minutes or until golden brown.

2 Mix turkey, onions, bacon and 1/4 cup mayonnaise. Spread over crust to within 1/4 inch of edge. Sprinkle with tomato and cheese.

3 Bake 5 to 6 minutes or until turkey mixture is hot and cheese is melted.

A NOTE *from* **DR. GHOSH**

Low-fiber foods are good for certain kinds of cancers because they don't cause intestinal distress, especially right after surgery. To make this recipe a low-residue option, too, omit the cheese, tomato and green onions.

High in calcium; low fiber

1 **SERVING:** Calories 490 (Calories from Fat 290); Fat 32g (Saturated 8g); Cholesterol 65mg; Sodium 910mg; Potassium 310mg; Carbohydrate 28g (Dietary Fiber 1g); Protein 23g **% Daily Value:** Vitamin A 8%; Vitamin C 4%; Calcium 24%; Iron 12%; Folic Acid 4%; Magnesium 8% **Diet Exchanges:** 2 Starch, 2 1/2 High-Fat Meat, 2 Fat

"I find that eating an early dinner allows for better digestion and sleep."

—MARY W.

"Simple foods that I grew up on, like pot roast, appealed to me the most."

Old-Fashioned Beef Pot Roast

8 servings   PREP: 10 min   •   COOK: 9 hr in slow cooker

4 medium potatoes, cut into chunks

2 pounds medium carrots, cut into chunks

1/4 cup water

1 can (10 3/4 ounces) condensed cream of chicken soup

1/2 package (2-ounce size) onion soup mix (1 envelope)

3-pound beef arm, blade or cross rib pot roast

1 Spray inside of 5- to 6-quart slow cooker with cooking spray. Place potatoes, carrots and water in cooker.

2 Mix chicken soup and onion soup mix in small bowl. Pour half of mixture over vegetables in cooker.

3 Place beef on top. Pour remaining soup mixture over beef. Cover and cook on low heat setting 8 to 9 hours or until beef and vegetables are tender.

A NOTE *from* **DR. GHOSH**

Broiling, braising and roasting are healthy techniques to use when preparing meats. Avoid charring meats so they appear blackened, and limit consumption of processed meats because of their nitrite and nitrate content, processes that are known cancer-causing agents.

High in iron, potassium and vitamin A; excellent source of fiber

1 **SERVING:** Calories 305 (Calories from Fat 100); Fat 11g (Saturated 4g); Cholesterol 65mg; Sodium 680mg; Potassium 960mg; Carbohydrate 30g (Dietary Fiber 5g); Protein 27g **% Daily Value:** Vitamin A 100%; Vitamin C 14%; Calcium 4%; Iron 20%; Folic Acid 8%; Magnesium 14% **Diet Exchanges:** 1 Starch, 3 Lean Meat, 3 Vegetable

Beef Fajita Bowls

4 servings PREP: 15 min • COOK: 15 min

FOOD *for*
THOUGHT

This beef recipe is a super source of both vitamin B$_{12}$, which is important for all body cells to function properly, and iron, a healing mineral that's vital for oxygen transfer in the blood. You cannot live without either of these vital nutrients.

1 cup uncooked regular long-grain rice

1 pound beef boneless sirloin steak

2 tablespoons vegetable oil

1 flour tortilla (8 inches in diameter), cut into 4 × 1/2-inch strips

1 bag (1 pound) frozen stir-fry bell peppers and onions

1/2 cup frozen whole kernel corn

1 cup thick-and-chunky salsa

2 tablespoons lime juice

2 tablespoons chili sauce

1/2 teaspoon ground cumin

2 tablespoons chopped fresh cilantro

1 Cook rice as directed on package. While rice is cooking, cut beef with grain into 2-inch strips; cut strips across grain into 1/8-inch slices.

2 Heat 12-inch nonstick skillet over medium-high heat. Add oil; rotate skillet to coat bottom. Cook tortilla strips in oil 1 to 2 minutes on each side, adding additional oil if necessary, until golden brown and crisp. Drain on paper towel.

3 Add beef to skillet; stir-fry over medium-high heat 4 to 5 minutes or until beef is brown. Remove from skillet.

4 Add bell pepper mixture and corn to skillet; stir-fry 1 minute. Cover and cook 2 to 3 minutes, stirring twice, until crisp-tender. Stir in beef, salsa, lime juice, chili sauce and cumin. Cook 2 to 3 minutes, stirring occasionally, until hot. Stir in cilantro.

5 Divide rice among bowls. Top with beef mixture and tortilla strips.

High in potassium, iron, folic acid and vitamins A and C; excellent source of fiber

1 **SERVING:** Calories 440 (Calories from Fat 80); Fat 9g (Saturated 2g); Cholesterol 60mg; Sodium 480mg; Potassium 790mg; Carbohydrate 65g (Dietary Fiber 5g); Protein 30g % **Daily Value:** Vitamin A 20%; Vitamin C 66%; Calcium 6%; Iron 30%; Folic Acid 36%; Magnesium 16% **Diet Exchanges:** 4 Starch, 2 Lean Meat, 1 Vegetable

"Stir-frying, sort of new to me, is a way of cooking that just feels healthy. I really felt like I was doing something good for myself and my family when I stir-fried meat and vegetables and ate them along with rice." —CATHERINE H.

Cheesy Beef Enchiladas

10 servings PREP: 10 min • BAKE: 20 min

1 pound extra-lean
ground beef

1/2 teaspoon salt

1/4 teaspoon pepper

1 medium onion, chopped
(1/2 cup)

1 cup sour cream

1 can (15 ounces) yellow and
white corn, drained

2 cups shredded Mexican
4-cheese blend (8 ounces)

8 flour tortillas (8 inches in
diameter)

1 can (10 ounces) hot
enchilada sauce

1 can (10 ounces) mild
enchilada sauce

1 Heat oven to 350°. Sprinkle beef with salt and pepper. Cook beef and onion in 10-inch skillet over medium heat 8 to 10 minutes, stirring occasionally, until beef is brown; drain. Stir in sour cream and corn.

2 Sprinkle 1 cup of the cheese in bottom of ungreased rectangular baking dish, 13 × 9 × 2 inches. Spoon about 2 tablespoons beef mixture onto each tortilla; top with a few drops hot enchilada sauce. Roll tortilla around filling; place seam side down on cheese in baking dish. Pour remaining hot and mild sauces over enchiladas. Sprinkle with remaining 1 cup cheese.

3 Bake uncovered about 20 minutes or until cheese is bubbly.

FOOD *for* THOUGHT

Try ethnic recipes; the different flavors, mix of ingredients and spices may appeal to your tastes. This Mexican-style dish is an excellent source of many important nutrients, like calcium, iron, potassium and magnesium.

High in calcium,
iron, potassium,
folic acid, magnesium
and vitamin A;
good source of fiber

1 SERVING: Calories 420 (Calories from Fat 170); Fat 19g (Saturated 9g); Cholesterol 60mg; Sodium 870mg; Potassium 540mg; Carbohydrate 43g (Dietary Fiber 3g); Protein 23g **% Daily Value:** Vitamin A 20%; Vitamin C 10%; Calcium 30%; Iron 20%; Folic Acid 24%; Magnesium 14% **Diet Exchanges:** 3 Starch, 2 High-Fat Meat

"I looked for foods rich in iron, and this recipe is iron-rich. An added plus is that my family thinks it tastes great, too!"

A NOTE *from* DR. GHOSH

A great source of iron, this recipe can help replenish red blood cells if you have anemia. Because maintaining iron stores during cancer treatment is very difficult, a multivitamin supplement containing iron can be used to enhance your diet.

Beef and Bean Dinner

6 servings (1 1/2 cups each)   PREP: 15 min • BAKE: 45 min

1 pound lean ground beef

1 medium onion, chopped (1/2 cup)

5 slices bacon

1 can (15 to 16 ounces) lima beans, drained

1 can (15 to 16 ounces) butter beans, drained

1 can (15 to 16 ounces) kidney beans, drained

1 can (28 ounces) baked beans

1/3 cup packed brown sugar

1/4 cup ketchup

2 tablespoons Worcestershire sauce

1 Heat oven to 350°. Cook beef and onion in 10-inch skillet over medium heat 8 to 10 minutes, stirring occasionally, until brown; drain. Place beef mixture in ungreased 3-quart casserole.

2 Cook bacon in same skillet over low heat 7 to 8 minutes, turning occasionally, until crisp and brown. Drain on paper towels; cool and crumble.

3 Stir beans, brown sugar, ketchup and Worcestershire sauce into beef in casserole. Top with bacon. Cover and bake 40 to 45 minutes or until hot and bubbly.

High in iron, folic acid, magnesium, potassium and vitamin A; excellent source of fiber

1 SERVING: Calories 505 (Calories from Fat 135); Fat 15g (Saturated 6g); Cholesterol 55mg; Sodium 1200mg; Potassium 1410mg; Carbohydrate 74g (Dietary Fiber 16g); Protein 34g **% Daily Value:** Vitamin A 28%; Vitamin C 6%; Calcium 12%; Iron 56%; Folic Acid 46%; Magnesium 32% **Diet Exchanges:** 4 Starch, 2 Lean Meat, 3 Vegetable

Beef and Bean Dinner

Beef-Barley Stew

6 servings   PREP: 10 min   •   BAKE: 1 hr 10 min

1 pound extra-lean
ground beef

1 medium onion, chopped
(1/2 cup)

2 cups beef broth

2/3 cup uncooked barley

2 teaspoons chopped fresh
or 1/2 teaspoon dried
oregano leaves

1/4 teaspoon salt

1/4 teaspoon pepper

1 can (14 1/2 ounces) whole
tomatoes, undrained

1 can (8 ounces) sliced
water chestnuts, undrained

1 package (10 ounces)
frozen mixed vegetables

1 Heat oven to 350°. Spray 10-inch nonstick skillet with cooking spray. Cook beef and onion in skillet over medium heat 7 to 8 minutes, stirring occasionally, until beef is brown; drain.

2 Mix beef mixture and remaining ingredients except frozen vegetables in ungreased 3-quart casserole, breaking up tomatoes.

3 Cover and bake 30 minutes. Stir in frozen vegetables. Cover and bake 30 to 40 minutes longer or until barley is tender.

A NOTE *from* DR. GHOSH

This stew is a great meal that you can store for leftovers for when you don't feel like cooking. Remember to refrigerate all leftovers right after eating because doing so will lengthen the time that the foods can be stored.

High in iron, vitamins A and C and potassium; excellent source of fiber

1 SERVING: Calories 250 (Calories from Fat 80); Fat 9g (Saturated 3g); Cholesterol 45mg; Sodium 610mg; Potassium 630mg; Carbohydrate 29g (Dietary Fiber 7g); Protein 20g % Daily Value: Vitamin A 32%; Vitamin C 24%; Calcium 6%; Iron 18%; Folic Acid 10%; Magnesium 12% Diet Exchanges: 1 Starch, 1 1/2 Lean Meat, 3 Vegetable

"Good food is especially warming and nurturing to the soul. At a time when control of my life seems an issue, being able to select and prepare tasty meals gives me a sense of control over my life."
—MARY W.

Breaded Pork Chops

8 servings PREP: 5 min • COOK: 10 min

1/2 cup Original Bisquick

12 saltine crackers, crushed
(1/2 cup)

1 teaspoon seasoned salt

1/4 teaspoon pepper

1 egg

2 tablespoons water

8 pork boneless loin chops,
1/2 inch thick (about
2 pounds)

1 Mix Bisquick, cracker crumbs, seasoned salt and pepper. Mix egg and water.

2 Dip pork into egg mixture, then coat with Bisquick mixture.

3 Spray 12-inch nonstick skillet with cooking spray; heat over medium-high heat. Cook pork in skillet 8 to 10 minutes, turning once, until slightly pink in center.

"I found this recipe so easy, my 13-year-old son could make it all by himself. My kids enjoyed making dinner on the days I felt most ill; they really thought they were helping, and they were!"

—ANNE R.

A NOTE *from* DR. GHOSH

This low-fiber, low-residue recipe is one to try when dietary restrictions apply, such as following stomach or intestinal surgery. It's so tasty, the whole family will enjoy it!

Low fiber; low residue

1 **SERVING:** Calories 220 (Calories from Fat 90); Fat 10g (Saturated 3g); Cholesterol 90mg; Sodium 380mg; Potassium 320mg; Carbohydrate 8g (Dietary Fiber 0g); Protein 24g % **Daily Value:** Vitamin A 0%; Vitamin C 0%; Calcium 2%; Iron 6%; Folic Acid 25%; Magnesium 6% **Diet Exchanges:** 1/2 Starch, 3 Lean Meat

Zesty Autumn Pork Stew

4 servings   PREP: 10 min • COOK: 20 min

1 pound lean pork tenderloin

2 medium sweet potatoes, peeled and cubed (2 cups)

1 medium green bell pepper, chopped (1 cup)

2 cloves garlic, finely chopped

1 cup coarsely chopped cabbage

1 teaspoon Cajun seasoning

1 can (14 1/2 ounces) chicken broth

1 Remove fat from pork. Cut pork into 1-inch cubes. Spray 4-quart Dutch oven with cooking spray; heat over medium-high heat. Cook pork in Dutch oven, stirring occasionally, until brown.

2 Stir in remaining ingredients. Heat to boiling; reduce heat. Cover and simmer about 15 minutes, stirring once, until sweet potatoes are tender.

A NOTE *from* DR. GHOSH

Most patients find comfort foods, such as stew, very satisfying. Savor hearty stews, creamy mashed potatoes or any other food that brings you comfort, and try to enjoy every moment of your meal.

"Stew has always been one of my favorites. Some people have said the smell of certain foods bothered them during treatment, but it has had the opposite effect for me. Just the smell of this stew simmering on the stove made me feel more like eating."   —MARY W.

High in potassium and vitamins A and C; good source of fiber

1 **SERVING:** Calories 240 (Calories from Fat 45); Fat 5g (Saturated 2g); Cholesterol 70mg; Sodium 730mg; Potassium 940mg; Carbohydrate 22g (Dietary Fiber 3g); Protein 29g % **Daily Value:** Vitamin A 100%; Vitamin C 44%; Calcium 4%; Iron 12%; Folic Acid 10%; Magnesium 12% **Diet Exchanges:** 1 Starch, 3 Very Lean Meat, 2 Vegetable

Set the Table, and Smell the Flowers

In the spirit of bringing back the joy of eating, when survivors created surroundings that were pleasant, they felt better and were able to eat more. Even little things can make a big difference.

1. **Dust off the good china.** Create a festive meal by setting the table with the nicest dishes you have—china or not! Use colorful pieces of dinnerware or festive disposable plates, even if they are mismatched (an eclectic mix can be fun). Try drinking your favorite warm or cold beverage from a favorite glass or mug.

2. **Embrace something new.** For fun, one family has a picnic in the middle of winter. They spread out a blanket on the floor and serve picnic foods like sandwiches and salads. Others create a backward dinner where dessert is served first or have a weekly pizza or pasta night.

3. **Improve the mood.** Light candles, use a small centerpiece, bring in unscented flowers, or unfold a colorful napkin in the middle of the table. Anything that cheers you and makes you feel better is worth a bit of extra effort.

4. **Bring the outside inside.** Open the window to breathe in the fresh air and gaze outside. If you do not have easy access to a window, place a picture of an outdoor scene nearby. Studies have shown that viewing an outdoor scene helps calm us and reminds us that we're part of a world that is magnificent.

5. **Celebrate the small stuff.** When you reach a treatment milestone or accomplish a small task, celebrate! Serve wine, sparkling water, juice or a nonalcoholic cocktail with the meal to put everyone in a festive mood. Serve a cake decorated to highlight your accomplishment.

6. **Enjoy each other's company.** "Surround yourself with your loved ones." Take time to share with each other. If you live alone, invite a friend or family over or ask to dine at their house. If it's too much trouble to provide a meal, ask your guests to pick up a takeout meal on the way over.

7. **Listen to music.** Music touches your emotions. And listening to certain types of music can help you to relax and feel more like eating. Choose classical, jazz, contemporary or whatever music helps to improve the mood and soothe.

8. **Walk on the wild side.** Venture outdoors, even if it's just to pick up the newspaper or to walk the dog. Take a short walk when you feel up to it. Visit a nearby pond, lake or river. Nature has a wonderful way of renewing and calming us. If a walk is too much, try simply sitting outside.

Realize, too, that there may be some days when you're not up to doing any of these suggestions. One solution is to ask others to help you with these things or to do them for you. Even small efforts can be helpful. And right now, you may need all the extra encouragement you can get to relax and nourish yourself.

Grilled Marinated Vegetables (page 202)

Comforting Side Dishes 7

Judy O. Shares her Recipe

*"My best friend sent me a note with the following words:
Yesterday is history, tomorrow is a mystery, today is a gift.
It hangs by my kitchen sink to remind me that today is
indeed a gift. Another gift is good food—I love making
these healthy grilled vegetables."*

A NOTE *from* DR. GHOSH

Folic acid is a nutrient needed for all cells. A diet rich in folic acid may also help to reduce heartburn and mouth sores.

High in iron, potassium, magnesium, vitamins A and C and folic acid; excellent source of fiber

1 SERVING: Calories 260 (Calories from Fat 90); Fat 10g (Saturated 1g); Cholesterol 0mg; Sodium 85mg; Potassium 1030mg; Carbohydrate 43g (Dietary Fiber 7g); Protein 6g % **Daily Value:** Vitamin A 66%; Vitamin C 100%; Calcium 6%; Iron 18%; Folic Acid 24%; Magnesium 18% **Diet Exchanges:** 2 Starch, 3 Vegetable, 1 Fat

Grilled Marinated Vegetables

8 servings (1 cup each) PREP: 20 min • MARINATE: 30 min • GRILL: 16 min

Zesty Garlic Marinade (below)

12 new potatoes

3/4 pound asparagus

2 bunches green onions

2 large portabella mushrooms, cut into 3/4-inch slices

2 large red bell peppers, cut into fourths

1 large zucchini, cut into 1/2-inch slices

1 large yellow summer squash, cut into 1/2-inch slices

4 roma (plum) tomatoes, sliced

Zesty Garlic Marinade

1/2 cup water

1/2 cup olive or vegetable oil

1 teaspoon sesame seed

2 teaspoons white vinegar

1 teaspoon Worcestershire sauce

1/2 teaspoon pepper

1/2 teaspoon chopped fresh parsley

1/2 teaspoon paprika

1/4 teaspoon salt

2 cloves garlic, finely chopped

1 Make Zesty Garlic Marinade.

2 Cut potatoes into fourths; place on microwavable plate. Cover with plastic wrap, folding back one edge 1/4 inch to vent steam. Microwave on High 5 minutes. Place potatoes and remaining ingredients in bag with marinade. Seal bag and refrigerate 30 minutes.

3 Heat coals or gas grill for direct heat. Grill half of the vegetables at a time 6 to 8 minutes, turning once, until vegetables are desired doneness.

Place all ingredients in 2-gallon resealable plastic food-storage bag. Seal bag and shake until ingredients are well mixed.

Pat Y. Shares *her Recipe*

"When I made easy, fast foods, I didn't have to be in the kitchen all day. This recipe is delicious as a side dish or served over baked potatoes. If you add meat, it's a main dish. Either way, it was a good choice for me and my family."

Easy Creamed Vegetables

4 servings (3/4 cup each) PREP: 2 min • COOK: 10 min

1 can (10 3/4 ounces) cream of celery or cream of mushroom soup

1 bag (1 pound) frozen broccoli, cauliflower and carrots (or other combination)

1 Heat soup to boiling in 2-quart saucepan over medium heat. Stir in frozen vegetables; reduce heat to low.

2 Cover and cook about 10 minutes, stirring occasionally, until vegetables are tender.

A NOTE *from* **DR. GHOSH**

If you decide to add meat to this dish, it is very important to chew your food well before swallowing for two reasons: (1) Your mouth has to do more of the digestion because your stomach and intestines may not be up to it right now, and (2) chewing and generating saliva can actually help prevent mouth sores and dry mouth.

High in vitamins A and C; good source of fiber

1 **SERVING:** Calories 85 (Calories from Fat 45); Fat 5g (Saturated 1g); Cholesterol 0mg; Sodium 580mg; Potassium 320mg; Carbohydrate 11g (Dietary Fiber 4g); Protein 3g % **Daily Value:** Vitamin A 66%; Vitamin C 32%; Calcium 8%; Iron 4%; Folic Acid 0%; Magnesium 6% **Diet Exchanges:** 2 Vegetable, 1 Fat

Marie E. **Shares** *her Recipe*

"Vegetable dishes without oil or cream appealed to me. These vegetables are a tasty low-fat option."

A NOTE *from* **DR. GHOSH**

Chopped fresh ginger-root, eaten raw, has been known to reduce nausea associated with chemo-therapy. If the taste is too bitter for you, try sucking on crystallized ginger, which has a sweeter taste.

Stir-Fried Vegetables

6 servings (1 cup each) PREP: 15 min · COOK: 6 min

1 tablespoon vegetable oil

1 tablespoon finely chopped gingerroot

1 clove garlic, finely chopped

1 medium onion, sliced

1 bag (16 ounces) coleslaw mix or 3 cups shredded cabbage

2 medium stalks celery, sliced diagonally (1 cup)

2 medium red bell peppers, cut into strips

1 medium green bell pepper, cut into strips

1 tablespoon soy sauce

1 teaspoon sugar

1/2 teaspoon salt

1/4 teaspoon pepper

1 Heat oil in 10-inch skillet over medium-high heat, rotating skillet to coat with oil. Add gingerroot, garlic and onion; stir-fry 1 minute.

2 Add coleslaw mix, celery and bell peppers; stir-fry about 5 minutes or until crisp-tender. Sprinkle with remaining ingredients.

High in vitamins A and C; good source of fiber

1 SERVING: Calories 60 (Calories from Fat 25); Fat 3g (Saturated 0g); Cholesterol 0mg; Sodium 380mg; Potassium 360mg; Carbohydrate 11g (Dietary Fiber 3g); Protein 2g % Daily Value: Vitamin A 50%; Vitamin C 98%; Calcium 4%; Iron 4%; Folic Acid 12%; Magnesium 4% Diet Exchanges: 2 Vegetable

Mashed Potatoes

4 to 6 servings PREP: 10 min • COOK: 30 min

6 medium round red or white potatoes (2 pounds)

1/3 to 1/2 cup milk

1/4 cup butter or margarine, softened

1/2 teaspoon salt

Dash of pepper

1 Place potatoes in 2-quart saucepan; add enough water just to cover potatoes. Heat to boiling; reduce heat. Cover and simmer 20 to 30 minutes or until potatoes are tender; drain. Shake pan with potatoes over low heat to dry (this will help mashed potatoes be fluffier).

2 Mash potatoes in pan until no lumps remain. Add milk in small amounts, mashing after each addition (amount of milk needed to make potatoes smooth and fluffy depends on kind of potatoes used).

3 Add butter, salt and pepper. Mash vigorously until potatoes are light and fluffy. If desired, sprinkle with small pieces of butter or sprinkle with paprika, chopped fresh parsley or chives.

"When the mouth sores were really bad, mashed potatoes were all I could manage to eat. I added whey powder with the butter, which made it into a meal that included a high-quality protein. It didn't change the taste, but it sure changed the nutritional benefit."

—ANNE R.

m

c

FOOD *for* THOUGHT

Mashed potatoes are easy to swallow, especially when there aren't any lumps. If you would like to add a little more milk to make them more moist, try adding 1 to 2 tablespoons at a time to get just the right consistency for you.

High in potassium; good source of fiber; low residue if skins are removed

1 SERVING: Calories 280 (Calories from Fat 110); Fat 12g (Saturated 7g); Cholesterol 35mg; Sodium 400mg; Potassium 760; Carbohydrate 45g (Dietary Fiber 4g); Protein 5g % **Daily Value:** Vitamin A 10%; Vitamin C 18%; Calcium 4%; Iron 12%; Folic Acid 4%; Magnesium 4% **Diet Exchanges:** 2 Starch, 1 Fruit, 1 1/2 Fat

Marilyn *Shares* her Recipe

"Adding more calories was important for me, to keep up my strength. This recipe helped me to do that."

A NOTE *from* DR. GHOSH

Broccoli is a great source of folic acid, which is essential in normal body functions. Excessive folic acid intake, however, can interfere with the effectiveness of a chemotherapy called methotrexate.

Easy Cheesy Broccoli Bake

6 servings (1 cup each) PREP: 5 min • BAKE: 55 min

1 bag (1 pound) frozen broccoli cuts, thawed and drained

1 can (10 3/4 ounces) cream of chicken or cream of celery soup

1 jar (8 ounces) process cheese sauce

1 medium onion, chopped (1/2 cup)

1 cup uncooked instant rice

1/4 cup milk

1/4 cup water

1/4 teaspoon pepper

1 Heat oven to 350°. Grease 3-quart casserole. Mix all ingredients in casserole.

2 Cover and bake 50 to 55 minutes or until rice is tender.

High in calcium, folic acid and vitamins A and C; good source of fiber

1 **SERVING:** Calories 260 (Calories from Fat 110); Fat 12g (Saturated 7g); Cholesterol 25mg; Sodium 1000mg; Potassium 330mg; Carbohydrate 29g (Dietary Fiber 3g); Protein 12g **% Daily Value:** Vitamin A 32%; Vitamin C 22%; Calcium 26%; Iron 8%; Folic Acid 20%; Magnesium 8% **Diet Exchanges:** 1 Starch, 1/2 High-Fat Meat, 3 Vegetable, 1 Fat

Enjoying Food during Cancer Treatment

During treatment, cancer patients often experience side effects of chemotherapy, radiation or surgery. Foods may taste metallic, patterns of hunger may be different, or, as several patients have commented, "Food just did not taste the way I remembered it before treatment."

There are ways you can bring back the joy of eating and eat well; try these suggestions.

1. **Start small.** Eat small quantities of food more often. You may feel full after eating only a little bit of food. Try eating a small amount, then try eating more food 30 minutes later.

2. **Eat big when you can.** Try eating your largest meal at a time when you are the least tired. If you are less tired in the morning or at noon, try eating your main meal then, instead of waiting until evening.

3. **Have someone else cook.** Food just seems to taste better when someone else cooks! Invite friends or family members to cook in your home, or pick a day when you're feeling better and try dining at their home.

4. **Dine at restaurants.** "If I choose good foods when eating out, it entices me to eat more because of the variety of choices," said a patient who ate many of her meals at restaurants.

5. **Choose comfort foods.** Everyone has a different version of comfort foods. Rice pudding, custard, mashed potatoes, oatmeal and macaroni and cheese conjure up pleasant, nostalgic thoughts, and are comforting and enjoyable for many. Use one of the many comfort food recipes in this book, or pull your favorites from your recipe collection.

6. **Eat foods at room temperature.** Because room-temperature foods have less aroma, this is of particular help when you are experiencing nausea.

7. **Eat away from the kitchen.** Avoid the smells associated with cooking by eating in a room other than the kitchen. Another environment can be quite helpful if you have nausea.

8. **Eat foods that are easy to swallow.** If you have mouth sores or dry mouth, this is key. "Soups, mashed potatoes and oatmeal went down easily," suggests one patient.

9. **Avoid greasy or fried foods.** Difficult for anyone to digest, greasy or fatty foods are particularly difficult to digest if you have an upset stomach or are feeling nauseated.

10. **Eat foods that agree with you.** Trial and error is the only way to know which are the best foods for your system right now. Start with small tastes of foods to see how well you tolerate them and if they taste good to you before you opt for a larger serving.

11. **Enhance eating.** Find simple ways to add pleasure to your dining experience. Try using colored plates, lighting candles or adding fresh flowers to improve your mood and help make you feel more like eating.

"So easy to make and so satisfying when I was tired."

A NOTE *from* **DR. GHOSH**

Tasty sunflower nuts are an excellent source of vitamin E. Working as an antioxidant, vitamin E protects body cells from damaging substances. Avoid seeds and nuts if you have an ostomy (where a portion of the intestine is brought up to the skin).

Broccoli-Bacon Salad

6 servings (1 cup each) PREP: 10 min • CHILL: 2 hr

1/2 cup mayonnaise or salad dressing

2 tablespoons sugar

2 tablespoons white vinegar

1 pound broccoli, cut into flowerets (5 cups)

1/4 cup chopped red onion

1/4 cup chopped yellow onion

1/4 cup sunflower nuts

6 slices bacon, crisply cooked and crumbled

1 Mix mayonnaise, sugar and vinegar in large bowl. Stir in broccoli and onion; toss until coated. Cover and refrigerate 2 hours to blend flavors.

2 Sprinkle with nuts and bacon before serving.

High in vitamin C

1 SERVING: Calories 240 (Calories from Fat 190); Fat 21g (Saturated 4g); Cholesterol 15mg; Sodium 260mg; Potassium 260mg; Carbohydrate 10g (Dietary Fiber 2g); Protein 5g **% Daily Value:** Vitamin A 12%; Vitamin C 74%; Calcium 4%; Iron 6%; Folic Acid 12%; Magnesium 8% **Diet Exchanges:** 2 Vegetable, 4 Fat

Broccoli-Bacon Salad

Bulgur Pilaf

6 servings (1/2 cup each)   PREP: 15 min · COOK: 25 min

2 tablespoons butter or margarine

1/2 cup slivered almonds

1 medium onion, chopped (1/2 cup)

1 medium carrot, chopped (1/2 cup)

1 can (14 1/2 ounces) chicken broth

1 cup uncooked bulgur

1/4 teaspoon lemon pepper seasoning, salt or pepper

1/4 cup chopped fresh parsley

1 Melt 1 tablespoon of the butter in 12-inch skillet over medium-high heat. Cook almonds in butter 2 to 3 minutes, stirring constantly, until golden brown. Remove almonds from skillet.

2 Add remaining 1 tablespoon butter, the onion and carrot to skillet. Cook about 3 minutes, stirring occasionally, until vegetables are crisp-tender.

3 Stir in broth, bulgur and lemon pepper seasoning salt. Heat to boiling; reduce heat. Cover and simmer about 15 minutes or until bulgur is tender and liquid is absorbed. Stir in almonds and parsley.

FOOD for THOUGHT

Bulgur is made from wheat berries that have been partially cooked and cracked. It imparts a nutty, whole wheat flavor with plenty of nutrients such as phosphorus and iron.

"A change of pace sometimes perked up my appetite. Double this recipe for tasty leftovers."
　　　　　　　—Mary W.

High in magnesium and vitamin A; excellent source of fiber

1 SERVING: Calories 175 (Calories from Fat 80); Fat 9g (Saturated 3g); Cholesterol 10mg; Sodium 350mg; Potassium 300mg; Carbohydrate 23g (Dietary Fiber 6g); Protein 7g % Daily Value: Vitamin A 44%; Vitamin C 4%; Calcium 4%; Iron 6%; Folic Acid 4%; Magnesium 18% Diet Exchanges: 1 Starch, 2 Vegetable, 1 Fat

Savory Black-Eyed Peas with Bacon

4 servings (1 1/2 cups each)   PREP: 20 min • COOK: 1 hr 15 min

4 slices bacon, cut into 1-inch pieces

2 1/2 cups chicken broth

1 cup dried black-eyed peas (8 ounces), sorted and rinsed

2 medium stalks celery, sliced (1 cup)

1 large onion, chopped (1 cup)

1 1/2 tablespoons chopped fresh or 1 1/2 teaspoons dried savory leaves

1 clove garlic, finely chopped

3 medium carrots, thinly sliced (1 1/2 cups)

1 large green bell pepper, cut into 1-inch pieces

1/2 cup shredded Monterey Jack cheese with jalapeño peppers (2 ounces)

1 Cook bacon in 10-inch skillet over medium heat, stirring occasionally, until crisp. Remove bacon with slotted spoon; drain. Drain fat from skillet.

2 Heat broth, black-eyed peas, celery, onion, savory and garlic to boiling in same skillet. Boil uncovered 2 minutes; reduce heat. Cover and simmer about 40 minutes, stirring occasionally, until peas are almost tender (do not boil or peas will fall apart).

3 Stir in carrots and bell pepper. Heat to simmering. Cover and simmer about 13 minutes, stirring occasionally, until vegetables are tender; stir. Sprinkle with cheese and bacon.

"This very comforting and flavorful dish is easy to eat, even with mouth sores. Doing some of the prep work early in the day when I had more energy made dinnertime easier for me. Cooking the bacon and chopping the celery, onion, garlic and pepper are all tasks that can be done ahead of time."   —ANNE R.

FOOD *for* **THOUGHT**

Be sure to include foods in your diet, such as this dish, that are nutrient-dense, meaning rich in healing nutrients—potassium, magnesium, iron, and calcium—that can aid in your recovery.

High in iron, potassium, magnesium, folic acid and vitamins A and C; excellent source of fiber

1 SERVING: Calories 255 (Calories from Fat 80); Fat 9g (Saturated 4g); Cholesterol 20mg; Sodium 870mg; Potassium 840mg; Carbohydrate 36g (Dietary Fiber 11g); Protein 19g % **Daily Value:** Vitamin A 100%; Vitamin C 38%; Calcium 16%; Iron 22%; Folic Acid 68%; Magnesium 20% **Diet Exchanges:** 2 Starch, 1 1/2 Lean Meat, 1 Vegetable

Kathy S. Shares *her Recipe*

"Eating small quantities made a big difference. Whenever I got hungry, I ate, no matter what time the clock said. This stuffing made a tasty snack."

A NOTE *from* **DR. GHOSH**

Walnuts and peanuts are great sources of magnesium. Surgery and chemotherapy deplete the body of many essential nutrients, including magnesium, so it's important to eat foods to help replace what is lost.

Wild Rice Stuffing

5 servings (1 cup each)   PREP: **10 min** • COOK: **50 min** • BAKE: **1 hr**

1 cup uncooked wild rice

2 1/2 cups water

1/3 cup butter or margarine, melted

1 cup orange juice

1 medium tart cooking apple, peeled and cut into 1-inch chunks

1 cup dry bread crumbs

1/2 cup raisins

1/2 cup chopped walnuts

1 Heat oven to 325°. Heat wild rice and water to boiling in 2-quart saucepan, stirring occasionally; reduce heat. Cover and simmer about 45 minutes or until wild rice is tender; drain.

2 Mix butter and orange juice in 2-quart casserole. Stir in apple, wild rice, bread crumbs, raisins and walnuts. Cover and bake about 1 hour or until apple is tender.

High in magnesium; excellent source of fiber

1 SERVING: Calories 480 (Calories from Fat 200); Fat 22g (Saturated 9g); Cholesterol 35mg; Sodium 280mg; Potassium 470mg; Carbohydrate 66g (Dietary Fiber 5g); Protein 10g % **Daily Value:** Vitamin A 10%; Vitamin C 16%; Calcium 8%; Iron 16%; Folic Acid 0%; Magnesium 20% **Diet Exchanges:** 3 Starch, 1 Fruit, 4 Fat

Wild Rice Stuffing

Barley and Asparagus

8 servings (1/2 cup each) PREP: 15 min • COOK: 20 min

2 tablespoons butter or margarine

1 medium onion, chopped (1/2 cup)

1 medium carrot, chopped (1/2 cup)

1 cup uncooked quick-cooking barley

2 cans (14 1/2 ounces each) chicken broth, heated

8 ounces asparagus (8 to 10 stalks), cut into 1-inch pieces

2 tablespoons shredded Parmesan cheese

1/4 teaspoon dried marjoram or thyme leaves

1/8 teaspoon pepper

1 Melt butter in 12-inch skillet over medium heat. Cook onion and carrot in butter 1 to 2 minutes, stirring occasionally, until crisp-tender. Stir in barley. Cook and stir 1 minute.

2 Pour 1 cup of the hot broth over barley mixture. Cook uncovered about 5 minutes, stirring occasionally, until liquid is absorbed. Stir in asparagus. Cook 15 to 20 minutes longer, adding broth 1 cup at a time and stirring frequently, until barley is tender and liquid is absorbed; remove from heat. Stir in remaining ingredients.

FOOD *for* THOUGHT

Combining grains and vegetables makes an interesting and good-for-you side dish, one that's fancy enough to serve to company but easy enough to make so you don't feel exhausted. Enjoy the time you save with loved ones.

"If your appetite is small, make a meal of this side dish." —MARY W.

High in vitamin A; excellent source of fiber

1 SERVING: Calories 130 (Calories from Fat 35); Fat 4g (Saturated 2g); Cholesterol 10mg; Sodium 520mg; Potassium 240mg; Carbohydrate 23g (Dietary Fiber 5g); Protein 6g % Daily Value: Vitamin A 32%; Vitamin C 4%; Calcium 4%; Iron 6%; Folic Acid 8%; Magnesium 6% Diet Exchanges: 1 Starch, 2 Vegetable

"I found that fresh fruit appealed to me the most. This fruit salad was great to have on hand because I could eat it whenever I craved something sweet."

Orange-Pineapple Fruit Salad

8 servings (1 cup each) PREP: 30 min • STAND: 2 hr • COOK: 5 min

3 medium oranges, sectioned

1 can (20 ounces) pineapple chunks in juice, drained and juice reserved

1/4 cup sugar

1 tablespoon lemon juice

1 tablespoon cornstarch

2 bananas, sliced

1 pint (2 cups) strawberries, sliced

1 cup seedless red grapes, cut in half

2 kiwifruit, sliced or cut into chunks

1 Place orange sections and pineapple chunks in colander in medium bowl; sprinkle with sugar. Pour reserved pineapple juice over fruit, allowing juice to drain into bowl; let stand 2 hours.

2 Pour juice from bowl into 1-quart saucepan. Stir in lemon juice and cornstarch. Heat to boiling over medium heat, stirring constantly. Boil and stir 1 minute; cool.

3 Place oranges, pineapple, bananas, strawberries, grapes and kiwifruit in large bowl. Pour sauce over fruit and gently stir. Serve immediately or chill before serving.

A NOTE *from* **DR. GHOSH**

Eat this salad with a meat that's high in iron, because the vitamin C makes the iron more readily absorbed into the body. Sprinkling a little sugar over the top will add sweetness and increase the number of calories. Remember: Every calorie counts!

High in vitamin C; good source of fiber

1 SERVING: Calories 160 (Calories from Fat 10); Fat 1g (Saturated 0g); Cholesterol 0mg; Sodium 5mg; Potassium 460mg; Carbohydrate 40g (Dietary Fiber 4g); Protein 2g **% Daily Value:** Vitamin A 4%; Vitamin C 100%; Calcium 4%; Iron 4%; Folic Acid 10%; Magnesium 8% **Diet Exchanges:** 2 1/2 Fruit

"This recipe was so easy. I mixed the fruit ahead of time. Then I drizzled on the dressing and added the cheese whenever I needed a little pick-me-up."

A NOTE *from* DR. GHOSH

This salad is a great healthy snack; small meals are better tolerated during chemotherapy and radiation therapy and after surgery. Substitute process cheese for the feta cheese during times of neutropenia, when the white blood cell count is low; neutropenia usually occurs seven to fourteen days after chemotherapy.

High in vitamin C; good source of fiber

1 SERVING: Calories 170 (Calories from Fat 35); Fat 4g (Saturated 2g); Cholesterol 15mg; Sodium 400mg; Potassium 410mg; Carbohydrate 34g (Dietary Fiber 4g); Protein 4g **% Daily Value:** Vitamin A 14%; Vitamin C 100%; Calcium 10%; Iron 6%; Folic Acid 16%; Magnesium 6% **Diet Exchanges:** 1/2 High-Fat Meat, 2 Fruit

Easy Fresh-Fruit Salad

6 servings (1 1/2 cups each)   PREP: 20 min

1 medium pineapple, cut into 1-inch chunks

1 pint (2 cups) strawberries, sliced

1 pint (2 cups) blueberries

1 small bunch (2 cups) seedless green grapes

1 bunch leaf lettuce

1/2 cup raspberry vinaigrette dressing

3 to 4 ounces feta cheese, crumbled

1 Mix pineapple, strawberries, blueberries and grapes in large bowl.

2 Serve fruit mixture on lettuce. Drizzle with dressing. Top with cheese.

Country Fruit Cobbler (page 220)

Treat-Yourself Desserts 8

Ellen T. Shares *her Recipe*

"This was the easiest dessert to put together, and it's so good served warm with whipped cream or ice cream. Sometimes I made this with drained canned peaches if I didn't have fresh fruit on hand."

A NOTE *from* **DR. GHOSH**

Scientists are uncovering more antioxidants every day. Berries contain natural antioxidants that may help protect the body from certain diseases, such as cancer and heart disease. Orange-colored fruits such as peaches and apricots are rich in beta-carotene and a good source of folic acid.

Country Fruit Cobbler

6 servings   PREP: 10 min • BAKE: 1 hr

1/4 cup butter or margarine

1 cup all-purpose flour

1 cup sugar

2 teaspoons baking powder

1/4 teaspoon salt

3/4 cup milk

4 cups fresh or frozen (thawed and drained) blueberries, raspberries, sliced peaches or strawberries (or combination of fruit)

1 Heat oven to 350°. Melt butter in 1 1/2-quart casserole in oven. Mix flour, sugar, baking powder, salt and milk in medium bowl. Pour batter into casserole onto butter without mixing with butter. Pour fruit over batter.

2 Bake uncovered about 1 hour or until top is golden brown. Serve warm.

Good source of fiber

1 **SERVING:** Calories 415 (Calories from Fat 100); Fat 11g (Saturated 6g); Cholesterol 30mg; Sodium 400mg; Potassium 190mg; Carbohydrate 78g (Dietary Fiber 4g); Protein 5g % **Daily Value:** Vitamin A 10%; Vitamin C 12%; Calcium 16%; Iron 8%; Folic Acid 8%; Magnesium 4% **Diet Exchanges:** Not recommended

Anne R. Shares her Recipe

"The best diet for me includes small meals and enough protein to help me heal and feel good during treatments. I use protein powder to boost the protein in foods that I can eat, as in these lemon bars. For a zestier lemon flavor, I add grated lemon peel to the filling."

Easy Lemon Bars

16 bars PREP: 25 min • BAKE: 30 min • COOL: 2 hr

1 package (1 pound 0.5 ounces) lemon bar mix

Juice of 1 whole lemon (about 3 tablespoons)

1/2 cup vanilla-flavored protein powder

1 container (8 ounces) fat-free, cholesterol-free egg product

Powdered sugar, if desired

1 Heat oven to 350°. Press dry crust from lemon bar mix in bottom of square pan (8 × 8 × 2 or 9 × 9 × 2 inches). Bake 10 minutes.

2 Add enough water to lemon juice to equal 1/2 cup. Place filling from lemon bar mix and protein powder in large bowl. Stir in egg product and lemon juice mixture with wire whisk until smooth. Pour filling over hot crust.

3 Bake 25 to 30 minutes or until top just begins to brown and center is set. Cool completely, about 2 hours. Sprinkle with powdered sugar. For bars, cut into 4 rows by 4 rows.

A NOTE *from* **DR. GHOSH**

These bars are a great snack or mini-meal when you are on the go! A daily dose of light exercise for 30 minutes can help combat your fatigue and lift your spirits.

Low fiber; low residue

1 BAR: Calories 180 (Calories from Fat 65); Fat 7g (Saturated 2g); Cholesterol 10mg; Sodium 60mg; Potassium 70mg; Carbohydrate 28g (Dietary Fiber 1g); Protein 2g **% Daily Value:** Vitamin A 6%; Vitamin C 2%; Calcium 2%; Iron 6%; Folic Acid 6%; Magnesium 4% **Diet Exchanges:** 1 Starch, 1 Fruit, 1 Fat

Catherine H. *Shares* *her Recipe*

"I have always baked a lot of cookies, and my favorite recipes contained oatmeal, coconut, dried fruits or nuts, which did not fit my low-residue diet restrictions. This recipe and the following one are low residue."

A NOTE *from* DR. GHOSH

Pumpkin is rich in beta-carotene, a form of vitamin A. Studies show that vitamin A, an antioxidant vitamin, may reduce the risk of certain types of cancer.

Pumpkin Drop Cookies

About 4 dozen cookies PREP: 10 min • BAKE: 10 to 12 min per sheet

1/2 cup butter or margarine, softened

3/4 cup granulated sugar

3/4 cup packed brown sugar

2 eggs

1 can (15 ounces) pumpkin (not pumpkin pie mix)

2 1/2 cups all-purpose flour

2 1/2 teaspoons baking powder

1 teaspoon baking soda

1 teaspoon salt

1 teaspoon ground cinnamon

1/4 teaspoon ground allspice

1/4 teaspoon ground nutmeg

1 cup raisins

1 Heat oven to 375°. Grease cookie sheet with shortening. Mix butter and sugars in large bowl with spoon. Beat in eggs. Stir in pumpkin. Stir in remaining ingredients except raisins. Fold in raisins.

2 Drop dough by tablespoonfuls about 2 inches apart onto cookie sheet.

3 Bake 10 to 12 minutes or until set and golden. Cool 1 to 2 minutes; remove from cookie sheet to wire rack.

Low fiber; low residue

1 COOKIE: Calories 80 (Calories from Fat 20); Fat 2g (Saturated 1g); Cholesterol 15mg; Sodium 120mg; Potassium 65mg; Carbohydrate 15g (Dietary Fiber 1g); Protein 1g **% Daily Value:** Vitamin A 30%; Vitamin C 0%; Calcium 2%; Iron 2%; Folic Acid 2%; Magnesium 0% **Diet Exchanges:** 1 Fruit, 1/2 Fat

Great Gifts

What are the best gifts for cancer patients? Not what you might expect. Try these favorites from cancer survivors.

What to Bring

Gift certificates—Give a gift certificate to a favorite restaurant or department store or for a mani-cure, pedicure or massage. Create a homemade certificate for a dinner you will make when the patient is home or well enough to enjoy eating, or for a household task. A certificate's under-lying message that you think the patient will eventually be well brings hope.

Books—Choose books with spiritual, uplifting messages or those with a humorous tone. Cartoons, comics and magazines are also good choices for reading when concentration may be difficult. Keep the patients' interests in mind—a mystery or the latest best-seller may be just what he or she wants for distraction.

Balloons—Colorful get-well balloons usually last a long time and let the recipient know you are thinking of him or her. Mylar balloons make the best choice because they have no smell and stay inflated for a long time.

Music—Cancer patients can listen at their leisure to music CDs or healing tapes to calm them or for inspiration.

Fruit and vegetable basket—Fresh fruits and vegetables are always good choices. They contain important nutrients for healing and are easy to snack on (just rinse and enjoy). Dried fruits are a good option, too. Be wary of any produce that has a strong aroma, which might be a problem.

Patient requests—Is there something in particular the patient wants? Funny slippers, body lotion, the latest gossip from the office? Being able to grant the patient's wish may indeed be the best gift. And sometimes, he or she may just want your company!

What Not to Bring

Fresh flowers—Flowers with a strong odor are not the best gift for patients who often feel nause-ated from cancer, medication or treatment. Ask the florist to suggest varieties (like some orchids) that offer little or no scent. Or bring a green plant to liven things up.

Candy—Cancer patients need to eat as healthfully as possible to keep up their strength. Eating even a couple of candies may not leave an appetite for lunch or dinner. Some patients on chemotherapy have said that chocolate now just tastes sweet without the chocolate flavor.

Anything with a strong aroma—Scented candles, bath salts and gels, lotions, powders or per-fumes that are very aromatic are not the best gift choices right now. If you can find unscented versions of these gifts, the cancer patient may be more pleased.

Catherine H. *Shares* her Recipe

"Something sweet after a meal was quite appealing. I would make up a batch of these cookies between treatments and freeze them, so it didn't take any effort to have a simple dessert or snack, even while I was on chemo."

A NOTE *from* DR. GHOSH

Pay special attention to where and at what temperature you store foods. Keep foods covered to increase storage time and to reduce odors in your kitchen. Make large quantities when you can and continue to eat, even when your appetite is down.

Rosalie's Orange Butter Cookies

About 3 1/2 dozen cookies   PREP: 10 min   •   BAKE: 8 to 10 min per sheet   •   COOL: 30 min

2/3 cup butter or margarine, softened

3/4 cup sugar

1 egg

Grated peel of 1 large orange (about 2 tablespoons)

1/2 cup orange juice

2 cups all-purpose flour

1/2 teaspoon baking powder

1/2 teaspoon baking soda

1/2 teaspoon salt

Orange Butter Frosting (below)

1 Heat oven to 350°. Mix butter, sugar and egg in large bowl with spoon until creamy and well blended. Stir in orange peel and orange juice. Stir in remaining ingredients except Orange Butter Frosting.

2 Drop dough by tablespoonfuls about 2 inches apart onto ungreased cookie sheet.

3 Bake 8 to 10 minutes or until light brown around edges. Cool 1 to 2 minutes; remove from cookie sheet to wire rack. Cool completely, about 30 minutes. Frost with Orange Butter Frosting.

Orange Butter Frosting

1 1/2 cups powdered sugar

2 tablespoons butter or margarine, softened

Grated peel of 1 large orange (about 2 tablespoons)

1 1/2 tablespoons orange juice

Mix all ingredients.

Low fiber, low residue

1 COOKIE: Calories 90 (Calories from Fat 35); Fat 4g (Saturated 2g); Cholesterol 15mg; Sodium 65mg; Potassium 20mg; Carbohydrate 13g (Dietary Fiber 0g); Protein 1g % **Daily Value:** Vitamin A 2%; Vitamin C 0%; Calcium 0%; Iron 2%; Folic Acid 2%; Magnesium 0% **Diet Exchanges:** 1 Fruit, 1 Fat

Rosalie's Orange Butter Cookies,
Pumpkin Drop Cookies (page 222)
and Easy Lemon Bars (page 221)

Orange-Cream Frosty

6 servings PREP: 5 min

1/2 gallon orange, vanilla or peach frozen yogurt

1 can (6 ounces) frozen (thawed) calcium-fortified orange juice concentrate

1 cup milk

1 Place half each of the frozen yogurt, juice concentrate and milk in blender. Cover and blend on medium speed about 45 seconds, stopping blender occasionally to scrape sides, until thick and smooth. Pour into 3 glasses.

2 Repeat with remaining yogurt, juice concentrate and milk.

FOOD *for* THOUGHT

The coolness of this dessert and the combination of juice and yogurt may be helpful during times when foods taste metallic or you're having difficulty swallowing.

"This was so refreshing and went down easily when I had problems swallowing other foods. For variety, I used grape juice concentrate instead of orange juice concentrate."
—CAROL N.

High in potassium, calcium, vitamin C and folic acid; low fiber

1 **SERVING:** Calories 350 (Calories from Fat 25); Fat 3g (Saturated 2g); Cholesterol 10mg; Sodium 170mg; Potassium 890mg; Carbohydrate 69g (Dietary Fiber 1g); Protein 14g % **Daily Value:** Vitamin A 8%; Vitamin C 100%; Calcium 46%; Iron 2%; Folic Acid 24%; Magnesium 14% **Diet Exchanges:** 3 Fruit, 2 Skim Milk

Randie N. Shares her Recipe

"I made gelatin recipes often——they helped my nausea. This one is cool and comforting."

Raspberry-Banana Gelatin Dessert

8 servings (1 cup each) PREP: 10 min • CHILL: 3 hr 30 min

2 cups boiling water

1 package (6 ounces) raspberry-flavored gelatin

2 cups vanilla ice cream

1 can (20 ounces) crushed pineapple in juice, drained

2 medium bananas, thinly sliced

1 Pour boiling water on gelatin in medium bowl; stir until gelatin is dissolved. Stir in ice cream. Refrigerate about 30 minutes or until partially set.

2 Spray 2-quart mold with cooking spray. Stir pineapple and bananas into gelatin. Spoon into mold. Cover and refrigerate at least 3 hours until firm. Unmold gelatin onto serving plate.

A NOTE *from* DR. GHOSH

During times of nausea, gelatin can help settle the stomach. To lessen the nausea, avoid acidic, sweet and high-fat foods. Crackers and dry toast can help combat nausea in the morning. Drinking plenty of fluids can also be a big help.

Low fiber

1 **SERVING:** Calories 185 (Calories from Fat 35); Fat 4g (Saturated 2g); Cholesterol 15mg; Sodium 55mg; Potassium 270mg; Carbohydrate 35g (Dietary Fiber 1g); Protein 3g **% Daily Value:** Vitamin A 4%; Vitamin C 16%; Calcium 6%; Iron 2%; Folic Acid 2%; Magnesium 6% **Diet Exchanges:** 2 Fruit, 1 Fat

A NOTE *from* DR. GHOSH

Molasses is a great source of iron and magnesium, plus gingerbread offers big taste from the spices. If you're not up to preparing the meringue, serve it with applesauce for an afternoon snack.

High in iron, magnesium and potassium; low fiber

1 SERVING: Calories 435 (Calories from Fat 125); Fat 14g (Saturated 4g); Cholesterol 25mg; Sodium 400mg; Potassium 650mg; Carbohydrate 72g (Dietary Fiber 1g); Protein 6g **% Daily Value:** Vitamin A 0%; Vitamin C 0%; Calcium 10%; Iron 20%; Folic Acid 10%; Magnesium 26% **Diet Exchanges:** Not recommended

Gingerbread with Brown Sugar Meringue

9 servings PREP: 15 min • BAKE: 1 hr

2 1/3 cups all-purpose flour

1/2 cup butter or margarine

1/3 cup sugar

1 cup full-flavor or mild-flavor molasses

3/4 cup hot water

1 teaspoon baking soda

1 teaspoon ground ginger

1 teaspoon ground cinnamon

3/4 teaspoon salt

1 egg

Brown Sugar Meringue (below)

Brown Sugar Meringue

2 egg whites

1/4 teaspoon cream of tartar

1/2 cup packed brown sugar

1 Heat oven to 325°. Grease bottom and side of springform pan, 9 × 3 inches, or square pan, 9 × 9 × 2 inches, with shortening; lightly flour. Beat all ingredients except Brown Sugar Meringue in large bowl with electric mixer on low speed 30 seconds, scraping bowl constantly. Beat on medium speed 3 minutes, scraping bowl occasionally. Pour into pan.

2 Bake about 50 minutes or until toothpick inserted in center comes out clean. Meanwhile, make Brown Sugar Meringue.

3 Increase oven temperature to 400°. Spread meringue over hot gingerbread. Bake 8 to 10 minutes or until meringue is light brown. Serve warm. Store covered in refrigerator.

Beat egg whites and cream of tartar in medium bowl with electric mixer on high speed until foamy. Beat in brown sugar, 1 tablespoon at a time; continue beating until stiff peaks form and mixture is glossy. Do not underbeat.

"Gingerbread. Ginger cookies. Ginger ale. Who knew they could lessen nausea so much? My mom makes me ginger cookies every time I have chemo. My neighbor brings over gingerbread. These foods sure hit the spot now." —ANNE R.

Gingerbread with Brown Sugar Meringue

Fudge Pudding Cake with Ice Cream

9 servings PREP: 15 min • BAKE: 40 min • STAND: 15 min

A NOTE *from* DR. GHOSH

Dessert can be an important part of a meal because it often provides plenty of calories per bite. If you are too full to eat dessert after a meal, try eating it as a snack between meals. Enjoy!

1 cup all-purpose flour

3/4 cup granulated sugar

2 tablespoons baking cocoa

2 teaspoons baking powder

1/4 teaspoon salt

1/2 cup milk

2 tablespoons vegetable oil

1 teaspoon vanilla

1 cup chopped nuts

1 cup packed brown sugar

1/4 cup baking cocoa

1 3/4 cups boiling water

1/2 cup vanilla ice cream per serving

1 Heat oven to 350°. Mix flour, granulated sugar, 2 tablespoons cocoa, the baking powder, and salt in ungreased square pan, 9 × 9 × 2 inches. Stir in milk, oil and vanilla with fork until smooth. Stir in nuts. Spread evenly in pan.

2 Mix brown sugar and 1/4 cup cocoa; sprinkle over batter. Pour boiling water over batter.

3 Bake 40 minutes. Let stand 15 minutes. Spoon cake and sauce into individual dishes. Top with ice cream.

MICROWAVE DIRECTIONS: Mix flour, granulated sugar, 2 tablespoons cocoa, the baking powder and salt in 2-quart microwavable casserole. Stir in milk, oil and vanilla. Stir in nuts. Spread evenly in casserole. Mix brown sugar and 1/4 cup cocoa; sprinkle over batter. Pour boiling water over batter. Microwave uncovered on Medium (50%) 9 minutes; rotate casserole 1/2 turn. Microwave uncovered on High 5 to 7 minutes or until top is almost dry.

High in calcium; good source of fiber

1 SERVING: Calories 480 (Calories from Fat 180); Fat 20g (Saturated 6g); Cholesterol 30mg; Sodium 240mg; Potassium 340mg; Carbohydrate 72g (Dietary Fiber 3g); Protein 6g % **Daily Value:** Vitamin A 6%; Vitamin C 0%; Calcium 18%; Iron 12%; Folic Acid 6%; Magnesium 14% **Diet Exchanges:** Not recommended

"After surgery, when I was shown the list of foods not on the low-residue/ low-fiber diet, I was devastated. Then I noticed chocolate. I said to my doctor, 'As long as I can eat chocolate, I'll be okay!' I can't live without my dose of chocolate every day." —ANNE R.

Fudge Pudding Cake with Ice Cream

Baked Custard

6 servings PREP: 10 min • BAKE: 45 min • COOL: 30 min

3 eggs, slightly beaten

1/3 cup sugar

1 teaspoon vanilla

Dash of salt

2 1/2 cups very warm milk

Ground nutmeg

1 Heat oven to 350°. Mix eggs, sugar, vanilla and salt in medium bowl. Gradually stir in milk. Pour into six 6-ounce custard cups. Sprinkle with nutmeg.

2 Place cups in rectangular pan, 13 × 9 × 2 inches, on oven rack. Pour very hot water into pan to within 1/2 inch of tops of cups.

3 Bake about 45 minutes or until knife inserted halfway between center and edge comes out clean. Remove cups from water. Cool about 30 minutes. Unmold and serve warm, or refrigerate and unmold before serving. Store covered in refrigerator.

A NOTE *from* DR. GHOSH

Custard is easy to swallow when other foods just won't go down or when you're suffering from mouth sores. The smooth and soothing texture may be just what you're looking for in a dessert or snack.

"This is so good, so smooth and creamy and so nutritious with all those eggs. I love this pudding when my mouth is sore. Sometimes I have a banana with it. Reminds of Grandma's banana cream pie. Mmm, good."

—ANNE R.

Low fiber

1 SERVING: Calories 135 (Calories from Fat 45); Fat 5g (Saturated 2g); Cholesterol 115mg; Sodium 120mg; Potassium 190mg; Carbohydrate 16g (Dietary Fiber 0g); Protein 7g **% Daily Value:** Vitamin A 6%; Vitamin C 0%; Calcium 14%; Iron 2%; Folic Acid 4%; Magnesium 4% **Diet Exchanges:** 1 Skim Milk, 1 Fat

Kathy S. Shares her Recipe

"I've returned to eating many of the foods I ate as a child. It's funny, my granddaughter and I are now eating the same foods."

Rice Pudding

7 servings (1/2 cup each)   PREP: **15 min**   •   COOK: **20 min**

1 cup uncooked regular
long-grain rice

2 cups water

2/3 cup sugar

1 tablespoon cornstarch

1/2 teaspoon salt

2 cups milk

2 eggs, beaten

1 teaspoon vanilla

Ground cinnamon or nutmeg

Slivered almonds, if desired

1 Heat rice and water to boiling in 2-quart saucepan, stirring once or twice; reduce heat to low. Cover and simmer 14 to 15 minutes (do not lift cover or stir). All water should be absorbed.

2 Mix sugar, cornstarch and salt in 3-quart saucepan; gradually stir in milk. Cook over medium heat, stirring constantly, until mixture thickens and boils. Boil and stir 1 minute. Gradually stir at least half of the hot mixture into eggs, then stir back into hot mixture in saucepan. Boil and stir 1 minute; remove from heat. Stir in rice and vanilla.

3 Serve warm sprinkled with cinnamon and almonds, or cover and refrigerate about 3 hours until chilled. Store covered in refrigerator.

A NOTE *from* DR. GHOSH

Puddings, custards and shakes are great comfort foods to include during cancer treatment. If you need extra protein, 2 tablespoons of protein powder can be stirred in with the cornstarch to boost the protein level of this pudding.

Low fiber

1 SERVING: Calories 235 (Calories from Fat 25); Fat 3g (Saturated 1g); Cholesterol 65mg; Sodium 220mg; Potassium 150mg; Carbohydrate 46g (Dietary Fiber 0g); Protein 6g **% Daily Value:** Vitamin A 4%; Vitamin C %; Calcium 10%; Iron 6%; Folic Acid 14%; Magnesium 4% **Diet Exchanges:** 2 Starch, 1 Fruit, 1/2 Fat

Easy Menus During Treatment

MEAL AND MENU PLANNING can be difficult and time consuming, especially when you aren't feeling well. In the following pages, you'll find ideas for healthy, quick meals and snacks that meet a cancer patient's needs, all based on eating smaller meals six times a day.

The seven-day menus list meal and daily nutrient totals and include foods that are rich in the following healing nutrients: calcium, iron, magnesium and potassium. For maximum healing, it's important to consume more than 1,000 milligrams of calcium, more than 18 milligrams of iron, more than 500 milligrams of magnesium and more than 1,000 milligrams of potassium per day. In addition, a fiber intake of 25 to 35 grams each day is suggested. We've also included the meal and daily calorie levels. Instead of focusing on calories during treatment, focus on getting the minerals your body needs at this time.

You can mix and match meals and snacks from different days to add variety to your eating and to adjust for foods you may not like or may not be able to eat right now.

The menus listed are intended to be a guide for you. On days when you are not feeling well, you may look at the menus and realize you can't eat that much. That's okay, just do your best to eat whatever you can. And on the days you are feeling better, try to eat as often as you feel up to it. *Remember*, during treatment, your survival is linked to your ability to eat and replenish lost nutrients.

In addition to the seven days of menus, we've provided a two-day menu for each of the four most common side effects: constipation, diarrhea, mouth sores and nausea. And because finding food sources that provide enough iron can be difficult, we've included high-iron food choices in a neutropenia menu. Read on to learn about your eating options.

Menu 1

Breakfast
- 1 serving **Cinnamon-Raisin Morning Mix** (*page 59*)
- 1 serving **Citrus-Peach Smoothie** (*page 103*)

Calories	Calcium (mg)	Iron (mg)	Magnesium (mg)	Potassium (mg)
295	212	8.5	43	482

Snack
- 1/2 bagel with 1 tablespoon cream cheese

Calories	Calcium (mg)	Iron (mg)	Magnesium (mg)	Potassium (mg)
129	33	1	9	46

Lunch
- 1 serving **Hot Turkey Sandwiches** (*page 90*)
- 10 baby-cut carrots with 2 tablespoons **Roasted Vegetable Dip** (*page 80*)
- 1 cup fat-free (skim) milk

Calories	Calcium (mg)	Iron (mg)	Magnesium (mg)	Potassium (mg)
484	401	3	105	1237

Snack
- 2 **Rosalie's Orange Butter Cookies** (*page 224*)
- 1 cup fat-free (skim) milk

Calories	Calcium (mg)	Iron (mg)	Magnesium (mg)	Potassium (mg)
259	321	1	32	441

Dinner
- 1 baked pork chop
- 1 serving **Wild Rice Stuffing** (*page 212*)
- 1/2 cup spinach salad with 2 tablespoons ranch dressing

Calories	Calcium (mg)	Iron (mg)	Magnesium (mg)	Potassium (mg)
831	143	4	116	875

Snack
- 6 ounces fruited low-fat yogurt
- 1 cup apple-cranberry juice

Calories	Calcium (mg)	Iron (mg)	Magnesium (mg)	Potassium (mg)
337	276	0.3	30	397

DAILY TOTAL

Calories	Calcium (mg)	Iron (mg)	Magnesium (mg)	Potassium (mg)
2337	1386	18	336	3478

Menu 2

Breakfast
· Milk and Rice "Soup" *(page 39)*
· 1/2 cup berries
· 1 cup fat-free (skim) milk

Calories	Calcium (mg)	Iron (mg)	Magnesium (mg)	Potassium (mg)
411	519	2	87	1062

Snack
· Crunchy Fruit Snack Mix *(page 43)*
· 1 cup Chai Tea *(page 108)*

Calories	Calcium (mg)	Iron (mg)	Magnesium (mg)	Potassium (mg)
246	280	6	53	532

Lunch
· 1 serving Orange-Pineapple Fruit Salad *(page 215)*
· 1 roast beef sandwich with 2 slices whole wheat bread and 2 teaspoons mayonnaise and/or mustard
· 1 cup raw broccoli flowerets and cauliflowerets
· 1 cup hot tea or coffee

Calories	Calcium (mg)	Iron (mg)	Magnesium (mg)	Potassium (mg)
532	133	5	127	1186

Snack
· 1 serving String Cheese Sticks *(page 86)*
· 1 cup fat-free (skim) milk

Calories	Calcium (mg)	Iron (mg)	Magnesium (mg)	Potassium (mg)
389	604	1.5	51	598

Dinner
· 1 serving Turkey Tetrazzini *(page 188)*
· 1 serving Corn and Black Bean Salad *(page 140)*
· 1 serving Raspberry-Banana Gelatin Dessert *(page 227)*

Calories	Calcium (mg)	Iron (mg)	Magnesium (mg)	Potassium (mg)
774	356	6	132	1047

Snack
· 1 cup red or green seedless grapes

Calories	Calcium (mg)	Iron (mg)	Magnesium (mg)	Potassium (mg)
114	18	0.4	10	296

DAILY TOTAL

Calories	Calcium (mg)	Iron (mg)	Magnesium (mg)	Potassium (mg)
2466	1910	21	460	4721

Menu 3

Breakfast
· 1 serving Home-Style Oatmeal with Raisins *(page 57)* sprinkled with 2 tablespoons brown sugar
· 1 cup fat-free (skim) milk

Calories	Calcium (mg)	Iron (mg)	Magnesium (mg)	Potassium (mg)
539	588	3	118	1266

Snack
· Hot Fruit Compote *(page 37)*
· 1 cup hot herbal tea

Calories	Calcium (mg)	Iron (mg)	Magnesium (mg)	Potassium (mg)
223	32	1.5	28	436

Lunch
· 1 serving Cream of Broccoli Soup *(page 13)*
· 1 serving Onion and Rosemary Focaccia Wedges *(page 83)* with 1 to 2 teaspoons butter or margarine
· 1 medium pear

Calories	Calcium (mg)	Iron (mg)	Magnesium (mg)	Potassium (mg)
488	285	3.5	63	856

Snack
· 1/2 cup cottage cheese
· 2 tablespoons sunflower nuts

Calories	Calcium (mg)	Iron (mg)	Magnesium (mg)	Potassium (mg)
200	82	1	62	199

Dinner
· 1 serving Potato-Tomato-Tofu Dinner *(page 130)*
· 1 slice whole wheat or white bread
· Romaine salad with 2 tablespoons French dressing
· 1 cup fat-free (skim) milk

Calories	Calcium (mg)	Iron (mg)	Magnesium (mg)	Potassium (mg)
447	455	4	104	1097

Snack
· 1 serving Orange-Cream Frosty *(page 226)*

Calories	Calcium (mg)	Iron (mg)	Magnesium (mg)	Potassium (mg)
362	448	0.4	49	604

DAILY TOTAL

Calories	Calcium (mg)	Iron (mg)	Magnesium (mg)	Potassium (mg)
2259	1888	13	423	4457

Menu 4

Breakfast
- 1 serving **Baked French Toast with Strawberry-Rhubarb Sauce** *(page 74)*
- 1 cup calcium-fortified orange juice

Calories	Calcium (mg)	Iron (mg)	Magnesium (mg)	Potassium (mg)
534	596	5	76	865

Snack
- 1 or 2 slices **Banana Bread** *(page 62)* or **Easy Brown Bread** *(page 63)*
- 1 cup **Sugar 'n Spice Green Tea** *(page 107)*

Calories	Calcium (mg)	Iron (mg)	Magnesium (mg)	Potassium (mg)
194	24	1	19	228

Lunch
- 1 serving **Zesty Autumn Pork Stew** *(page 198)*
- 1 kiwifruit
- 1 cup fat-free (skim) milk

Calories	Calcium (mg)	Iron (mg)	Magnesium (mg)	Potassium (mg)
388	368	2.5	99	1599

Snack
- 1 serving **Tomato Bruschetta** *(page 84)*

Calories	Calcium (mg)	Iron (mg)	Magnesium (mg)	Potassium (mg)
229	96	1.7	17	107

Dinner
- 1 serving **Extra-Easy Baked Ziti** *(page 162)*
- Mixed-greens salad with 2 tablespoons Caesar dressing
- 1 serving **Easy Fresh-Fruit Salad** *(page 216)*

Calories	Calcium (mg)	Iron (mg)	Magnesium (mg)	Potassium (mg)
522	348	4	79	805

Snack
- 1 serving **Easy Salmon Spread** with crackers *(page 102)*

Calories	Calcium (mg)	Iron (mg)	Magnesium (mg)	Potassium (mg)
237	138	1	23	229

DAILY TOTAL

Calories	Calcium (mg)	Iron (mg)	Magnesium (mg)	Potassium (mg)
2104	1570	15	313	383

Menu 5

Breakfast
- 1 serving **Poached Eggs in Milk** *(page 53)*
- 1/4 cup raisins or dates
- 1 cup fat-free (skim) milk

Calories	Calcium (mg)	Iron (mg)	Magnesium (mg)	Potassium (mg)
632	650	4	88	1167

Snack
- 1 serving **Creamy Caramel Dip with Fruit** *(page 100)*
- 1 cup calcium-fortified orange juice

Calories	Calcium (mg)	Iron (mg)	Magnesium (mg)	Potassium (mg)
357	451	2	49	770

Lunch
- 1 serving **Cantaloupe and Chicken Salad** *(page 120)*
- 1 whole wheat dinner roll with 2 teaspoons butter or margarine

Calories	Calcium (mg)	Iron (mg)	Magnesium (mg)	Potassium (mg)
597	90	3.5	73	500

Snack
- 2 **Pumpkin Drop Cookies** *(page 222)*
- 1 cup fat-free (skim) milk

Calories	Calcium (mg)	Iron (mg)	Magnesium (mg)	Potassium (mg)
249	350	1	40	538

Dinner
- 1 serving **Layered Tuna Casserole** *(page 181)*
- 1 cup steamed green beans
- 1/2 cup melon cubes
- 1 serving **Easy Lemon Bars** *(page 221)*

Calories	Calcium (mg)	Iron (mg)	Magnesium (mg)	Potassium (mg)
562	293	6.5	116	798

Snack
- 1/2 English muffin with 1 teaspoon peanut butter
- 1/2 cup apple juice

Calories	Calcium (mg)	Iron (mg)	Magnesium (mg)	Potassium (mg)
157	60	1.3	18	221

DAILY TOTAL

Calories	Calcium (mg)	Iron (mg)	Magnesium (mg)	Potassium (mg)
2554	1894	18	385	3994

Menu 6

Breakfast

1 serving **Rise 'n Shine Muffins with Creamy Orange Glaze** *(page 64)*

1 cup calcium-fortified orange juice

Calories	Calcium (mg)	Iron (mg)	Magnesium (mg)	Potassium (mg)
298	86	3	68	572

Snack

· 1 serving **Quick Quesadillas** *(page 93)*

· 1/4 cup **Fresh Salsa** *(page 98)*

Calories	Calcium (mg)	Iron (mg)	Magnesium (mg)	Potassium (mg)
290	263	2	26	227

Lunch

· 1 serving **Broccoli-Bacon Salad** *(page 208)*

· 1 dinner roll with 2 teaspoons butter or margarine

· 1 serving **Rice Pudding** *(page 233)*

· 1 cup fat-free (skim) milk

Calories	Calcium (mg)	Iron (mg)	Magnesium (mg)	Potassium (mg)
738	485	3.5	93	870

Snack

· 1 soft breadstick with 2 teaspoons butter or margarine

· 1 cup tomato juice

Calories	Calcium (mg)	Iron (mg)	Magnesium (mg)	Potassium (mg)
196	50	2	36	574

Dinner

· 1 serving **Hash Brown Frittata** *(page 178)*

· 1 serving **Easy Creamed Vegetables** *(page 203)*

· 1/2 cup mixed fresh fruit

Calories	Calcium (mg)	Iron (mg)	Magnesium (mg)	Potassium (mg)
540	366	9	97	1188

Snack

· 1 serving **Baked Custard** *(page 232)*

· 1 cup hot herbal tea

Calories	Calcium (mg)	Iron (mg)	Magnesium (mg)	Potassium (mg)
161	168	0.6	22	248

DAILY TOTAL

Calories	Calcium (mg)	Iron (mg)	Magnesium (mg)	Potassium (mg)
2222	1417	20	342	3678

Menu 7

Breakfast

· 1 serving **Blueberry Brunch Cake** *(page 66)*

· 1 cup raspberries or 1 pear

· 1 cup fat-free (skim) milk

Calories	Calcium (mg)	Iron (mg)	Magnesium (mg)	Potassium (mg)
425	400	2	58	668

Snack

· 1 medium banana

· 1 cup fat-free (skim) milk or hot or iced tea

Calories	Calcium (mg)	Iron (mg)	Magnesium (mg)	Potassium (mg)
194	309	0.5	62	873

Lunch

· 1 serving **Beef and Bean Dinner** *(page 194)*

· 1 orange, tangerine or clementine

· 1 cup hot herbal tea or coffee

Calories	Calcium (mg)	Iron (mg)	Magnesium (mg)	Potassium (mg)
618	190	10	164	1676

Snack

· 1 cup cranberry juice

· 1 cup pretzels

· 1/4 cup raisins

Calories	Calcium (mg)	Iron (mg)	Magnesium (mg)	Potassium (mg)
413	55	3	49	643

Dinner

· 1 serving **Crispy Baked Fish with Tropical Salsa** *(page 182)*

· 1 baked potato with 2 tablespoons sour cream or butter

· 1 whole-grain or white dinner roll with 2 teaspoons butter or margarine

· 1 cup fat-free (skim) milk or water

Calories	Calcium (mg)	Iron (mg)	Magnesium (mg)	Potassium (mg)
853	474	5	191	1917

Snack

· 2 graham crackers with 1 tablespoon peanut butter

· 1 cup fat-free (skim) or low-fat milk

Calories	Calcium (mg)	Iron (mg)	Magnesium (mg)	Potassium (mg)
291	315	1	62	561

DAILY TOTAL

Calories	Calcium (mg)	Iron (mg)	Magnesium (mg)	Potassium (mg)
2794	1743	22	568	6339

A Two-Day Suggested Eating Plan for Constipation

Day 1

Eating high-fiber foods and drinking plenty of liquids, at least eight glasses of water daily, is important. Drink a hot beverage about half an hour before your usual time for a bowel movement. See page 36 for other tips on handling constipation. Here's a sampling of foods to assist you when you're feeling constipated:

Breakfast
· Rise 'n Shine Muffins with Creamy Orange Glaze *(page 64)*
· 1 cup hot herbal tea

Snack
· Hot Fruit Compote *(page 37)*
· 1 cup water

Lunch
· Spaghetti and "Meatballs" *(page 171)*
· 1/2 cup fat-free (skim) milk

Snack
· 1/4 cup dried apricots or raisins
· 2 or 3 tablespoons toasted soybeans
· 1 cup water

Dinner
· Corn and Black Bean Salad *(page 140)*
· 1 slice whole-grain bread
· 1 cup fruit juice

Snack
· Easy Fresh-Fruit Salad *(page 216)*
· 1 cup mineral water

Day 2

Breakfast
· Potato Pancakes with Cinnamon Apples *(page 70)*
· 1/2 cup prune juice

Snack
· 1 kiwifruit
· 1 cup water

Lunch
· Barley and Asparagus *(page 214)*
· Stir-Fried Vegetables *(page 204)*
· 1 cup hot tea

Snack
· 1/3 to 1/2 cup high-fiber cereal with milk
· 1 cup water

Dinner
White Turkey Chili *(page 154)*
· Whole-grain breadsticks or bread
· 1 cup fat-free (skim) milk

Snack
· Creamy Caramel Dip with Fruit *(page 100)*
· 1 cup fruit juice

A Two-Day Suggested Eating Plan for Diarrhea

Replenishing lost fluids is of great importance when you have diarrhea. One way to ensure fluid replacement is to drink plenty of water and other liquids throughout the day, at least eight glasses. If you can, consume foods and beverages that contain extra potassium and sodium, because these nutrients are lost during bouts of diarrhea. See page 38 for hints on helping to calm diarrhea. Below is a sampling of foods that may help soothe diarrhea:

Day 1

Breakfast
· Milk and Rice "Soup" *(page 39)*
· 1 cup water

Snack
· 1 or 2 slices **Banana Bread** *(page 62)*
· 1/2 cup apple juice

Lunch
· 1 baked potato with sour cream or butter
· 1 scrambled egg
· 1 slice white bread, toasted
· 1 cup fat-free (skim) milk

Snack
· 1 container (6 ounces) fruited yogurt
· 1/2 cup sports drink

Dinner
Salmon Burgers *(page 180)*
· 1/2 cup **Orange-Pineapple Fruit Salad** *(page 215)*, canned mandarin orange segments or pineapple chunks
· 1 cup orange juice

Snack
· Saltine crackers with creamy peanut butter
· 1 cup fat-free (skim) milk

Day 2

Breakfast
· Home-Style Oatmeal with Raisins *(page 57)*
· 1 cup fat-free (skim) milk

Snack
· 1 banana
· 1 cup grape juice

Lunch
· Cantaloupe and Chicken Salad *(page 120)*
· 1 slice French bread
· 1 cup tomato juice

Snack
· Citrus-Peach Smoothie *(page 103)*
· 1 cup water

Dinner
· Old-Fashioned Beef Pot Roast *(page 191)*
· 1 slice white bread
· 1 cup water

Snack
· Rice Pudding *(page 233)*
· 1 cup hot herbal tea

A Two-Day Suggested Eating Plan for Mouth Sores

See page 42 for hints to help you soothe your mouth sores. Here's a sampling of foods that may also be of help:

Day 1

Breakfast
· Poached Eggs in Milk *(page 53)*
· 1/2 cup applesauce
· 1/2 cup apple juice

Snack
· Watermelon-Kiwi-Banana Smoothie *(page 104)*
· 1 cup water

Lunch
· Cream of Broccoli Soup *(page 134)*
· Crackers moistened with soup
· 1 cup fat-free (skim) milk

Snack·
· 1 banana
· 1 frozen ice pop
· 1 cup water

Dinner
· Loaded Potatoes (puree if necessary) *(page 132)*
· 1 cup fat-free (skim) milk

Snack
· Baked Custard *(page 232)*
· 1 cup hot herbal tea

Day 2

Breakfast
· Home-Style Oatmeal with Raisins *(page 57)*
· 1 cup fat-free skim milk

Snack
· 1/2 cup cottage cheese
· 1 cup peach or apricot nectar

Lunch
· Easy Salmon Spread *(page 102)*
· Soft crackers
· 1/2 cup watermelon

Snack
· Creamy Caramel Dip with Fruit *(page 100)* with canned peaches or pears as dippers
· 1 cup water

Dinner
· Acorn Squash and Apple Soup *(page 175)*
· 1 or 2 soft breadsticks
· 1/2 cup mashed or pureed vegetables, such as peas or carrots

Snack
· Raspberry-Banana Gelatin Dessert *(page 227)*
· 1 cup water

A Two-Day Suggested Eating Plan For Nausea

Though you may not feel like eating when you have nausea, it's important to keep eating. Eating will actually help you regain your strength and your appetite as well. If your doctor has prescribed antinausea medicine, be sure to take it, and drink plenty of clear liquids. See pages 32 and 77 for specific hints on easing nausea. Listed below is a sampling of foods that you may eat for two days when nausea strikes:

Day 1

Breakfast
· Fruit Parfaits *(page 60)*
· 1 cup water

Snack
· 1 or 2 slices toast dry, or with a small amount of butter or margarine
· 1/2 cup fat-free (skim) milk

Lunch
· Chicken Soup with Homemade Noodles *(page 152)*
· Oyster crackers
· 1/2 cup fat-free (skim) milk

Snack
· 1 container (6 ounces) low-fat fruited yogurt
· 1/2 glass sparkling water or soda

Dinner
· Dijon Chicken *(page 146)*
· Mashed Potatoes *(page 205)*
· 1/2 cup canned green beans, corn or peas
· 1/2 cup fat-free (skim) milk

Snack
· 1/2 cup frozen sherbet
· 1 cup sparkling water or soda

Day 2

Breakfast
· Home-Style Oatmeal with Raisins *(page 57)*
· 1/2 cup fat-free (skim) milk

Snack
· Pretzels
· 1/2 cup apple-cranberry juice

Lunch
· Macaroni Pasta "Soup" *(page 133)*
· Rice Pudding *(page 233)*

Snack
· Canned peaches, pears or other canned bland fruit
· 1/2 glass sparkling water

Dinner
· 3 ounces baked or boiled chicken, without skin
· Baking Powder Biscuits *(page 68)*
· Easy Creamed Vegetables *(page 203)*
· 1 cup water

Snack
· Orange-Cream Frosty *(page 226)*
· 1/2 cup apple juice

A Two-Day Suggested Eating Plan For Neutropenia

Approximately seven to fourteen days after receiving chemotherapy, developing an abnormally low white blood cell count is common; this is called *neutropenia*. When your blood cell counts drop, you need to get plenty of iron from the foods you eat. In addition, your doctor may suggest you take iron supplements to be certain you're getting enough iron. A sampling of some high-iron foods to eat during neutropenia is listed below:

Day 1

Breakfast
· Cinnamon-Raisin Morning Mix *(page 59)*
· Berry-Banana Smoothie *(page 29)*

Snack
· Roasted Vegetable Dip *(page 80)* with broccoli flowerets and cauliflowerets

Lunch
· Chicken and Vegetable Stir-Fry *(page 185)*
· 1 cup tomato juice

Snack
· Savory Black-Eyed Peas with Bacon *(page 211)*
· 1/2 cup cooked spinach
· 1 cup fat-free (skim) milk

Dinner
· Beef and Bean Dinner *(page 194)*
· 1 cup fat-free (skim) milk

Snack
· Gingerbread with Brown Sugar Meringue *(page 228)*
· 1 cup orange juice

Day 2

Breakfast
· Tropical Pancakes *(page 69)*
· 1/2 cup strawberries
· 1 cup fat-free (skim) milk

Snack
· 1/3 cup raisins
· 1/2 cup pretzels
· 1 cup sparkling water

Lunch
· Philly Beef Sandwiches *(page 92)*
· Canned mandarin orange segments

Snack
· Streusel-Topped Fruit Brunch Cake *(page 65)*
· 1 cup fat-free (skim) milk

Dinner
· Crowd-Size Minestrone *(page 156)*
· Soft breadsticks
· 1 cup water

Snack
· 2 graham crackers with peanut butter
· 1 cup apple juice

Recipes to Use After Treatment

The **ABCs for a Healthy Lifestyle** after cancer treatment are discussed on pages 23–25. They include Aiming for Fitness, Building a Healthy Base and Choosing Foods Sensibly. Many of the recipes in this cookbook fit these guidelines and can be useful even after treatment. (And they also taste great!) Following is a list of recipes that offer many nutrients:

Chapter 1

Berry-Banana Smoothie *(page 29)*

Hot Fruit Compote *(page 37)*

Milk and Rice "Soup" *(page 39)*

Creamy Seafood Risotto *(page 41)*

Crunchy Fruit Snack Mix *(page 43)*

Lentil-Rice Casserole *(page 45)*

Roasted Garlic Mashed Potatoes *(page 47)*

Chapter 2

Country Eggs in Tortilla Cups *(page 52)*

Poached Eggs in Milk *(page 53)*

Cheesy Ham and Asparagus Bake *(page 54)*

Home-Style Oatmeal with Raisins *(page 57)*

Cinnamon-Raisin Morning Mix *(page 59)*

Fruit Parfaits *(page 60)*

Tropical Pancakes *(page 69)*

Cheesy Pear Oven Pancake *(page 73)*

Baked French Toast with Strawberry-Rhubarb Sauce *(page 74)*

Make-Ahead Waffles with Peanut Butter Spread *(page 78)*

Chapter 3

Roasted Vegetable Dip *(page 80)*

Easy Chicken Nuggets *(page 91)*

Philly Beef Sandwiches *(page 92)*

Chicken Salad in Pitas *(page 94)*

Mozzarella and Tomatoes *(page 97)*

Creamy Caramel Dip with Fruit *(page 100)*

Spinach Dip in Bread Bowl *(page 101)*

Citrus-Peach Smoothie *(page 103)*

Watermelon-Kiwi-Banana Smoothie *(page 104)*

Orange-Pineapple Smoothie *(page 106)*

Chapter 4

Fettuccine with Asparagus and Mushrooms *(page 112)*

Mediterranean Couscous and Beans *(page 113)*

Angel Hair Pasta with Avocado and Tomatoes *(page 114)*

Creamy Quinoa Primavera *(page 116)*

Honey-Mustard Turkey with Snap Peas *(page 118)*

Caribbean Chicken Salad *(page 119)*

Cantaloupe and Chicken Salad *(page 120)*

Spinach-Shrimp Salad with Hot Bacon Dressing *(page 122)*

Chutney-Salmon Salad *(page 123)*

Savory Scallops and Shrimp *(page 124)*

Chopped Vegetable and Crabmeat Salad *(page 126)*

Fiesta Taco Salad *(page 129)*

Loaded Potatoes *(page 132)*

Cream of Broccoli Soup *(page 134)*

Easy Beef Stroganoff *(page 136)*

Caramelized Pork Slices *(page 137)*

For more great-tasting healthy
recipes, see *Betty Crocker's*
HEALTHY NEW CHOICES
cookbook

Nutrition and Medical Glossary

Medical and nutrition terms can sometimes be confusing, so we have gathered definitions of the nutrition and medical terms used in this cookbook.

Acupuncture—The insertion of needles into specific points on the body to help the body heal.

Alternative therapies—Treatment options that include thoughts and emotions as an integral part of healing. These may be used in combination with conventional forms of treatment.

Antioxidant—A substance that inhibits oxidation in plant and animal cells. Scientists believe that having a diet high in antioxidants may contribute to reducing disease.

Aromatherapy—The use of essential oils to increase relaxation, improve mood, and enhance circulation.

Ayurveda—An ancient medical practice that originated in India, based on the concept that energy keeps the mind and body alive.

Body Mass Index (BMI)—A measure used to compare the height and weight of adult men and women to their risk of disease.

Bodywork—A catchall term for a variety of techniques that treat ailments and promote relaxation through proper movement, posture, exercise or massage.

Calcium—A mineral found in dairy foods that is important for maintaining strong bones and teeth and proper nerve and muscle function. Calcium aids recovery.

Cancer—The abnormal growth of any cells in the body.

Carbohydrates—Providing quick energy, they are the body's favorite fuel source. The carbohydrate content of each recipe in this book is listed under the recipe.

Chemotherapy—Systemic drugs that target and kill rapidly dividing cells, including cancer cells.

Chi—The flow of energy; based on the belief that energy flows between body organs along channels. Healing occurs when the flow of energy in the entire body is balanced.

Cholesterol—Fatlike substance, found primarily in animal foods, that is important for cell structures, hormones and nerve coverings. It is also manufactured in our bodies.

Complementary therapies—See "Alternative therapies."

Coronary Heart Disease (CHD)—A buildup of fatty, cholesterol-filled deposits in the arteries that block the normal flow of blood and can ultimately cause a heart attack.

Cruciferous—Vegetables from the cabbage family, including broccoli, cabbage, cauliflower and Brussels sprouts, which are thought to be somewhat protective against certain types of cancer when eaten as part of a low-fat, healthy diet.

Diet Exchanges—Developed by the American Dietetic Association and the American Diabetes Association, Diet Exchanges categorize foods based on their nutritional content.

Dietary Guidelines for Americans—Developed in May 2000 by the U.S. Departments of Agriculture and Health and Human Services, these guidelines help educate people about how to develop a healthy lifestyle.

Fat—A necessary nutrient, fat helps build new cells, shuttles vitamins through the body and makes certain hormones that regulate blood pressure.

Fiber—The type of carbohydrate in a food that is not broken down before passing through to the stool.

Food Guide Pyramid—A nutrition education guide developed to help people learn how to eat a healthy balance of a variety of foods.

Herbs—Specific plants or parts of plants that impart flavor and have medicine-like qualities.

High blood pressure (hypertension)—A condition that occurs when blood pressure is equal to or greater than 140/90 millimeters of mercury.

Iron—A mineral that carries much-needed oxygen to body cells, is vital for life and aids recovery. Iron is found in meats, spinach and fortified cereal.

Liquid diet—A clear liquid diet is mainly comprised of liquids and provides only about 500 calories per day. It should be used for only short lengths of time.

Low-residue diet—A diet made up of foods that, when eaten, leave little material in the colon after digestion. Cancer patients who have had stomach or colon surgery may need to eat a low-residue diet.

Magnesium—A nutrient (mineral) that helps release carbohydrate energy from foods and aids recovery. Magnesium is found in nuts and spinach.

Massage—The manipulation of soft tissue to relieve sore muscles and promote relaxation.

Meditation—Quiet forms of contemplation and mindfulness used to establish a sense of peace, inner calm and relaxation.

Minerals—Organic compounds, needed in very small amounts, that help the body with many functions. Minerals beneficial to cancer treatment are calcium, iron, magnesium and potassium.

Naturopathy—With an emphasis on preventive care, it takes advantage of the body's natural healing powers.

Neuropathy—Tingling and numbness in the fingers and toes that can develop in cancer patients when undergoing chemotherapy.

Neutropenia—A condition that occurs when white blood cell counts fall below 500 cells per cubic millimeter of blood; often occurs seven to ten days after beginning chemotherapy treatment.

Nutrient—Catchall term that describes substances necessary for life that build, repair and maintain body cells. Protein, carbohydrates, fats, water, vitamins and minerals are all examples of nutrients.

% Daily Value—A standard for nutrition labeling of foods that is based on a 2,000-calorie daily diet. It applies to healthy people of various ages and represents the highest recommended level of each nutrient. It replaces the former U.S. Recommended Daily Allowance (RDA).

Potassium—A nutrient (mineral) that helps maintain the body's fluid balance and aids recovery. Potassium is found in fruits, vegetables and dairy foods.

Phytochemicals—Umbrella term used to describe many naturally occurring substances found in plant foods that may have disease-fighting properties.

Protein—This nutrient helps build new cells, makes hormones and enzymes that keep the body functioning and generates antibodies to fight off infection. During cancer treatment, the body has an increased need for protein.

Radiation (radiotherapy)—The use of concentrated energy to target and kill cancer cells.

Residue—The material left in the colon after digestion, including intestinal cells and breakdown products such as fiber from the foods you eat.

Saturated fat—Solid at room temperature, these fats tend to elevate blood cholesterol levels and usually come from animal sources, such as beef, pork, poultry, eggs and dairy foods including cheese, whole milk and butter. Also included are palm oil and coconut oil, even though they are liquids.

Shiatsu—A form of Japanese acupressure that uses finger pressure on specific body sites to increase circulation and improve energy flow.

Unsaturated fat—Liquid at room temperature, these fats do not tend to elevate blood cholesterol levels. They usually come from plant sources such as olive oil, sunflower oil, corn oil, nuts and avocados.

Vitamins—A group of vital nutrients, found in small amounts in a variety of foods, that are key to developing cells, controlling body functions and helping release energy from fuel sources. Vitamins are different from minerals in that they contain the element carbon; minerals do not.

Yoga—An ancient practice and philosophy first developed and practiced in India, yoga is based on stretching and strengthening exercises, ethical beliefs and dietary restrictions to balance the mind, body and spirit.

Additional Resources

BOOKS AND PUBLICATIONS

Cancer Talk: Voices of Hope and Endurance from "The Group Room," the World's Largest Cancer Support Group. Schimmel, Selma R., with Barry Fox, Ph.D. New York: Broadway Books, 1999.

It All Begins with Hope: Patients, Caregivers, and the Bereaved Speak Out. Jevne, Ronna Fay. Philadelphia, PA: Innisfree Press, 1991.

Eating Hints for Cancer Patients: Before, During, and After Treatment. Leonard, Barry, ed. National Institutes of Health, National Cancer Institute, 1999.

CANCER RESOURCES WEB SITES

American Cancer Society: www.cancer.org

American Institute for Cancer Research: www.aicr.org

National Cancer Institute: www.nci.nih.gov

Oncology.com: www.oncology.com

Women's Cancer Network: www.wcn.org

NUTRITION RESOURCES WEB SITES

American Dietetic Association: www.eatright.org

Beltsville Human Nutrition Research Center, USDA: www.barc.usda.gov/bhnrc

Helpful Nutrition and Cooking Information

We provide nutrition information for each recipe that includes calories, fat, cholesterol, sodium, carbohydrate, fiber and protein and essential vitamins and minerals for healing. Individual food choices can be based on this information.

Recommended intake for a daily diet of 2,000 calories as set by the Food and Drug Administration		
	Total Fat	Less than 65g
	Saturated Fat	Less than 20g
	Cholesterol	Less than 300mg
	Sodium	Less than 2,400mg
	Total Carbohydrate	300g
	Dietary Fiber	25g

Criteria Used for Calculating Nutrition Information
- The first ingredient was used wherever a choice is given (such as 1/3 cup sour cream or plain yogurt).
- The first ingredient amount was used wherever a range is given (such as 3- to 3-1/2–pound cut-up broiler-fryer chicken).
- The first serving number was used wherever a range is given (such as 4 to 6 servings).
- "If desired" ingredients and recipe variations were not included (such as sprinkle with brown sugar, if desired).
- Only the amount of a marinade or frying oil that is estimated to be absorbed by the food during preparation or cooking was calculated.

Ingredients Used in Recipe Testing and Nutrition Calculations
- Ingredients used for testing represent those that the majority of consumers use in their homes: large eggs, 2% milk, 80%-lean ground beef, canned ready-to-use chicken broth and vegetable oil spread containing not less than 65 percent fat.
- Fat-free, low-fat or low-sodium products were not used, unless otherwise indicated.
- Solid vegetable shortening (not butter, margarine, nonstick cooking sprays or vegetable oil spread as they can cause sticking problems) was used to grease pans, unless otherwise indicated.

Equipment Used in Recipe Testing
We use equipment for testing that the majority of consumers use in their homes. If a specific piece of equipment (such as a wire whisk) is necessary for recipe success, it is listed in the recipe.
- Cookware and bakeware without nonstick coatings were used, unless otherwise indicated.
- No dark-colored, black or insulated bakeware was used.
- When a pan is specified in a recipe, a metal pan was used; a baking dish or pie plate means ovenproof glass was used.
- An electric hand mixer was used for mixing only when mixer speeds are specified in the recipe directions. When a mixer speed is not given, a spoon or fork was used.

Beat: Mix ingredients vigorously with spoon, fork, wire whisk, hand beater or electric mixer until smooth and uniform.

Boil: Heat liquid until bubbles rise continuously and break on the surface and steam is given off. For rolling boil, the bubbles form rapidly.

Chop: Cut into coarse or fine irregular pieces with a knife, food chopper, blender or food processor.

Cube: Cut into squares 1/2 inch or larger.

Dice: Cut into squares smaller than 1/2 inch.

Grate: Cut into tiny particles using small rough holes of grater (citrus peel or chocolate).

Grease: Rub the inside surface of a pan with shortening, using pastry brush, piece of waxed paper or paper towel, to prevent food from sticking during baking (as for some casseroles).

Julienne: Cut into thin, matchlike strips, using knife or food processor (vegetables, fruits, meats).

Mix: Combine ingredients in any way that distributes them evenly.

Sauté: Cook foods in hot oil or margarine over medium-high heat with frequent tossing and turning motion.

Shred: Cut into long thin pieces by rubbing food across the holes of a shredder, as for cheese, or by using a knife to slice very thinly, as for cabbage.

Simmer: Cook in liquid just below the boiling point on top of the stove; usually after reducing heat from a boil. Bubbles will rise slowly and break just below the surface.

Stir: Mix ingredients until uniform consistency. Stir once in a while for stirring occasionally, often for stirring frequently and continuously for stirring constantly.

Toss: Tumble ingredients (such as green salad) lightly with a lifting motion, usually to coat evenly or mix with another food.

Metric Conversion Guide

Volume

U.S. Units	Canadian Metric	Australian Metric
1/4 teaspoon	1 mL	1 ml
1/2 teaspoon	2 mL	2 ml
1 teaspoon	5 mL	5 ml
1 tablespoon	15 mL	20 ml
1/4 cup	50 mL	60 ml
1/3 cup	75 mL	80 ml
1/2 cup	125 mL	125 ml
2/3 cup	150 mL	170 ml
3/4 cup	175 mL	190 ml
1 cup	250 mL	250 ml
1 quart	1 liter	1 liter
1 1/2 quarts	1.5 liters	1.5 liters
2 quarts	2 liters	2 liters
2 1/2 quarts	2.5 liters	2.5 liters
3 quarts	3 liters	3 liters
4 quarts	4 liters	4 liters

Weight

U.S. Units	Canadian Metric	Australian Metric
1 ounce	30 grams	30 grams
2 ounces	55 grams	60 grams
3 ounces	85 grams	90 grams
4 ounces (1/4 pound)	115 grams	125 grams
8 ounces (1/2 pound)	225 grams	225 grams
16 ounces (1 pound)	455 grams	500 grams
1 pound	455 grams	1/2 kilogram

Note: The recipes in this cookbook have not been developed or tested using metric measures. When converting recipes to metric, some variations in quality may be noted.

Measurements

Inches	Centimeters
1	2.5
2	5.0
3	7.5
4	10.0
5	12.5
6	15.0
7	17.5
8	20.5
9	23.0
10	25.5
11	28.0
12	30.5
13	33.0

Temperatures

Fahrenheit	Celsius
32°	0°
212°	100°
250°	120°
275°	140°
300°	150°
325°	160°
350°	180°
375°	190°
400°	200°
425°	220°
450°	230°
475°	240°
500°	260°

Index

Note: *Italicized* page references indicate photographs.

Complete your cookbook library with these *Betty Crocker* titles

Betty Crocker's A Passion for Pasta

Betty Crocker's Best Bread Machine Cookbook

Betty Crocker's Best Chicken Cookbook

Betty Crocker's Best Christmas Cookbook

Betty Crocker's Best of Baking

Betty Crocker's Best of Healthy and Hearty Cooking

Betty Crocker's Best-Loved Recipes

Betty Crocker's Bisquick® Cookbook

Betty Crocker's Bread Machine Cookbook

Betty Crocker's Cook It Quick

Betty Crocker's Cookbook, 9th Edition - *The* **BIG RED** *Cookbook*™

Betty Crocker's Cookbook, Bridal Edition

Betty Crocker's Cookie Book

Betty Crocker's Cooking and Coping with Cancer

Betty Crocker's Cooking Basics

Betty Crocker's Easy Slow Cooker Dinners

Betty Crocker's Eat and Lose Weight

Betty Crocker's Entertaining Basics

Betty Crocker's Flavors of Home

Betty Crocker's Good & Easy Cookbook

Betty Crocker's Great Grilling

Betty Crocker's Healthy New Choices

Betty Crocker's Indian Home Cooking

Betty Crocker's Italian Cooking

Betty Crocker's Kids Cook!

Betty Crocker's Kitchen Library

Betty Crocker's Low-Fat Low-Cholesterol Cooking Today

Betty Crocker's New Cake Decorating

Betty Crocker's New Chinese Cookbook

Betty Crocker's Picture Cook Book, Facsimile Edition

Betty Crocker's Slow Cooker Cookbook

Betty Crocker's Southwest Cooking

Betty Crocker's Vegetarian Cooking